Cognitive Discourse Analys

Analysing language data systematically and looking closely at how people formulate their thoughts can reveal astonishing insights about the human mind. Without presupposing specific subject knowledge, this book gently introduces its readers to theoretical insights as well as practical principles for systematic linguistic analysis from a cognitive perspective. Drawing on Thora Tenbrink's twenty years' experience in both linguistics and cognitive science, this book offers theoretical guidance and practical advice for doing Cognitive Discourse Analysis. It covers areas of analysis as diverse as attention, perspective, granularity, certainty, inference, transformation, communication, and cognitive strategies, using inspiring examples from many different projects. Simple techniques and tools are used to allow readers new to the subject easy ways to apply the methods, without the need for complex technologies, whilst the cross-disciplinary approach can be applied to a diverse range of research purposes and contexts in which language and thought play a role.

THORA TENBRINK is a Reader in Cognitive Linguistics at Bangor University. Her previous books include *Space, Time, and the Use of Language* (2007) and three co-edited books on spatial language and cognition.

Cognitive Discourse Analysis

An Introduction

Thora Tenbrink

Bangor University

CAMBRIDGE
UNIVERSITY PRESS

CAMBRIDGE
UNIVERSITY PRESS

University Printing House, Cambridge CB2 8BS, United Kingdom

One Liberty Plaza, 20th Floor, New York, NY 10006, USA

477 Williamstown Road, Port Melbourne, VIC 3207, Australia

314–321, 3rd Floor, Plot 3, Splendor Forum, Jasola District Centre, New Delhi – 110025, India

79 Anson Road, #06–04/06, Singapore 079906

Cambridge University Press is part of the University of Cambridge.

It furthers the University's mission by disseminating knowledge in the pursuit of education, learning, and research at the highest international levels of excellence.

www.cambridge.org
Information on this title: www.cambridge.org/9781108422666
DOI: 10.1017/9781108525176

First published 2020

Printed in the United Kingdom by TJ International Ltd, Padstow Cornwall

A catalogue record for this publication is available from the British Library.

Library of Congress Cataloging-in-Publication Data
Names: Tenbrink, Thora, 1969– author.
Title: Cognitive discourse analysis : an introduction / Thora Tenbrink, Bangor University.
Description: Cambridge, UK ; New York : Cambridge University Press, 2020. | Includes bibliographical references and index.
Identifiers: LCCN 2019030553 (print) | LCCN 2019030554 (ebook) | ISBN 9781108422666 (hardback) | ISBN 9781108525176 (epub)
Subjects: LCSH: Discourse analysis – Psychological aspects. | Cognition.
Classification: LCC P302.8 .T4856 2020 (print) | LCC P302.8 (ebook) | DDC 401/.41–dc23
LC record available at https://lccn.loc.gov/2019030553
LC ebook record available at https://lccn.loc.gov/2019030554

ISBN 978-1-108-42266-6 Hardback
ISBN 978-1-108-43684-7 Paperback

Contents

List of Figures   *page* vii
List of Tables   viii
Preface   ix
Acknowledgements   x

Introduction   1

1   Background and Scope   7
   1.1   How Language Relates to Thought   8
   1.2   Areas of Application for CODA   12
   1.3   Reliability, Generalisability, and Limits of CODA   26

2   Language as a Representation of Thought   32
   2.1   Research on the Use of Language to Represent Thought: A Brief Overview   33
   2.2   How Psycholinguists Analyse Language Use in Relation to Cognition   37
   2.3   How Cognitive Psychologists Analyse Language Use in Relation to
       Cognition   41

3   Resources   57
   3.1   Cognitive Linguistics   57
   3.2   Discourse Analysis   72
   3.3   Functional Grammar   83

4   Identifying Cognitive Orientation   92
   4.1   Attention   92
   4.2   Perspective   103

5   Identifying Cognitive Depth   117
   5.1   Granularity   117
   5.2   Certainty   128

6   Identifying Cognitive Constructiveness   142
   6.1   Inference   142
   6.2   Transformation   155

7   Using Language to Convey Thoughts   168
    7.1   Communication   169
    7.2   Cognitive Strategies   181

8   CODA Procedures   194
    8.1   Preliminary Considerations   195
    8.2   Experimental Design   197
    8.3   Verbal Data Elicitation   201
    8.4   Data Preparation   208
    8.5   Practical Steps of Data Analysis   210
    8.6   Qualitative Insights   220
    8.7   Quantitative Patterns   222

9   Beyond CODA   226
    9.1   Triangulation: Combinations with Other Methods   226
    9.2   Practical Purposes within and outside Academia   240
    9.3   Conclusion   248

Register of Linguistic Features   251
References   255
Index   269

Figures

1.1 Furniture item arrangement used in Andonova et al. (2010) and Tenbrink et al. (2011b). *page* 17

3.1 Profiled meanings in Langacker (2002:6). 65

4.1 The different profiles of semantically similar sentences (following Langacker, 1986). 96

4.2 Screenshot of a tunnel during the virtual journey in the tunnel task used in Schönebeck et al. (2001), followed by a set of arrows shown when emerging from the tunnel. 108

5.1 Example for paths chosen by novices and experts (Tenbrink et al., 2011a). 139

6.1 Screenshot from the film in Tenbrink et al. (2016), showing a tilted view with artificial horizon. 154

7.1 An example for a dialogue situation modelled by COR (Shi et al., 2010). 177

8.1 Screenshot of Excel-based analysis done in Tenbrink and Taylor (2015). 215

8.2 Spreadsheet for the analysis in Tenbrink and Taylor (2015). 223

9.1 A process model of writing (Flower & Hayes, 1981). 235

Tables

3.1 Examples of Chinese characters that represent their meaning
to a degree. *page* 59

Preface

This book is the result of twenty years of engagement with a seemingly simple idea: we use language to express our thoughts. At first glance, you might find this rather trivial: isn't this what language is for, what we do all the time? But then you might wonder how much research is really out there that examines discourse in order to identify people's thoughts. There is some, but there could be more – after all, what could be more fascinating than the human mind? This train of thought is what motivated me to look more closely into methodology and develop Cognitive Discourse Analysis (CODA).

Initially inspired by a few fascinating studies that used language to access central human concepts, I started experimenting with this approach myself. Over the years, I benefited tremendously from collaborating with experts across various disciplines, who shared the desire to learn something specific about the human mind – and trusted me enough to believe my suggestion that language provides a unique way of accessing it. Each of my collaborators has contributed in their own way to the refinement of CODA as it is presented here. I am grateful to all of them, as well as to the generations of students who have done linguistic analysis in my classes and tutorials, creating ever-new perspectives on how language represents thought. Based on this personal experience and the host of relevant literature now available, I strongly believe that CODA is useful for gaining insights about the human mind across disciplines. I hope this book will help to spread the method and develop it further.

Acknowledgements

I am greatly indebted to my colleagues, friends, and collaborators for their continuous support as this book took shape. Several people have read and commented on every single chapter; others provided critical feedback on individual parts. Many, many thanks go to Holly Taylor, whose inspiration, collaboration, and friendship have been absolutely invaluable, right from the very early stages of using the method. My heartfelt thanks further extend to Jago (Anwen Williams) for her reliable constructive criticism and support throughout, and likewise to Josie (Sarah J. Ryan), Harry (Yu Hui), Saskia Kuliga, Katja Egorova, Sharon Miller, Colin Burns, Asterios Chardalias, Charlotte Danino, Davood Gozli, Rick Moore, Katharina Stoltmann, and Phillip Wadley. I am sure the book wouldn't be the same without their feedback and inspiring comments. I also thank Bangor University for granting me a teaching-free semester to finish this book, and I am grateful for support by the publisher, Cambridge University Press, particularly Andrew Winnard and Stephanie Taylor.

Introduction

There is a paradox here – a delicious one – which I cannot resolve: if there is indeed a fundamental difference between experience and description, between direct and mediated knowledge of the world, how is it that language can be so powerful? Language, that most human invention, can enable what, in principle, should not be possible. It can allow all of us, even the congenitally blind, to see with another person's eyes.

Oliver Sacks, The Mind's Eye (2010:240)

Imagine you are trying to find your friend who is waiting for you in the cafeteria of a large hospital. The building is complex, and you don't see any signs that would help you find the way. You ask the receptionist, who advises, 'Well, try the big staircase over there, it must be there somewhere!' What do you make of this? Almost certainly, you'd be well aware (and probably very surprised) that the receptionist doesn't really know where the cafeteria is. Nevertheless, you might try the staircase as advised.

But – how do you know this? Where does your awareness of the receptionist's lack of knowledge come from? Can you read her mind? She never mentioned any uncertainty explicitly, and you probably wouldn't be able to state her ignorance as a given fact. Nevertheless, your knowledge of language, and of the principles of conventional language use, enable you to make this inference. The receptionist's uncertainty was communicated implicitly, not explicitly – not in *what* was said, in terms of the information conveyed, but in *how* it was said, in terms of linguistic features.

With a closer look, you will find evidence in the receptionist's short answer to support your intuition. To start with, you may note what was *not* said: she didn't, as might be expected, give you precise directions to the cafeteria. Instead, there are various indications of vagueness and uncertainty. The initial discourse marker *well* provides a first hint, followed by the term *try*, which points to an activity that should not be necessary while following an expertly given route description. Referring to the main staircase as 'the big staircase over there' seems odd, and the modal verb *must* indicates a degree of uncertainty. Finally, the term *somewhere* isn't sufficiently specific to serve as expert guidance. Quite likely, the receptionist's utterance also *sounded* hesitant with

1

regard to prosody and fluency, which you would recognise as additional subtle indicators.

Any adult native speaker of a language will intuitively recognise features such as these. In everyday life, we absorb this kind of implicit information subtly, swiftly, and effortlessly. This book demonstrates how to use these insights and intuitions systematically for research on human cognition, based on a wealth of findings on the relationship between language and thought. Cognitive Discourse Analysis – CODA – is a method designed to reveal how speakers' thoughts and concepts are reflected in language, both explicitly and implicitly. CODA looks at linguistic data, at spoken or written language (i.e. discourse) produced in situations relevant to thinking. Closely related to traditional discourse analysis methods, CODA means doing discourse analysis with a focus on concepts and thought processes.

In a very basic sense, speaking is based on thinking. Without concepts and thoughts there would be no language. Sounds and noises may be produced without cognition, but meaning cannot. Also, language seems to be the most direct medium available to humans for expressing our thoughts; almost inevitably, we will answer the everyday question 'What are you thinking?' through language rather than any other medium.

Linguistic research, across various subfields, is accumulating an ever-increasing wealth of insights about the ways in which language relates to cognition. In cognitive linguistics, various theories address the relationship between language and the mind (e.g. Evans, 2009a, 2009b; Langacker, 2000; Talmy, 2000, 2007; Tomasello, 2003). In particular, lexicogrammatical structures in language appear to be systematically related to cognitive structures and processes. This structural fact carries over to principles of language in use: the way we think is related to the way we talk. This is true both generally in terms of what we can do with language (or with a particular language in contrast to another), and specifically with respect to what we actually do.

The relationship between language and thought may not be simple, but it is nevertheless systematic. For instance, how a speaker describes a scene reflects what they are currently attending to in the scene, in contrast to other aspects of the scene that are not mentioned or remain in the background. Thus, *the car next to the tree* conveys a different focus of attention to *the tree next to the car*, even though the spatial relationship is identical. In both cases, other objects in the scene, and aspects such as the car's colour or the type of tree, are not represented at all.

Linguistic choices reflect crucial aspects of the speakers' concepts and strategies at the time of speaking, along with their relevance in a communicative context. Some of these strategies may be intentional, but most of our linguistic choices while speaking happen too quickly to be completely conscious. Because of these phenomena, discourse analysis provides a good pathway to access various layers of cognition, assuming the necessary expertise regarding relevant features of language. This book offers the conceptual tools needed for this. It will enable researchers to reveal aspects of human thought through a close analysis of language.

CODA primarily uses language as data that more or less directly expresses thoughts and concepts: for example, when people describe a complex scene or event, think aloud while solving a problem or making a difficult decision, or explain a complicated process to a friend. All of these situations involve cognitive challenges that will find their way into language in systematic ways, depending on the specific features of the situation.

Some aspects concerning human thoughts are directly reflected in content, and researchers have used this fact for many decades in cognitive science (Ericsson & Simon, 1993). For instance, when asked to think aloud, people will say what they are thinking about and consider their task-related observations explicitly. Verbal protocols can therefore reveal the cognitive steps that humans take to solve a complex problem. However, language reflects more than this, beyond the content that speakers express directly. For instance, in an utterance like 'Have you still not finished reading?', the marker *still* subtly conveys the speaker's underlying expectations. Likewise, in 'I have heard about it, too,' the term *too* reflects the speaker's knowledge about not being the only one to which the utterance applies.

Other aspects that have been established through linguistic research may be less obvious to a non-expert. For instance, the prepositions *in* and *on* convey more than the geometric properties that they denote: they also suggest a sense of control, as illustrated by 'the painting is on the wall', or 'the flowers are in the vase'. Although the flowers are not fully contained in the vase, the term *in* can be used because the vase controls the flowers' location; the flowers will move with the vase when carried to another place in the room.

Subtle markers such as these are well known in linguistics, and they represent a vast resource of insights about human thought. CODA offers a comprehensive way of applying these insights through systematic analysis of human language use. The goal is to illuminate underlying concepts and thought processes that may go beyond conscious reflection by individual speakers, and that may not necessarily be directly observable in linguistic content. This is because speakers are typically not aware of the underlying network of options that allows for a range of linguistic choices besides their own. This network only becomes evident by considering a larger data set collected under controlled circumstances. To identify the conceptual significance of these choices, CODA draws on rigorous data collection procedures and involves systematic analysis measures. Equipped with the necessary tools, as described in this book, the researcher can reveal systematic aspects of human thought by a close look at language use in relation to the context of production.

The book is structured as follows. The first three chapters provide general background and discuss the approach from an interdisciplinary perspective.

- Chapter 1 sets the stage by outlining the background and scope for CODA: what does the method build on, what is it intended for, why and where is it useful, and what are the limits of this approach to cognition?
- Chapter 2 discusses the relationship between language and thought from a variety of perspectives. This further elaborates on the background for CODA by relating the methodology to approaches in psycholinguistics and cognitive psychology.
- Chapter 3 turns to insights that support the analysis from three different fields: cognitive linguistics, discourse analysis, and functional grammar. Each of them offers a host of resources for analysts to draw on: practical insights as well as theoretical findings to relate to in order to make sense of linguistic patterns found in the data. This concludes the set of general background chapters.

Chapters 4–7 address specific cognitive aspects that have frequently been addressed using CODA, and that illustrate the kinds of phenomena that CODA can identify. The eight aspects discussed in these chapters can be regarded as possible analysis perspectives that complement each other, and that serve as examples of ways to analyse language in relation to cognition. Linguistic data will normally not be analysed with respect to all of these aspects at once, nor only from a single one. Instead, awareness of the wide range of possible analysis perspectives will allow the analyst to identify particularly interesting phenomena in their data that are relevant to their research question.

- Chapter 4 discusses two central aspects of cognitive orientation, namely *attention* and *perspective*. Whenever we describe something, what we say will reflect what we attend to; aspects that we barely think about will rarely be reflected in our descriptions. Also, while we often describe things from our own point of view, other perspectives are possible, such as our interaction partner's standpoint. While we don't often say explicitly which perspective we're using, our language will reflect the underlying viewpoint in systematic ways.
- Chapter 5 turns to cognitive depth, another aspect of our thinking that is regularly reflected in the way we formulate our thoughts. On the one hand, we can think things through, and formulate them in language, in much detail or we can remain on the surface, sticking to the mere essentials. On the other hand, we can be more or less certain about what we describe, reflecting our expertise or the uncertainty of the subject matter itself. Both aspects, *granularity* and *certainty*, work together, as experts will often be able to look into things in much more depth than novices – but on the other hand they don't always need to, as they quickly recognise patterns that they have come across before.

- Chapter 6 addresses two ways in which our minds can be constructive: either by making inferences on the basis of what's already there – filling in gaps of information – or by transforming what's there into something new. This twofold ability of the human mind to construct is basic to our existence, enabling us to go beyond what we encounter around us. The way we talk reflects both *inference* and *transformation* processes systematically.
- Chapter 7 turns to a set of aspects around the formulation of thought. On the one hand, whenever we put our thoughts into words, we do this for a specific purpose – typically for the benefit of an interaction partner. The first half of Chapter 7 discusses *communication* and dialogic interaction. The second half addresses the idea of *cognitive strategies*, which are the main target of think-aloud protocol analysis in traditional problem-solving studies. These are not intended to be primarily formulated for an addressee but instead represent the structure of cognitive processes in temporal sequence.

This concludes the set of chapters addressing analysis perspectives. The remaining two chapters offer more practical insights.

- Chapter 8 provides a detailed account of practical steps and advice for doing CODA. Starting with preliminary considerations as to the purpose of individual CODA studies, it discusses relevant procedures step by step, including experimental design aspects, data collection, data preparation, practical steps of data analysis, and considerations pertaining to qualitative and quantitative analysis methods.
- Chapter 9 looks beyond CODA in two ways. On the one hand, CODA is only one among many established ways to examine human thought; linguistic analysis can be easily and fruitfully combined with other methods. On the other hand, CODA is rarely used purely for its own sake; more often than not, linguistic analysis is part of a wider goal. Therefore, the second half of Chapter 9 concludes the book with a discussion of practical uses for the methodology in academia and beyond, in applied fields such as architecture and artificial intelligence.

With this overall scope, I am confident this book will be of interest to readers from various academic fields, and indeed readers beyond academia in areas where insights about human ways of thinking would be welcome. While this book was primarily written for researchers in their early career stages onwards, there is no prerequisite for doing CODA. Anybody who speaks a language well enough to have clear intuitions about the network of options available in that language can do a CODA study. The only prerequisite is a readiness to do systematic analysis, as this will allow for significant insights based on speakers' choices in situations where thoughts are relevant.

So the book is open to all – but different readers come with different backgrounds and might be interested in different aspects of the book. My own background is a combination of linguistics and cognitive science, and it is quite possible that this has some reflection in my writing. Perhaps those with a similar background will be the ones most interested in reading the book cover to cover. Many readers will already be familiar with CODA from their own research, or from having read the shorter introductory article in Tenbrink (2015); they might wish to access further information about specific aspects of CODA in the book.

Other readers might be more selective. Academics with a firm background in linguistics, especially those aspects covered in the book, may quickly skim through the earlier chapters or jump directly to the various analysis perspectives starting in Chapter 4. In contrast, cognitive scientists with little background in linguistics might find the first three chapters particularly enlightening, together with the procedural Chapter 8 and the final Chapter 9 on extensions. They may also develop their own ideas for analysis perspectives rather than relying solely on those outlined in Chapters 4–7.

Some researchers interested in language and cognition from a more theoretical perspective might get inspiration from the first three chapters alone. Conversely, some may focus entirely on practical aspects, perhaps in order to gain insights into doing systematic discourse analysis as part of a larger project; they may find Chapters 8 and 9 to be entirely sufficient. Finally, it is possible to use the book as a handbook rather than a textbook to read, and simply access it sporadically to find specific information on some aspect of language in relation to the mind. The Register of Linguistic Features and the Index provided at the end of this book should be helpful for this kind of use.

Whichever way you use this book, I hope you find it inspiring and helpful for your own purposes. It is my firm belief that language is an excellent medium that represents our thoughts systematically in accessible and analysable ways – and I cannot imagine anything more fascinating than the human mind, with all its complexities and diversities.

1   Background and Scope

Language and thought: they belong together, they are intricately related. Can you speak (or write) entirely without thinking? Can you think without language? Perhaps you aren't sure; perhaps your answer is a hesitant *Yes* to either or both of these questions. Even so, it is fairly obvious that there are limits to the *Yes*. Producing language without thought would be restricted to mindless babble or repetition of words. Thinking without language is more interesting: this might be closer to intuition, emotion, and other functions that the mind might perform. You might clearly visualise images in your head that you find difficult to describe in words. Your mind might explore colours, shapes, sensations, and the like; it could relate them to each other, and relate them to the real world. Perhaps this depends on who you are, or what your profession is. For example, artists or engineers might develop special skills in 'thinking without language'.

But what does it actually mean, to *think* – in relation to language? The analysis of language produced to express thoughts (in CODA) hits upon this question in several respects. One central aspect will be explored in Section 1.3 in this chapter, namely the limits of *verbalisability*. This concept reflects the fact that not all of our thoughts can be put into words, in speaking or writing, in a straightforward way. Some things going on in our minds lack a precise word to describe them (such as mixed emotions), and other things may simply happen too fast or are too complex and evasive to be verbalisable, even in retrospect. These phenomena naturally limit the scope of what language analysis can tell us about thought. There will always be more things going on in our minds, beyond language – and these things may or may not be regarded as 'thinking'.

Despite the limits of language in the representation of thought, language undoubtedly remains one of the most important ways – or perhaps *the* most important way – for us to express our thoughts. At a very young age, we *learn to think* through language. Parents put their understanding of the world into words for their children, and they often respond by repeating these words. And then, they reuse the words in situations where they *think* they can be applied in the same way.

Often, children *think aloud* as they discover the world, playing with the words they have heard others say in similar contexts. They do this creatively, and it is fascinating to watch them try out where words may fit. Frequently children will end up overusing a word, as they tend to overgeneralise categories (Tomasello, 2003). Then, not just *Toby* is a *dog*, but also *Kitty* (the cat) – and perhaps even the hare seen on the field. Such effects reveal thought processes that make logical sense, but do not correspond to the way the words are normally used.

As children grow up, they learn to use language to communicate thoughts to others. They learn that parents cannot read their minds, and that they must express what they are thinking or feeling in order to get a desired reaction. This remains the most important use of language throughout adult life: the communication of thoughts and ideas, feelings, and observations. Sure, there are other ways of communicating: through actions, through non-linguistic gestures, through facial expressions. But there are many things that can't be expressed in those ways – and that's when we need language. Language becomes even more crucial when we're not in the same room while communicating, which is now rather common and easy in the modern Internet-connected world. Indeed, the limits of language become apparent in such a situation, and therefore Internet users creatively develop additions to language in the form of emojis and emoticons. These are increasingly perceived and integrated as a proper part of linguistic communication in the modern world (Gülşen, 2016).

Generally, the relationship between language and thought has fascinated researchers for a long time, and the topic has been looked at from many different perspectives. This chapter will look at three aspects relevant to CODA. First, it will provide a brief overview of the study of language in relation to thought. Then, it will show ways in which CODA can be applied across different areas in which thought is represented. Finally, it will address the limitations of linguistic data analysis in relation to thought, outlining the extent to which we can 'trust' that the language we analyse actually does represent thoughts and thought processes.

1.1   How Language Relates to Thought

Language and thought: how do they relate to each other, and how does language relate to other cognitive functions or 'modules' (Fodor, 1983)? The debate in the academic literature is as old as the study of language itself; indeed, linguistics originated as a branch of psychology, reflecting the close link to the human mind or 'psyche'.

Human thought is fundamentally linked to its environment. We understand the world simply because we live in it with our bodies and perceive it with our senses (Anderson, 2003; Lakoff & Johnson, 1999; Wilson, 2002). The fact that we're *embodied* in the world affects the way we think in many ways – including language. To learn language, to understand how a word refers to an object in the world, a child needs to interact with the object or perceive it in relation to the overall context, and understand how the word relates to it. We process linguistic input on the basis of our physical experience (Fischer & Zwaan, 2008). The entire language system can be best understood on the basis of the features and needs we encounter in the real world (Feldman, 2010).

What happens in our minds when we comprehend language – when we listen to what someone is saying, or read what others have written? Our minds are good at forming mental images or 'models' out of language-based input (Johnson-Laird, 1983). We hear a story about a character travelling through a landscape; the landscape is sketched in the story – and before we know it, we can 'see' it emerging in our mind's eye, without ever having actually been there. Or we hear somebody moan how their legs are aching from climbing a steep hill – and we can sympathise and perhaps even feel our own muscles, just from imagining the action.

It sounds like magic, but our minds can do it because we have experienced the world physically, and we can easily imagine being in various parts of it, given only a few sketched hints through language. As a result, we will likely 'see' and 'feel' a lot more than has actually been said, in our mind's eye. We fill in the gaps, use whatever information we can gain – including some specific previous experiences of our own, or that we've heard about, and expectations that we build up on this basis. A simple word like *poor*, in the context of a suburban area, directly makes us think of houses that have seen better times, of ragged clothes, perhaps beggars in the street. Our mind is full of associations of this kind, and after a very short time we may not be able to tell whether something has actually been described directly, or whether we have simply been making assumptions based on what was said. The existence of cultural stereotypes and cognitive biases towards certain ways of thinking reinforces these effects.

If we build up mental models and fill in gaps from what we hear and read, how does this relate to other kinds of input? How do language-based representations relate to other information sources? Consider an everyday example: is it better to listen to a verbal route description, or to look at a map? Surprisingly, it seems like both kinds of input are equally suitable for wayfinding (Meilinger & Knauff, 2008). Likewise, Tversky and Lee (1999) found that people put pretty much the same kind of information into verbal route descriptions as they would do when sketching the route on a piece of paper. What we need for wayfinding seems to be restricted to a few basic pieces of information, called 'skeletal' by Denis (1997) – something like Example 1.1.

Example 1.1   Turn left at the church, carry on for a few minutes, till you see the goal on the left.

Further information can be supplied – through language or through a sketch map – such as the angle of the left turn, or the exact distance in metres. But this type of additional information is not essential for finding the route. This would explain why, in this kind of scenario, language can be equal to maps. Some additional information would be more easily conveyed through language, such as a reference to past developments or personal experience; other things can best be shown on the map, such as the relationship to other places in the vicinity. While such information can support the wayfinding process, it is typically not part of an everyday route description given by a stranger in the street, and we can find our way without it.

In general, it seems that human cognition is fairly flexible with respect to different types of input. The modules in our minds can skilfully use information from diverse sources and then come up with similar outcomes (more or less) independent of the representation format. This is not to say that it doesn't matter if we haven't got access to some kind of input. Blind people, for instance, are hampered by the lack of vision simply because visual information is incredibly rich and ubiquitous; it is notoriously hard to compensate for this through other sources.

As long as the same information is equally presented through different media, the mind can cope with it equally. This may mean improved performance in other areas, such as better listening skills with blind people (Röder & Rösler, 2003). In reality, it is unfortunately rather hard to provide the exact same information through different channels. Vision manages to capture many details at once, while auditory or tactile information must necessarily be presented piecemeal, sequentially, in what can be a laborious and awkward process.

In addition, there are various elements inherent to language that make language different from mental concepts (Levinson, 1997). Languages differ in how they express reality, and they sometimes leave unexpected gaps for expression. Not all kinds of thoughts (or knowledge) can easily be put into words. Try to describe a family member's face, which you know really well and will be able to recognise in milliseconds. Or try to capture a strongly emotional experience adequately: you will soon find that the few terms in the lexicon that are available to express emotions are ridiculously inadequate.

Clearly, language and thoughts aren't the same. We can think and feel things for which we have no words, and different input modes facilitate different types of thoughts. In that sense, language is just one way of evoking, or expressing, thoughts and thought processes. Arguably however, it is the most complex and developed one – accessible to everyone on the planet in one form or other, and used incessantly for the communication of thoughts, and more. While the limitations of language can't be denied, no other medium of communication has proved equally flexible and useful for a multitude of purposes.

But how do language and thought interrelate? Does a person's language perhaps even *shape* the way the person thinks, as Whorf (1941) suggested? Whorf's idea was that language provides us with a set of patterns that determine the way we think. He suggested that if a language represents the world in a particular way, this will fundamentally affect how the speakers of this language think about and understand the world. In a nutshell, Whorf suggested that our minds and thought processes are constrained by our language, conditioned by its structure.

This general idea has been debated at length in many different ways (e.g. Nuyts & Pederson, 1997). And many of the insights that inform the interpretation of discourse in CODA have been inspired by Whorfian ideas in some way or other (see Chapter 3). CODA, as such, is about how language represents thought rather than how thought is shaped or constrained by language, but both aspects belong together: the relationship between thought and language is complex and bidirectional; neither can be fully understood entirely without the other.

To take just one example, Lakoff and Johnson (1980) famously showed how much our thinking is affected by *metaphors* in our language. In English (and related languages), we consistently talk about *arguments* in terms of *war*, *time* in terms of *space*, *love* in terms of a *journey*, and so on – and these concepts shape the way we conceive of them, the way we organise our lives. Even prepositions like *on* and *over* have certain associations that are carried over to more abstract domains (Tyler & Evans, 2003), for instance when we say *on the job* or *over £100*. All of these insights feed into the question of how we *think* in relation to *language*, and how the study of linguistic structures and usage preferences can guide our understanding of human cognition.

By now, much insight has been gained as to how languages differ in representing thought, and in representing how humans understand the world. After nearly eighty years of research in the wake of Whorf's (1941) suggestions, it is now undeniable that language and cognition are intricately connected and interdependent, yet obviously distinct. The mutual influence is strong and has been confirmed and specified in many areas. The way humans think influences the way language has evolved, and the language used in a culture affects thought in that culture. Effects of these processes can be seen through increasing evidence that cognitive flexibility is enhanced through *bilingualism* (Adesope et al., 2010). Learning and speaking more than one language does not only increase metalinguistic awareness, but comes with a range of other benefits for thinking, such as better attention and working memory.

Most research on language and thought deals with linguistic *structure* in relation to conceptual structure, that is, with the general ways in which language resembles thought, across speakers and typically abstracting from individual differences. CODA takes these rich and varied insights as resources that enable a close, well-informed look at specific uses of language: the analysis of language *use* in relation to *current* cognitive phenomena. If previous research shows that a particular type of linguistic construction reflects a particular way of thinking *in general*, then any *specific* instance of using this construction (such as talking about love in terms of a journey) reflects that this way of thinking is *currently* relevant, currently being activated by the speaker.

Altogether, we can conclude that language and thought are deeply interconnected. Our language may not strictly determine the way we think, but it certainly matters for our thoughts what kind of repertory our language makes available in a certain context. The next section will look at the areas where such considerations can lead to further insights about the nature of human cognition, using language analysis in specific situations rather than focusing on generalised linguistic phenomena.

1.2   Areas of Application for CODA

If language is closely related to thought, it must be useful to look at language in order to find out about thought – use language, to an extent, as a window to the mind. This is the basic tenet in cognitive linguistics, which primarily looks at language as a system – and it is also the starting point for CODA, which looks at how we *use language* to express our thoughts. In the following we will start with general considerations about using language, and then outline the two main areas for CODA applications – mental representations and complex cognitive processes.

1.2.1   Using Language to Express Our Thoughts

Whenever we use language, we make a choice from the general repertory of the language we are using, based on the ways in which our language represents our thought patterns in general. Such a choice will always be meaningful, as pointed out by linguists across various theoretical approaches (e.g. Brennan & Clark, 1996; Fontaine, Bartlett, & O'Grady, 2013). In particular, our linguistic choices relate systematically to the ways in which we *think* about the things we *talk* about. Consider the difference in the following two positive answers to the same question about 'Johnny':

Example 1.2   Johnny is a well-educated, friendly person with polite manners and a lot of knowledge.

Example 1.3   Johnny? Oh, Johnny. He's my best friend! What would I do without him?

While the number of words in the two utterances is the same, and both appraisals are clearly positive, there is a fundamental difference here that any speaker of English will immediately notice. Intuitively, it is strikingly obvious – though it isn't said directly – that the relationship between the speaker and Johnny must be a lot closer in Example 1.3 than in Example 1.2. Somehow the description seems very distant in Example 1.2, despite the emphasis on positive character traits, and despite the fact that we actually get more information about Johnny in Example 1.2 than we do in Example 1.3. To gain a clearer idea about why this intuition jumps at the reader, we need to go beyond word counts (equal), feature polarity (everything is positive), or content (more information details are given in the more *distant* version). What kinds of factors, exactly, reflect the difference in interpersonal distance that the reader intuitively perceives?

The answer lies in a close look at combinations of linguistic features that include syntactic (or *mood*) structure, lexical choices, reference types, and modality. Example 1.2 has a relatively complex declarative clause structure that invokes the idea of formal, written language, whereas Example 1.3 has a series of brief exclamations, with only one short declarative sentence fol-lowed by an exclamation mark. Example 1.2 employs a coherent series of formal lexical items that share the semantic field of positive personal judge-ment (well-educated, friendly, polite, a lot of knowledge), whereas Example 1.3 does very little to evaluate the person himself, other than as a 'friend'. Example 1.2 refers to Johnny just once, whereas Example 1.3 mentions the name twice and adds two further references through personal pronouns (he/him), thus emphasising the link to the person linguistically. And, perhaps unexpectedly, we can spot the additional use of two first-person pronouns (my/I), despite the fact that the question concerned Johnny, not the speaker: this supports the conceptual connection. Example 1.2 represents factual infor-mation in a concise manner, whereas Example 1.3 uses the modal 'would' to construe an alternative world – leaving it to the addressee to infer how miser-able such a world would be.

Together, these linguistic features convey a crucial fact about the speaker's mind that does not get direct expression in language: that the speaker does not only think positively about Johnny, but actually *feels close to him*. This is what speakers of English would intuitively grasp, based on their knowledge of the linguistic system in English: if the speaker of Example 1.3 felt less close to Johnny, they would not make these linguistic choices; they would find other ways of talking positively about him, as done in Example 1.2. How this implicit communication of thoughts or emotions works can be derived from a close look at the linguistic choices made. This is facilitated by the contrast between two distinct examples, because the contrast highlights the system of choices avail-able in this situation.

This short example illustrates the basic tenet in CODA: the idea that speakers always make choices whenever they use language. They choose from the network of available options whatever seems most fitting for the situation at hand. This will also depend on who they are. Johnny's best friend would only choose Example 1.2 for an answer in a fairly formal context, whereas someone who has only spoken to Johnny a couple of times would typically not dream of using Example 1.3 in any situation.

There are, of course, limits to this logic. We do not, in all situations, simply represent our thoughts and feelings using the most accurate set of linguistic choices and features. We sometimes make errors, and there are certain general limits to our ability and readiness to 'speak our minds'. The strongest mediating factor, arguably, can be subsumed in terms of *communicative intent*. Whatever we say has a lot to do with whatever we want to communicate to our interaction partner in a given situation. For this reason, it is entirely possible to use Example 1.3 in spite of feeling rather distant to Johnny. Example 1.3 could be used sarcastically, or with the intention of creating a false impression.

Communication affects our linguistic choices at all levels, at all times. Language use without communication is difficult to imagine; there are not many occasions where we speak without intending to communicate. Communicative intent therefore needs to be taken into account in any language analysis – including CODA, despite the fact that CODA primarily looks at the *cognitive* aspects of language use. Nevertheless, this is not a book about communication; there are numerous very useful publications available on this topic (e.g. Clark, 1996; Sperber & Wilson, 1986; Wachsmuth et al., 2013, and many others).

CODA is typically applied for situations in which the communication aspect is kept at a minor level or controlled, either because communication is not relevant (see Chapters 7 and 8), or because the parameters of communication are narrowly defined by the researcher. This is true for the two core application areas of CODA: *mental representation* and *complex cognitive processes*, which we will deal with shortly. However, CODA can also be used to address the interplay of cognitive and communicative aspects in dialogue. This is a major extended application area of CODA that adds another layer to the analyst's challenge. We will return to these issues in Chapter 7.

So what exactly is this method good for? Broadly speaking, anything that can be meaningfully verbalised by speakers can be meaningfully analysed using systematic linguistic methods. However, two main areas stand out as particularly relevant for CODA: mental representations and complex cognitive processes. *Mental representation* means how we think about a scene, how we perceive or remember events, and the like. *Complex cognitive processes* pertain to more complicated challenges such as problem solving or decision making. When we express our thoughts while dealing with such a challenge, our language will reflect what aspects we think about first, what kinds of things we take seriously, and so on.

Both of these areas have rich traditions in research, going in very different directions (see Chapter 2); CODA adds another perspective to them. Studies in both of these areas have often related to language in some way, but traditionally they rarely include a systematic analysis of linguistic choices.

In sum, we can identify each instance of discourse as a meaningful choice from a network of options, namely the repertory of the linguistic system in the speaker's mind. Choices reflect aspects of thoughts and feelings, along with communicative intent and relevance in a specific context. This is particularly relevant when we use language to express mental representations or complex cognitive processes. We will now look more closely at each of these areas in turn.

1.2.2   Mental Representations

Understanding mental representations means understanding how we make sense of what we see or hear, and how we remember things. This is a very broad field, which opens up a wide range of interesting questions to ask and things to discover. We can confront speakers with any kind of scene, shown in the real world or depicted on a piece of paper or on a screen; it can be a static scene or an event that unfolds gradually, perhaps involving a series of pictures or a continuous film. We can ask them to describe what they see, to explain it to somebody else, to remember and later recall, or to suggest changes to what they see. In each case, features of the perceived situation will systematically affect the linguistic representation.

However, simply looking at the language used will not lead to any deeper insights unless there is a theoretical reason for looking at certain aspects of the language. That is, any study in the area of mental representation must be based on a clear research question that can be addressed by language analysis.

With CODA, a very basic underlying research goal across all application areas is to find out more about how humans *think*. In the area of mental representation, CODA opens up new perspectives by adding to and combining insights from traditional approaches. For instance, there is little overlap between the three traditions of psycholinguistics, cognitive linguistics, and systemic functional linguistics (SFL). Studies that take a psycholinguistic experimental approach rarely draw from insights in theoretical cognitive linguistics that could illuminate the conceptual implications of certain empirical results. And because the idea of systemic choice is not as prominent in psycholinguistics as it is in SFL, psycholinguistic experimental designs often severely restrict the choices that speakers can make in the first place. This makes it impossible to explore the significance of meaningful choice patterns across speakers, beyond those preselected by the researcher.

Let's look at an example. If we consider the world around us, we almost inevitably need to think about *space*. Our world consists of space filled by objects and people; their relationships change over time, and they may have a huge relevance to humans in their everyday life, depending on the contexts and situations in which they occur. Spatial relationships are everywhere, and they matter to us. Within cognitive science, the understanding of spatial relationships is central.

Traditionally, research in psycholinguistics and psychology aims to reduce the natural complexity of spatial relationships to highly abstract scenes and situations. For instance, Franklin, Henkel, and Zangas (1995) positioned participants in a circular room and asked them to point to objects in various directions, as well as to describe their positions. Such a scenario provides a controlled environment in which particular factors that influence the outcomes can be determined. This is highly informative for assessing some aspects of human concepts of space. However, language production studies in this tradition are not designed to highlight speakers' choices out of the entire range of available options. Instead, the range of what participants are allowed to say is typically restricted; for instance, in Franklin et al.'s (1995) study, they were not allowed to use compass or clock directions.

Some studies do allow for language use in a less restricted way, and this brings them closer to the tenets of CODA. For instance, Ehrich and Koster (1983) identified systematic patterns in speakers' descriptions of living room arrangements, and Carroll and von Stutterheim (1993) presented a cross-linguistic comparison of speakers' preference when describing spatial configurations. Taking these insights as a starting point, we (Andonova, Tenbrink, & Coventry, 2010; Tenbrink, Coventry, & Andonova, 2011b) looked further into spatial relationships in complex situations, as follows.

We were particularly interested in how people describe where objects are within a complex configuration, and also how they are oriented (for instance *facing the wall*). Our scenario involved fifteen pieces of doll's house furniture that were arranged on a tray. The tray was placed in front of participants, and they were asked to describe the arrangement so that another person would be able to rearrange the pieces in the same way. This task may sound easy, but actually it involves quite a few challenges, such as structuring the description in a useful way, and deciding on a perspective that would work for each object. Consider the following example description, translated from our original German data:

Example 1.4   Okay, so on the left side of the room there is an armchair with a yellow cushion in the bottom left corner. And in front of this armchair there is a rack with red rungs. And behind this rack there is a sofa with a yellow cushion. To the right of this sofa, not very far away, there is a red chair. And below this red chair there is, again, another red chair.

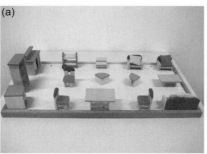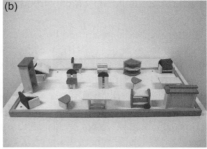

Figure 1.1 Furniture item arrangement used in Andonova et al. (2010) and Tenbrink et al. (2011b).
The arrangement in (a) includes some functionally meaningful groups of objects, but the one in (b) doesn't.

And so on. Were you able to follow this description, so far? Would you be able to arrange the items, and would you be confident that they are placed correctly? If not, you're not alone. It is very difficult to create a spatial description that is entirely clear and unambiguous, and which doesn't leave some questions open, such as: how far are the objects apart? Which perspective is used with the words *in front of* – is it in front of the armchair's seat, or do I use my own view on the scene? What is meant by *below* – should I be stacking the objects on top of each other? Just as in other contexts, language doesn't always solve these problems in a very direct way; utterances are underspecified and ambiguous in many ways (Carston, 2002). No matter how you put it, there may always be other (and possibly better) ways of saying it. Therefore, it is very interesting to look at the choices that speakers make in spatial description.

What helps us in our everyday life, when we talk about spatial relationships, is the fact that objects are sometimes functionally related to each other (Carlson & van der Zee, 2005; Coventry & Garrod, 2004). For instance, if chairs are arranged around a table, it is very easy to think of the whole group of objects as a dining-room arrangement. In a description, people would therefore describe the group as a whole, rather than as individual, unrelated objects. We thought that this aspect could be very relevant for our study, and so we used two different configurations of furniture items. In one case (Figure 1.1(a)), some groups of objects were arranged in a meaningful way, such as a living room table with several armchairs around it. In the other case (Figure 1.1(b)), no such functional relationships were included. And indeed, we found that this influenced the descriptions in interesting ways. If objects were arranged in meaningful groups, they were described in a different order than if there were no functional relationships. Also, the amount of detail was affected, and whether people mentioned in which direction objects were facing (Andonova et al., 2010).

After we had determined how functional relationships affected descriptions in Andonova et al. (2010), we then wondered what other kinds of thought patterns we might find reflected in the linguistic data. In Tenbrink et al. (2011b) we started by spelling out the whole range of what speakers did in this scenario, and then showed how often they made specific linguistic and conceptual choices. What kinds of information did they provide about location and orientation of objects? What kinds of things did they relate specific objects to in order to describe where they are? For instance, they could refer to another object, as in *the chair is to the left of the table*, or they could refer to the room's shape or features, as in *the chair is on the left side* (or *wall*). What kinds of perspective did they use – did they stick to their own point of view, or did they sometimes use an object's sides, such as the front side of a chair for *in front of the chair*?

By looking closely at speakers' typical choices in these respects, we could identify frequent strategies of description – and also several cases where individual speakers did something completely different. For instance, most speakers very clearly went with their own perspective throughout most of their descriptions, without changing to any other perspective out of the overall range of options. This was independent of whether the array included functional relationships or not.

However, sometimes this unwritten rule was broken locally, based on particular features within the configuration. If objects had very clear intrinsic front and back sides, they often prompted speakers to disregard their own perspective – but only when these objects were facing towards the right or left, from the speaker's point of view. Thus, if a cupboard's doors faced to the speaker's right, the speaker might mention a *table in front of the cupboard* – even though the table would be on the *right* of the cupboard from the speaker's point of view. And another interesting exception was one single speaker who very rarely used his own perspective at all, because he actually used compass directions such as *north* and *south*; this was totally unexpected in this table-top scenario. These were very interesting deviations from an otherwise consistent description strategy across speakers, which we could not have predicted from earlier research in the area.

People not only typically used one consistent perspective, but they also had a range of other systematic preferences. For instance, they usually described objects in relation to the room and its walls, as well as objects mentioned directly before. Other, earlier-mentioned objects were rarely used for reference, and speakers also did not often refer to their own position. Interestingly, this pattern was reversed when describing where objects were facing. Although speakers rarely said *the chair is in front of me*, they did very often say things like *the chair is facing towards me*. Clearly, they were aware that basically all objects were located more or less in front of them, so this wouldn't have been very informative. In contrast, the objects' orientation could be described in this way without leading to any obvious ambiguity.

Altogether, these two publications report a wide range of qualitative and quantitative analyses based on our corpus of doll's house furniture arrangement descriptions. This helps us to understand better how people perceive and think about the spatial relationships in a complex scene, to the extent that this is reflected in language. Note that these descriptions of doll's house furniture arrangements did not involve a dialogue partner; however, we (Tenbrink et al., 2008, 2017) also carried this line of research further to address how people describe dolls' house furniture arrangements to each other (see Chapter 7 for details).

As we can see in this example, the verbal expression of mental representations can get quite complex and intricate, especially with increasing complexity of the situation that is represented. And so far, we have only talked about static *scenes*. Observing, memorising, and describing dynamic *events* can add various exciting layers to this kind of analysis. For instance, when people report and describe events, they usually do so by providing causal links – not just temporal order. If events are described as following each other, they very often do so for a reason: if Peter sees Mary on the opposite side of the road and *then* starts walking across the road, this is probably *because* he wants to talk to her.

However, this does not always get expressed in language directly. People might just say things like *When Peter saw Mary on the other side of the road, he walked across to her.* This would typically imply that Peter walked across to her *because* (not just, coincidentally, *when*) he saw Mary. Such causal inferences happen in the minds of humans, they are made very easily and very quickly, whether consciously or subconsciously. The language people use reflects such inferences to some extent. In fact, some linguistic items such as *after* very often imply causal connections, even though they only represent the temporal aspects directly (Tenbrink & Schilder, 2003).

Generally, analysing verbal descriptions of perceived or remembered events can provide a wide range of insights about how such events are represented in the speakers' minds. For instance, Zacks, Tversky, and Iyer (2001) looked into the ways in which people think about the structure of events shown in videos. They found that the participants structured the events in their minds in a hierarchical way, guided by the goals that were achieved within a scene. Since overarching goals can normally be achieved by sequentially completing some relevant subtasks, a hierarchical structure helps to understand purposes of actions – or the 'meaning' of events and sub-events in context. This hierarchical structure was reflected both by how people segmented the videos and by how they described them verbally.

In sum, the analysis of mental representations is a very broad field, which encompasses static scenes as well as events, and pertains to perception as well as memory. Across these diverse scenarios, CODA can be used to enhance the understanding of how we mentally represent the world we perceive and remember.

1.2.3   Complex Cognitive Processes

So far, we have looked at how people conceptualise and describe things they perceive or remember. Such mental representations can be complex, yet they do not involve what psychologists would call *complex cognitive processes*. This is because mental representations simply concern how we naturally conceive of things, without needing to solve a problem or make a decision. In other words, there is no directly associated challenge or *action* in the mind. We can observe a complex scene or an entire film completely passively, without a care in the world, without trying to get at some solution in any sense. The only task in such situations is the task given to the participants in our experimental studies, designed to obtain an external representation of the internal concepts that we develop in our minds, based on what we perceive. This kind of task does not normally pose any challenge to experimental participants.

In the case of complex cognitive processes, in contrast, people actively seek some kind of solution, depending on the task. This involves developing relevant thoughts over time, as they come to mind while accomplishing the task. In cognitive psychology, such sequential thought processes have been of great interest for many decades, and researchers have sought to identify relevant patterns of thought related to a range of different tasks. Mainly, these tasks fall into the two areas of *problem solving* (Newell & Simon, 1972) and *decision making* (Ranyard, Crozier, & Svenson, 1997). These areas are interrelated, but not identical: making a decision, such as which company to invest in, can come with a range of sub-problems to solve. And solving a problem, such as how to cross a river without a bridge, might involve a range of decisions along the way. Understanding how people solve problems and make decisions is central to understanding who we are: it explains how and why we do the things we do, based on decisions we make, related to the everyday challenges and problems in life.

When solving complex tasks of problem solving and decision making, people are normally to a large extent aware of their thought processes, and so they find it relatively easy to put them into words. (Try it out: how many windows are there in a house that you know very well, for instance the one you grew up in? Say your thoughts out loud until you come up with a number.) For this reason, research in psychology has an extensive tradition of using language data to access solution paths to complex cognitive tasks. This is done by asking people to *think aloud* during such tasks, or to provide a *retrospective report* of what they remember thinking while they solved the problem. The resulting language data are called *verbal protocols*; the methodology is described in depth in Ericsson and Simon (1993) and is based on early work by Newell and Simon (1972).

It is important to note that the method involves a range of well-considered procedures, going well beyond simply (informally) asking people how they solved the task at hand. We will get back to relevant methodological concerns in Chapter 8. The method spelled out by Ericsson and Simon (1993) has over the past decades been widely used across many different domains, including spatial cognition (Gugerty & Rodes, 2007), medical areas (Kuipers, Moskowitz, & Kassirer, 1988), design studies (Purcell & Gero, 1998), reading research (Afflerbach & Johnston, 1984), usability (Krahmer & Ummelen, 2004), and many more.

Conventionally, analysing verbal protocols in psychology means focusing (primarily) on content. Such analysis targets precisely those aspects that the speakers are themselves aware of (or 'heed', in the words of Ericsson & Simon, 1993), such as specific thought processes, strategies, problem-solving steps, or criteria for making decisions. Chapter 2 will take a closer look at what these are – what kinds of cognitive processes can be expected to be found in verbal protocols. Experts in a particular problem domain who are familiar with theoretical insights and prior findings in the field can often gain very specific insights just by examining the content of verbal reports. There are specific methods for doing this systematically (Krippendorff, 2012 – we will take a closer look in Chapter 8). Thorough content analysis should always be the first step when analysing verbal protocols, and this often leads to well-founded specific insights about the cognitive processes involved (see, for instance, a detailed script analysis in Kuipers & Kassirer, 1984).

However, content is not all that we can gain from verbal protocols. Just as with verbal representations of visual scenes and events, *how* people formulate their thoughts might be as revealing as *what* they say. In traditional verbal protocol analysis, linguistic structure has rarely been taken into account. Since most researchers in this tradition have been trained as psychologists, not linguists, there is typically little awareness of the implications of particular ways of saying things. Here, CODA provides a substantial step forward from established verbal protocol analysis procedures, and enhances them in several ways. CODA points to the cognitive significance of specific linguistic features that are used to express certain contents. These insights can be used to operationalise, validate, and interpret content categories: if a particular type of content is expressed regularly in a particular way, this can be used as evidence that this is indeed a conceptual category of its own.

The identification of linguistic markers can help to make content category annotation more objective, less dependent on the individual annotator's intuitions (see Chapter 8 for procedural details). Also, insights about the language used to express a particular content category can provide valuable insights about the underlying concepts in the speaker's minds, adding to the interpretation of the content category. Apart from supporting content analysis in this way, CODA further extends the scope of analysis *beyond* content. Systematic linguistic choices can reveal cognitive aspects that are not necessarily consciously available to the speakers, and therefore do not get to be verbalised explicitly. This opens up avenues for addressing research issues that have not yet been investigated using verbal data so far.

Consider a simple example from Ericsson and Simon (1993:316ff). With respect to a task of sorting blocks on the basis of given information, a participant produced the following in the process of thinking aloud:

Example 1.5   *(. . .) a white block is further down than the black one*
and the black one is between the red and the green
white, red, black, green
I'll say then
but the green one is bottommost but one
then I'll say
white, green, black, red
instead
then the white one is bottommost (. . .)

Note that the sketchiness of this extract is fairly typical for think-aloud protocols; participants do not necessarily produce whole sentences (or readable, coherent text). Ericsson and Simon (1993) present a content-based analysis of this example, and show how the logic in the participant's thinking plays out. In particular, they distinguish the repetition of premises given in the task from novel inferences made by the speaker. They note, on the basis of this content, that most inferences start with *then*.

From a linguistic point of view, in contrast, it makes sense to start directly from the use of conjunctions such as *then*. Such markers are known to serve certain established purposes in discourse: for instance, *and* is additive, *but* is contrastive, *then* is consecutive, and so on, among other possibilities (Halliday & Matthiessen, 2014). If a speaker uses these conjunctions in the context of thinking aloud while solving a problem-solving task, this reflects how the speaker relates the verbalised insights to each other. Someone saying *then* expresses a consecutive logic between two thoughts.

Conjunctions can therefore be *expected* to yield relevant insights, and they can be used as *evidence*, based on the body of knowledge available in linguistics about such terms and structures. In this example, looking closely at where exactly the speaker says *then* could yield valuable insights concerning how the speaker conceives of decisions, insights, or actions during problem solving. Such a focus adopted in linguistic analysis provides cues to places where important cognitive steps can be expected to occur. This analysis perspective is based not just on intuition or on the common-sense interpretation of content, but relies on a straightforward operationalisation, using linguistic markers as cues.

To take another example, consider the following statement, taken from a route instruction in downtown Freiburg (Hölscher, Tenbrink, & Wiener, 2011). This was translated from a German description written by a participant; here we will treat it as though it was produced in English, to facilitate matters in our example, since it is a plausible part of an English route direction:

Example 1.6   *At the concert hall take the Sedanstraße in the direction of the theatre.*

Looking at content, the problem of how to get to the goal is solved by describing the path, referring to landmarks (concert hall) and streets. Route directions have been subject to wide-ranging analyses in spatial cognition research, as they reveal crucial aspects about how we think about space (e.g. Denis, 1997; Klein, 1979). Such analyses have primarily focused on the types of elements that are included in a route description, showing what kinds of information we need in order to find a route.

However, there's more to be gained from a route description. Take a closer look at Example 1.6. The statement starts from a reference to *the concert hall* – but where is the concert hall? This information is not part of the statement itself; the speaker must be assuming that the listener knows where it is – the location is *presupposed*, as indicated by the definite article '*the*'. There may be several reasons for such a presupposition; for instance, the location of the concert hall may be part of the earlier discourse, such as the previous sentence in the route description. More generally, a context can be assumed which has mentally disposed the speaker to start this sentence from this particular location, and to take it as *given*. As in this example, you might find it revealing to simply focus on articles when doing discourse analysis; the use of definite articles reveals what speakers take for granted in a particularly clear-cut and intuitive way.

The next reference in Example 1.6, *the Sedanstraße*, is the proper name of a street, and it is anchored within the statement (*at the concert hall*). Here the preposition *at* expresses how the speaker thinks of the relevant spatial relationship. As with many specific linguistic choices, the literature can help us determine their conceptual associations. Bateman et al. (2010) describe the preposition *at* as denoting functionally based proximity. Thus, the route describer refers to a very close connection between the concert hall and the Sedanstraße, with a functional association in the sense that the concert hall's location relates to a specific street address.

Next, the location of *the theatre* is again presupposed, which is striking as it occurs in the later part of the statement, where speakers normally package *new* information (Halliday & Matthiessen, 2014). This indicates that the theatre's location is firmly anchored in the speaker's mind, but it is not made explicit in the linguistic representation. Nevertheless, the reference to *the theatre* is used to describe the direction of the next movement: the addressee is supposed to orient towards the theatre, but is given no further information about its location. The route giver probably assumes that the wayfinder, when reaching this particular location, will be able to identify the correct direction. This is often possible based on visual clues in the environment: the theatre may be visible once they get there, or there may be signs pointing to the theatre. It is also possible that there are no alternatives, such as if the Sedanstraße happened to extend in only one direction at this location.

If all this is not the case, the wayfinder may really have a problem – but the route giver is obviously not aware of this. The route is described just in the way that it comes to mind, and information is added as far as it seems to be relevant in this particular route-giving situation. There may be all sorts of reasons for why some facts and factors are deemed relevant in a given context (Sperber & Wilson, 1986). Clearly, any description will always come with certain limits – ways in which it may not be entirely complete.

This analysis suggests that presuppositions may be fairly crucial in route descriptions, as they reflect how the speaker thinks of distant buildings such as the *theatre*. A systematic CODA analysis of this aspect would mean identifying all relevant instances of a particular type of presupposition within the verbal data of all speakers collected in an experimental context. This could, for instance, be a definite article used along with references to the *theatre*. The use of definite articles in this context may depend on various aspects related to the scenario design, for instance, familiarity with the city at hand, the intended addressee, the complexity of the route, the discourse status (i.e. previous mention) of the theatre, and the like. Such structures can be detected by systematic annotation of relevant features. And changing these aspects in the design in another experimental condition will shed even more light on the particular role of the presupposition.

Further insights can be gained by looking more closely at other factors, such as the routes chosen for the description, features of the situational context, or features of the referent. For instance, if particular environmental aspects (for instance well-known public buildings such as the theatre) are systematically presupposed more often in route descriptions than other aspects (such as marginal side roads), this would suggest that speakers think differently about public buildings to how they think about marginal side roads.

In related research, a colleague and I were interested in the strategies that people use to reduce the complexity of a spatial planning task (Tenbrink & Seifert, 2011). Our participants were given a map of Crete or, in one version of the study, a similar island with a different shape, called Cretopia. The map showed spatial relationships plus some further information about activities that could be done at particular places. Participants were then asked to plan a holiday route for a friend, with the aim to include much variation in terms of getting around and doing various activities. They were allowed to draw the route on the map, and they wrote a list of targets to be visited in a particular order. Next, they wrote a retrospective report of the problem-solving process. The study was carried out in four different versions so as to gain insights about the impact of traveling mode (car vs. bike) or the shape of the island (Crete vs. Cretopia), and so on.

The written reports were first examined with respect to content: what kinds of planning strategies did the participants mention explicitly? Next, we looked at linguistic indicators for specific planning strategies, inspired by previous findings in the relevant literature, and also (post hoc) by the data at hand. Our results showed that participants used a number of planning heuristics that were very similar to strategies found in the literature in other spatial planning contexts. For instance, they oriented towards particular spatial regions and noted where places were close together. In other cases, they mentally imagined the travel route or the environment as a whole or in part, and they avoided line crossings and detours. We will return to this aspect of the study (mentally imagining a route, based on a map) in Chapter 7.

To sum up what was laid out in this section: CODA is suitable for analysing what people say in relation to what they think, or how they conceptualise certain aspects that they perceive, remember, or currently deal with. The main areas of application are mental representations and complex cognitive processes such as problem solving and decision making. Ideally, language data are collected by sets of speakers in a controlled experimental situation, which makes it easier to identify systematic patterns in the linguistic choices made by speakers (see Chapter 8). However, there is no direct limit to the kinds of language data that can be analysed using the principles of CODA. Meaningful patterns of linguistic features can also be identified in existing corpora such as mountaineering reports (Egorova, Tenbrink, & Purves, 2015), in the think-aloud data of a single speaker (Tenbrink, 2008), in joint-action dialogues (Tenbrink et al., 2017), and in any other context that enables systematic analysis in relation to a conceptual domain or challenge.

1.3   Reliability, Generalisability, and Limits of CODA

To what extent can we trust language data? Can we really trust what people say? As we all know, people don't always say what they mean. But even if you're willing to cooperate, you might sometimes find it difficult to express your thoughts. You might feel that you're not expressing what you're thinking or feeling very clearly. Perhaps you don't really want to, or perhaps you can't – perhaps you don't have the right words to express what you think. Your language might not have perfectly suitable words in its lexicon, or your language competence may be limited. As a matter of fact, not even adult native speakers are 'perfect' in their own language – nobody knows all the words, everybody makes mistakes in writing, and sometimes we get the grammar wrong, or we have different opinions about what is right (Dąbrowska, 2012). Also, you might get to the limits of your attention span when you speak along with a given task, and this might affect how well chosen your words are when representing your thoughts. And on top of that, there may be aspects to 'thought' that you are not aware of – very rapid or subconscious processes in the brain that you will never be able to report in language.

Because of all this, there are clearly limits to the kinds of insights that we can gain from systematic language analysis. In this section, we will take a closer look at the extent to which CODA yields reliable insights, what kinds of insights can be generalised, and where the analyst must stop in order to avoid over-interpretation.

As we saw in the previous section, language data have for a long time been used to gain insights about cognitive processes, both in the area of mental representations (primarily in psycholinguistics) and in the area of complex cognitive processes (primarily in cognitive psychology). Trying to capture the entire rationale for these wide research traditions would take a few more books, so we'll focus here on several central aspects that are particularly relevant to CODA.

1.3.1   What Kinds of Aspects of Language Use Can We Trust?

One of the main motivations for doing CODA is to add weight and reliability to the analysis of content. CODA means going beyond content analysis in a range of ways. That is, the primary contribution of CODA does not concern *what* people say, but rather, *how* they formulate their thought processes. If we collect data in a controlled experimental setting, and several speakers independently express a thought or thought process in a similar way, then there may be an interesting reason for that. If certain linguistic patterns are associated with a certain thought category, this means moving away from mere intuition when looking at what kinds of thoughts people express.

Patterns of linguistic features that are shared across a range of speakers are typically meaningful in relation to the given situation. This is especially clear if statistically significant differences can be identified, but a qualitative or descriptive pattern in itself can be meaningful, too (see Chapter 8 for more details). The interpretation of such patterns can be substantially supported by established findings on language, drawing on a wide range of relevant theoretical and empirical resources. This approach adds a substantial layer of reliability to the intuitive interpretation of verbalised thoughts.

1.3.2 Why Can We Trust Them?

People reporting their thoughts may not always wish to be entirely truthful or complete – there may be aspects in their thought processes that they do not wish to share. In such cases they might focus on other things to report. Crucially however, they will be unable to report anything that they have not even thought of. To take an extreme example, imagine a situation in which you are confronted with the problem of interpreting the following formula:

$$P_r = \frac{P_t \lambda^2 g_t g_r \sigma_b f^4}{(4\pi)^3 r^4}$$

Example 1.7   The Bistatic Radar Equation defines the received power when radio waves are transmitted from one site and reflected from an object before reaching the receiver.

Example 1.8   This must be a mathematic formula of some kind, I think it defines a value called P.

Would you be able to come up with anything resembling the statement in Example 1.7? Most likely, unless you're a genuine expert in the field, your interpretation of the formula would be far more general, perhaps rather like Example 1.8. Note that Example 1.7 is far more specific and far more confident in style, containing no linguistic markers of uncertainty like the items *must*, *some kind*, and *I think* in Example 1.8. While uncertainty can to some extent be feigned, expertise cannot: the level of specific knowledge that is reflected in Example 1.7, if accurate, must represent expert knowledge (unless the speaker had access to a reliable information source). The accuracy of expertise can be assessed based on the given task; the analyst will be able to determine to what extent a statement like Example 1.7 is correct.

Moreover, an expert trying to mislead the audience with respect to the given task would be more likely to provide different, misleading, content; people rarely 'lie' about linguistic uncertainty markers such as *must*, *some kind*, and *I think*. Nevertheless, it is advisable to err on the side of caution: if verbalisations remain general and vague, this does not necessarily mean that the speaker is unable to provide more detailed and specific responses. There might be other factors in the situation that keep them from doing that. However, it is still often enlightening in an empirical scenario to look at levels of specificity across speakers. If a factor in a particular condition (such as expertise or verbal ability) systematically leads to more specific and accurate responses, this does reflect a likely difference in the underlying conceptualisations. We will get back to issues related to granularity and certainty in Chapter 5.

Note also that experimental participants typically do try to comply with the researcher's aims, as experience over many decades of research in empirical settings shows (e.g. Ericsson & Simon, 1993). In fact, this assumption is the basis for doing any empirical research in the first place – if we couldn't trust participants at all, there would be little a researcher could do. If a person reports their thoughts during a problem-solving process, it is rather unlikely that they talk about a strategy that they actually find completely irrelevant and would never really use, while using a completely different one secretly in their minds, without mentioning it in any way.

In fact, the well-established central 'bottleneck' in attentional processes may make this virtually impossible (Pashler, 1984), pushing participants towards honesty. While they may be unable to put all of their thought processes adequately into words, the strategies that they do talk about must at least play a role in their problem-solving process – and any major strategy or problem-solving step that they are aware of will normally find their way into language in some way. If a participant aimed to consciously mislead the researcher, there would have to be a reason for that. In some scenarios participants may be more likely to aim to hide their real thoughts than normally – for instance, if asked about a sensitive issue that humans are typically ashamed of. Such issues need to be taken into account in any experimental design.

In addition, CODA means looking at aspects that participants will not be aware of, such as patterns in the features of linguistic choices. Consider the travel planning scenario described in Section 1.2.3 (Tenbrink & Seifert, 2011). A purposefully misleading response would have to include references to conceptual aspects that weren't actually relevant to the speaker. An utterance like 'I have decided to cross Crete on the coast west of Heraklion' indicates a cognitive focus on a spatial region (the coast west of Heraklion), among other aspects. It is hard to imagine that this participant actually used a different planning strategy in which spatial regions were completely irrelevant. This would not make sense in this context. This is primarily due to the fact that the *content* of this utterance (crossing Crete on the coast west of Heraklion) is not in the main focus of analysis, but rather the underlying concepts that get to be expressed in language – and these are hard to fake.

To take another example, imagine a researcher interested in the kind of perspective adopted when describing a spatial scene (similar to Tenbrink et al., 2011b, as shown in Section 1.2.2). If they directly *asked* participants about the perspectives that they adopt, they might get unreliable responses – people might not know which perspective they use, they might not understand the concept, or they might not want to say. However, if the researcher instead asks the participants to *describe* the scene, participants will automatically adopt a perspective, probably without thinking about it. The perspective they choose will be expressed in language, either explicitly (as in *The ball is to the right of the table from my point of view*) or (more likely) implicitly (as in *The ball is to the right of the table*). Through their knowledge of the scene, the analyst will then be able to derive the underlying perspective reliably.

1.3.3   To What Extent Can We Generalise CODA-Based Insights?

Whenever patterns of language are found in relation to a specific context, it is vital to specify the features of this specific context, and to remain aware of them throughout the interpretation of verbal data. It is very easy to fall into the trap of overgeneralising insights gained from experimental settings, as they are normally motivated from a more overarching background – and the setting is chosen to represent this more general idea. However, linguistic choices are made on the basis of the *exact* situation that is perceived by the speaker. Keeping the experimental context constant – including the exact wording used to explain the experimental task – is therefore essential wherever data are collected from more than one person. This is crucial in any empirical setting, but it might be even more crucial for CODA. Fine-grained systematic language data analysis across speakers makes most sense with a strict procedure, even though the content of speakers' verbalisations may roughly remain the same even if the instruction is worded slightly flexibly.

To take a famous example from the spatial domain, based on one seminal study by Linde and Labov (1975), it was widely believed for decades that speakers normally describe spatial scenes from the perspective of an 'imaginary wanderer' who walks through the scene. The limits of generalisability were unknown, and have remained largely unexplored to this day. However, our study described above (Tenbrink et al., 2011b) strongly suggests that the imaginary wanderer may at least depend on scale. In our table-top doll's house furniture scenario, none of the participants imagined walking through the scene, although it would have been possible to imagine mentally scaling up to a real furniture setting.

Many results gained through CODA are actually of a more qualitative nature, raising fewer concerns about generalisability. Qualitative analysis means showing that certain phenomena exist and how they work. For instance, in our route planning study (Tenbrink & Seifert, 2011) we demonstrated how participants used and combined a range of conceptual strategies that had so far only been identified for other kinds of tasks. Based on these insights, it is then a meaningful next step to ask under what (generalised) kinds of circumstances speakers regularly use these strategies, and when they don't; this is likely to reach far beyond the specific context of planning a holiday trip on Crete for a friend.

1.3.4   What Are the Limits of Language Analysis Using CODA?

Despite the wide range of things that we can learn through a close analysis of linguistic patterns beyond content, it is important to be aware of the kinds of cognitive processes that will not get any expression in language. This limits the scope of research questions that can be meaningfully addressed via language analysis. In general, in terms of cognitive neuroscience, only non-automatic cognitive processes will get into language in some way. Automatic cognitive processes are consciously inaccessible to such an extent that they won't ever be verbalised. This includes such things as memory retrieval – how, exactly, do we extract memories from our minds? Even when we do this consciously – trying to remember the details of an earlier experience – it is very hard to put into words what we are *doing* in order to retrieve these memories.

Or recognition – what are the cognitive processes that enable us to know that we have seen a person or object before? We may be able to identify features that we remember, or situations in which we have seen them. But the cognitive process of recognition itself will not be verbalisable.

Or automated procedures – what goes on in our minds when we ride a bicycle? If you have ever tried to explain how to ride a bike, you will have noticed how difficult it is to describe in words what our bodies achieve, or how exactly they achieve it. We learn to do such things by observation and practice, and then we just *know*.

Or sudden insights or realisations – what exactly led us to suddenly 'see' or understand something that we didn't a moment ago? Some of these cognitive effects can be reported after the fact, as far as we remember them, that is, to the extent that they leave a trace in short-term memory (Ericsson & Simon, 1993). Also, think-aloud data may to some extent reflect cognitively crucial moments by subtle features such as hesitation markers, pauses, changes in intonation, and the like. Such linguistic features do not directly express the low-level cognitive processes themselves, but they can certainly reflect that something important has been going on. However, such features are subtle and can have multiple reasons and purposes, both in terms of cognition and in terms of communication.

Because it is important to have a clear understanding of what one might expect to derive from verbal data through CODA, we will return to these issues in Chapter 2. For now, let's note that the overall field of cognitive science is rather wide; much research in the field concerns lower levels of cognitive processing that will not find any reflection in language, and will therefore need to be addressed in different ways.

There are also some limits within the realm of higher-level cognitive processes, of the kind that can in principle be reflected in language. Some participants may not actually be aware of the thought processes and strategies that they adopt, or they may first adopt them implicitly, and only later realise that they are doing so – which is when they start reporting them verbally (Siegler & Stern, 1998). However, this is where CODA can make a valuable contribution, because patterns of language use often reveal more than the speakers realise themselves, in particular if choices are related to specific (implicit) aspects of the task in ways that speakers are unaware of.

For instance, the situation may constrain preferred perspective choices, guide the cognitive focus of attention, and so on – as in the examples discussed in this chapter (and there will be many more in the following chapters). None of these pertain to directly verbalised conceptual strategies on the part of the speakers, and therefore the speakers do not actually need to be consciously aware of them, or be able to report them on request. On the other hand, these factors do not directly reflect mental activities at a neuronal level either. Implicit aspects such as these represent an intermediate cognitive level that is reflected in the structure of linguistic representations, and that is accessible to systematic analysis that takes into account the range of variability available to speakers.

To sum up, in this chapter we have explored the background for CODA and its motivation and scope in a range of ways. We have found that language is intricately related to thought, and that this has been recognised and utilised in a wide range of ways in the literature. We have taken a closer look at the kinds of linguistic data that can be meaningfully addressed using CODA; these fall into the main areas of mental representation and complex cognitive processes. Finally, we discussed the extent to which linguistic data analysis of this kind can be reliable in terms of informing us about what goes on in the human mind.

2   Language as a Representation of Thought

Chapter 1 laid out the general scope for CODA against the background of several approaches to the relationship between language and thought in the literature. As we saw, language analysis is often used as a 'window' to the mind to address a wide variety of research questions, many of which relate to mental representations or complex cognitive processes. This chapter explores the associated research and methodologies in more depth, in relation to CODA.

There are two main ways in which language is seen as a representation of thought. Either you can think of the *system* of language in a static way, or you can think of how the system is *used* by speakers to express their thoughts, and what happens in their minds as they do so. Looking at the system itself, some approaches primarily explore how linguistic structure represents cognitive structure; specific aspects of the linguistic system are identified as expressing specific aspects of thought. This leads to theories about language(s) and linguistic structure(s) in relation to the mind. For purposes of CODA, two of these theories are particularly useful, although they have rarely been combined, and they are also based on very different assumptions: cognitive linguistics and Systemic Functional Grammar. As these theories represent central resources for CODA, they will be addressed separately in the next chapter, along with a third: the broader field of discourse analysis, which includes a wide range of methods for analysing language in use, for diverse purposes besides accessing cognition. Doing discourse analysis to access cognition means doing CODA, bringing these various resources together; this is what this book is about.

In this chapter, we look at the wider range of approaches that explore *language in use* in order to access cognition, that is, that regard discourse as a representation of thought. We start with an overview of methodologies and look at some related projects and findings, and then return to the two major areas of research in which, as pointed out in Chapter 1, the use of language is regularly used to access aspects of cognition: psycholinguistics and cognitive psychology.

2.1 Research on the Use of Language to Represent Thought: A Brief Overview

This section will first take a brief look at the overall research field, and then zoom in to one particular domain: spatial language and cognition.

2.1.1 Sketching the Field

Language can be used and investigated in a vast range of ways. This includes spontaneous natural discourse, in all sorts of variations. Everything can be varied: how many people are talking? Who is talking to whom? Men to men, women to women, or a mix? What is their age, their social background, their culture? What are they talking about? Are they actually talking, or are they writing – or using digital media to chat or post messages? What is the situation, the context in which they are communicating? What are they looking at? What are they thinking about? What is relevant for the current speaker? And so on.

All of these factors will affect how people use language, how they speak or write, and how they choose their words. This has led to wide-ranging findings using methods of sociolinguistics, Critical Discourse Analysis, conversation analysis, pragmatics, and more. Typically, the aim in such work is to find out how people use language in specific situations or locations, often combined with a particular analysis perspective: what are the linguistic features of a particular text type? Do men talk differently from women? How do people use language to manipulate others? How do they display their power and superiority – or else their deference or lack of power? And so on.

Apart from looking at patterns in available resources of natural discourse, there is the option of collecting linguistic data in controlled experimental contexts, where the variability of language use is restricted in some ways for a particular research purpose. This is done, for instance, in experimental pragmatics (Noveck & Sperber, 2006) and in psycholinguistic approaches, which we will look at in Section 2.2. Clearly, as soon as some restriction is imposed on the speaker, their choices will be narrowed down; controlled studies seek this effect, but it doesn't necessarily correspond to natural language use. Also, the presence of a researcher collecting data will inevitably affect the language produced; this is known as the 'observer's paradox' or 'Hawthorne effect'. This cannot be entirely avoided, but it can be minimised (see Chapter 8). Any relevant effects need to be taken into account in the interpretation of language data collected in empirical studies.

Language plays a central role for many of the techniques used to gain insights about the human mind (see, e.g., Anderson, 2009), typically without building on linguistic expertise. For example, language is treated in laboratory contexts as a medium for accessing memory, mental representation, or other cognitive phenomena. This is achieved by restricting participants' responses to a set of predefined options, or by extracting decontextualised features of text that can be handled statistically. Such approaches abstract from the fine detail of linguistic structure and thus avoid dealing with the complexity of natural discourse and social implications (Edwards & Potter, 1992). It is for this reason that grounding in linguistic theory is not necessarily seen as essential for analysis in this area. Nevertheless, the widespread use of such methods bears witness to the many insights that can be gained by using language as an external representation of phenomena that would otherwise remain inaccessible within the human mind.

Going in the opposite direction, there is the option of largely ignoring situational factors by drawing on huge and varied data sets. This is done in methods of corpus linguistics (e.g. Biber, Conrad, & Reppen, 1998). Just like in controlled experimental studies, quantitative and inferential statistical methods are widely used in this type of research. Corpus linguistic methods are very useful for finding out how people speak in general – what is normal for them across a wide range of situations. This can be narrowed down to specific dialects or sociological regions, depending on how a corpus was collected.

Knowledge about such findings can be very useful for the interpretation of data collected in a specific setting. If we know how people speak in general, this will help us see the significance of their linguistic choices when they express their thoughts in a particular context. And corpus linguistic methodologies can also be useful as a tool to analyse a data set for CODA, as the collected data may actually be treated as a (small) corpus. Then, results from a large corpus can be compared to a small-group corpus collected in relation to thought (i.e. a CODA data set). We will return to this idea in Chapter 9.

As we can see, there is a broad range of diversity when it comes to investigating the use of language. Some of these approaches have their main focus on other aspects or a more or less purpose-free methodology, where the relationship between language and cognition is not central. However, there now is a strong and growing tradition of approaches directly targeting cognition through language analysis, with major research centres addressing relevant aspects in depth. For instance, the ways in which cognition and communication relate to each other have been explored in projects and institutes such as Cognition, Communication, and Learning[1] (e.g. Holsanova, 2008), Language, Communication and Cognition[2] (e.g. Maes, Arts, & Noordman, 2004), and the Cognition and Communication Research Centre at Northumbria University[3] (e.g. Bugmann, Coventry, & Newstead, 2007).

---

[1] https://ccl.ht.lu.se
[2] https://research.tilburguniversity.edu/en/organisations/language-communication-and-cognition
[3] www.northumbria.ac.uk/research/research-areas/psychology-psychiatry-and-neuroscience/cognition-communication-research-centre

This list could be expanded; the interface of cognition and communication continues to be exciting, and opens up ever more avenues to explore. Here, we can see how language represents and expresses thoughts or thought processes – and there is no limit to the kinds of insights to be discovered there. Also, the range of methods used to explore this interface is not limited as such; all of the methods for analysing language in use that we have briefly noted above can be adopted for looking at how thoughts are expressed by language and communicated to another person.

2.1.2 *Research on Language Used to Represent Spatial Cognition*

As already hinted in Chapter 1, space is central for human thinking: who we are, the way we think, and the way we talk – all of this depends on *where* we are. If we don't know where we are, we feel lost – a horrible experience for most of us. If we need to get somewhere, we need a clear idea of how to do so, to avoid losing our way. All of the many objects we use in our daily lives are located somewhere, and if we don't know where they are, that can be a major problem as well. Also, we meet people in certain places in order to live and to work, to interact and communicate. This need becomes somewhat reduced through the invention of 'virtual spaces', social networks that enable us to communicate without depending on spatial constraints. However, there definitely is something special about being co-present, being together in one place, within a room or outdoors in the city or in a beautiful natural setting.

Space matters, and our thinking is to a large extent influenced by this fact. We will see in Chapter 3 how cognitive linguistics has picked up on this: a substantial portion of the linguistic repertory is affected by spatial concepts. Much of our language starts from a spatial relationship and then gets transferred to something more abstract, as in the following two well-known examples:

Example 2.1   She's in *high* spirits today.

Example 2.2   Christmas is *around the corner.*

In both cases, spatial terms (*high* and *around the corner*) are used to express something that is definitely not meant in any direct spatial sense. Feelings and time are not spatial as such, but apparently our knowledge of space helps us to understand and talk about them. There are many ways in which language is based on physical experience. Experts debate the question as to whether cognition is achievable at all without this kind of embodiment (Wilson, 2002) – an interesting point to consider in relation to artificial intelligence.

For instance, research has revealed a range of things that we do when we do something as simple as finding our way around in everyday life: we choose a particular perspective when thinking and talking about a route (Tversky, 1999). We orient ourselves towards landmarks such as churches, well-known places, or highly visible landscape features (Denis, 1997; Egorova et al., 2015; Newman et al., 2007). We organise our route concepts sequentially, around decision points and spatial segments, guided by intersections and chunks of space that belong together in our minds (Klippel, 2003). All of these, and more, have been identified for language just as well as for non-linguistic cognition (e.g. Allen, 2000; Couclelis, 1996). Thus, the *language* of route descriptions can reveal very clearly how we *think* about routes – what is important for us when we consider how to get somewhere.

Not all descriptions are entirely correct or consistent, especially when they are given spontaneously by a stranger on the street when we ask them for the way. Perhaps the person doesn't know the way and is simply guessing; this would be quite normal. However, perhaps they would be perfectly able to find the way to the same location themselves. Even then, describing the route can be really difficult. This shows just how difficult it is for humans to describe something adequately that we know, or that we can do ourselves. We might have the procedural knowledge of getting somewhere, but may not be able to put it into words. Remembering all relevant aspects and concepts and representing them in suitable words can be challenging no matter what the context is, and spatial relationships are notoriously difficult in this respect.

But even with completely correct and consistent route descriptions, there are differences in quality. Denis (1997) showed that route descriptions are typically preferred that crisply represent the most essential elements that we use to find our way – landmarks, decision points, and the like. Other route descriptions were either judged as containing insufficient information – some elements are missing and people can get lost – or more information than is really useful. Getting too much information across in a route description can indeed be harmful, as the wayfinder will typically need to remember what they were told; irrelevant information can therefore overload memory and distract from the goal.

Intuitively, we share this kind of knowledge within a culture, as we will all have heard several route descriptions, and found our way on this basis, before we have to provide one ourselves. It is part of the common knowledge that we share, as we grow up with similar experiences. Our environment is for a large part shared, our thought processes about it are similar, and the descriptions we produce on this basis share systematic features.

Nevertheless, there are a number of challenges that come up every single time we describe a route. Besides the problems of remembering the details of the route and putting them into words, we need to make certain assumptions about the specific situation at hand: how much does the wayfinder already know? Can we, for instance, refer to the popular shop that used to be on that corner but is no longer there? Is the listener capable of following a complex description, or would they find this rather challenging? Do they have high spatial abilities? How detailed should the description be? How much should the listener be expected to remember?

Because we can only make best guesses according to what we know about our interaction partner, route descriptions can differ quite a lot according to familiarity. A stranger on the street might get very different advice to a friend. And it really matters whether a listener is actually present or only imagined, for instance when writing down a route description for a friend's or stranger's future trip. The impact of such considerations and factors has not been addressed in much detail so far, though a number of authors emphasise their importance (Filipi & Wales, 2004; Haddington, 2010). Further evidence for the role of this variability comes from more general research on discourse and dialogue (Clark, 1996; Pickering & Garrod, 2004; Schober & Brennan, 2003; and see Chapter 3).

As we can see, just looking at route descriptions – a seemingly small and limited research area – opens up a wide range of concerns and questions related to the ways in which language represents thought in this particular domain. And altogether, across the board, the range of insights that have been gained from analysing the use of language as a representation of cognition is continually expanding; a single book chapter would never be sufficient to outline the scope of the state of the art adequately in this regard. So this is not the goal here.

Importantly however, many of the individual studies carried out in these rich traditions fit into the scope of CODA, or are very closely related to the idea of CODA: discourse analysis (of some kind) is employed to access cognition. This includes, for instance, countless studies that address how factors of a situation affect how people use language to express their concepts in that situation. Thus, CODA is not a new invention, in spite of the fact that a coherent methodology had not been recognised and spelled out. To do so is the aim of this book: to bring to light what we are doing when we analyse discourse to access cognition – and to explore some well-established and systematic ways to do so.

We will now take a closer look at the two main established traditions within which language use is analysed to explore cognition: psycholinguistic methods that address mental representation, and verbal protocol analysis of complex cognitive processes in cognitive psychology. Both of these traditions have established clearly defined methodologies that are directly relevant to, and in part overlap with, CODA as a discourse analytic approach.

2.2   How Psycholinguists Analyse Language Use in Relation to Cognition

The wider field of psycholinguistics is understood to include areas such as child language acquisition, the study of how words are organised and accessed in the brain, how we manage to understand written and spoken language, and how we produce language (Aitchison, 1983; Altmann, 2001; Klabunde & von Stutterheim, 1999). Of these, psycholinguistic studies of language production are most closely related to CODA studies because CODA addresses how we *use* language. Like CODA, this kind of research also builds on the assumption that aspects of language production systematically reflect cognitive features. However, the purposes and analysis goals are rather different. While CODA looks at the significance of linguistic choices a speaker makes, psycholinguistic studies aim primarily to find out how words and sentences are processed in the brain. Because of this, they typically use a far more constrained approach to data collection than what is typically used in CODA studies. But nonetheless there are considerable links. Many findings from psycholinguistic studies are directly relevant to CODA research, and CODA studies may be directly informed by them, including methodological aspects.

A typical psycholinguistic experimental design involves a specific task setting that will highlight how language is produced under certain circumstances, related to the mental representation of a concept. Participants are given a clearly defined linguistic task, which is typically quick and easy and does not allow for many choices. They might be asked to choose an appropriate expression or phrase from a set of available options, or to fill a gap in a nearly complete sentence. Frequently, such studies do not only look at linguistic choices, but additionally involve related methods such as the analysis of eye movements, reaction times, acceptability judgements, and more. For instance, Corley and Scheepers (2002) asked speakers to complete sentences such as *The bank manager gave the cheque* ... They were interested in the grammatical choices that speakers made, and how they were influenced (primed) by what they did immediately before. In addition, they looked at response times, that is, how long it took the participants to start typing their answers.

Priming effects such as those addressed by Corley and Scheepers (2002) are widely researched in psycholinguistics, and this has led to profound insights as to how speakers access words and concepts in the brain, guided by what they have just accessed before. Pickering and Garrod (2004) even suggested that much of what happens in dialogue is actually quite automatic, triggered by the kinds of things that our minds have just connected to. As we listen to each other and produce language in response, we align to each other's use of language, and even align with the underlying concepts in the mind.

All of this is basically guided by the familiar effects of priming – one concept primes another, leading on to further thoughts that again prime related thoughts. This explains why we are so often able to complete each other's sentences, as shown very nicely by Clark and Wilkes-Gibbs (1986) and others – corresponding to our everyday life experience: *'Are you going ... ' – ' ... out? Yes, planning to!'* This kind of thing happens all the time – as if we could read each other's minds. In Pickering and Garrod's (2004) theory, dialogue is the most fundamental way of using language, since language was developed for communicating. Therefore, the production and comprehension of language in our minds can to a large extent be explained by such processes of interactive alignment, drawing on various priming mechanisms.

Priming is very relevant for CODA, even though CODA does not target the mechanisms of language production and comprehension in the mind. However, it is important to recognise that priming mechanisms are at work whenever people produce language. This may affect the analysis and interpretation of linguistic choices, as speakers may be primed by what they heard or read or did before. Choosing from the linguistic network of options is not necessarily an unbiased or completely open process – many factors may influence this choice, and priming can be an extremely strong factor in this regard. This is relevant in the context of task instructions in an experimental design – including giving examples, answering clarification questions, and so on (see Chapter 8) – and it is also centrally important in the context of communication (see Chapter 7).

For instance, Clark and Wilkes-Gibbs (1986) looked at how speakers work together in dialogue in order to agree on an object that they're talking about. They found that references to objects systematically change over time: they become shorter and shorter. When their participants referred to a tangram figure, they said the following in a sequence of different trials of the same experiment (Clark & Wilkes-Gibbs, 1986:12):

Example 2.3

1. All right, the next one looks like a person who's ice skating, except they're sticking two arms out in front.
2. Um, the next one's the person ice skating that has two arms?
3. The fourth one is the person ice skating, with two arms.
4. The next one's the ice skater.
5. The fourth one's the ice skater.
6. The ice skater.

This study, like many others in the psycholinguistic tradition of analysing dialogue, used a task design that is widely known as the *referential communication task*. In this task paradigm, two people are asked to solve a task together, and one person has more information than the other. In the study by Clark and Wilkes-Gibbs (1986), the partners had to arrange cards showing tangram figures in a particular order, and this task was repeated over a sequence of six trials. This setup led to the above finding: that references to the same object by the same set of speakers can have a certain life course.

Referential communication tasks resemble face-to-face conversations in many respects (Clark, 1996), and researchers widely agree that they provide a relatively naturalistic setting for dialogue – at least compared to monologic psycholinguistic task settings in which linguistic choices are restricted to a minimum. Nevertheless, studies in this paradigm vary rather widely with respect to the actual freedom given to the participants. In many such studies (e.g. Hanna, Tanenhaus, & Trueswell, 2003), one of the dialogue participants is a 'confederate' – a person who was secretly instructed by the experiment designers to act according to a script, enabling tight control of the dialogue. In contrast, in the study by Clark and Wilkes-Gibbs (1986), both dialogue participants were untrained; both were actually participating in the experiment, and all of their language was analysed afterwards. The data collected in studies of this kind is inevitably far more complicated and complex to analyse, as free dialogue can develop in complex and unforeseen ways. It certainly takes considerable effort and a good eye to identify meaningful overarching patterns in free-production dialogue data.

Understandably, many researchers shy away from this kind of challenge. One of the aims of this book is to make unwieldy linguistic data sets a little more accessible, by demonstrating feasible analysis perspectives that can be adopted meaningfully across a range of possible scenarios (Chapters 4–7), and by offering some practical tips for efficient analysis procedures (Chapter 8). Equipped with such tools, referential communication tasks can be very well suited as scenarios for CODA purposes. In fact, some of the analyses done in the psycholinguistic tradition are actually very close to CODA, in that they focus more on the linguistic choices made naturally by speakers than on the processing of language in the brain.

And some previous CODA studies are based on referential communication tasks. In a dialogue-based doll's house study that will be further explored in Chapter 7, Tenbrink, Andonova, and Coventry (2008) and Tenbrink et al. (2017) used a classic referential communication task design without confederates, in which one dialogue partner instructed the other to furnish a doll's house in order to match it to their own. The results gathered relate closely to those gained from earlier psycholinguistic studies, even though the motivation underlying data collection was somewhat different.

Altogether, there is no sharp dividing line between CODA and psycholinguistic approaches. Where the methods overlap, the difference is reduced to a subtle shift in focus: psycholinguistics is typically more concerned with accessing linguistic items in the mind (how much time does it take? what concepts are more readily available?), whereas CODA looks at the linguistic choices themselves (what words and constructions do speakers choose?), with respect to how they represent concepts in the mind. Sometimes, both aspects are informed by an analysis of speakers' linguistic preferences in a particular situation. However, there may be differences in the theoretical (motivating) background, which might also affect how results are interpreted and discussed in light of the literature.

2.3 How Cognitive Psychologists Analyse Language Use in Relation to Cognition

As with CODA, the primary aim of research in cognitive psychology is to understand how our minds work. This includes what is often referred to in terms of *higher-level cognitive processes*: namely, the kinds of processes that are based on knowledge and used to solve problems or make decisions, and the like. As mentioned in Chapter 1, these would often be processes that we recognise as our active thoughts, and that we can put into words in some way. Insights and methods in cognitive psychology are therefore highly relevant for CODA.

Verbal data can provide a range of insights that would not otherwise be accessible to the analyst. For instance, consider a situation where a participant makes a mistake – a behavioural result that is clearly visible to the analyst. However, it may be less easy to see what caused the mistake. Failures may occur on different levels, and all of these lead to less than optimal results. According to Reason (1990), errors can be ascribed to specific subprocesses of human planning actions. The intended plan itself may be faulty, or the execution of the plan is other than intended. Verbal data typically provide some insights concerning the participant's underlying intentions and thus contribute to understanding at which level the errors occurred.

The tradition of using verbal data to access cognitive processes, plans, intentions, problem-solving strategies, and the like is extremely widespread. The range of problems and cognitive challenges that can be addressed using verbal data is unlimited – just as our minds are not in any simple way limited, considering the vast range of things we can think about. In the following, we will look at various aspects related to this kind of research, with a view to how CODA can inform this tradition.

2.3.1 What Kinds of Complex Thought Processes Are Interesting for Cognitive Psychology Research?

Problems are abundant in our everyday life; they engross our thoughts about the big challenges just as well as the small ones, from a very young age. How can I reach the bowl of biscuits on the top shelf? How should I tie my shoes? How will I find my dream partner? How will I become happy for the rest of my life? How can I solve the riddle in the newspaper's entertainment section? How am I to obtain my dream profession? Not all of these problems are directly solvable, of course; accordingly, they don't lend themselves to research in any straightforward way. Research in cognitive psychology focuses on types of problems that fulfil some essential criteria.

First of all, the problem needs to be *manageable* within a limited amount of time, so that participants can be observed while solving it, and all relevant thoughts can be captured without missing out on decisive aspects. Deciding on a profession, for instance, is a long-term process that involves a host of thoughts and experiences and reasoning processes; the researcher would need to observe and interview the participant over a very long time to ensure that all relevant aspects are included. Doing this with a sufficient number of participants in order to identify systematic quantitative patterns is then a major challenge, and will typically not be feasible. In contrast, the problem of tying shoes is solvable fairly quickly, although it is cognitively challenging for a child.

Similarly, the problem needs to be *bounded*, that is, limited to clearly discernible factors. The aim is to reduce all distracting contextual factors that might come into play. For this reason, research tends to focus on a task that is clearly defined within the experimental context, drawing on as little prior background knowledge as possible. In this light, the problem of tying shoes turns into a question of observing how children learn to tie shoes. In order to capture this process in its entirety, the child's very first exposure to a shoe-tying process would need to be recorded and analysed, and this again makes this kind of problem unwieldy and impractical. In contrast, if participants are given a riddle, perhaps of the kind that appears in the newspaper's entertainment pages, the researcher will only need to make sure that they haven't seen or solved it before. If not, they can be reasonably sure that the problem is confined to the experimental setting.

However, this does not mean that the participant will not draw on any prior knowledge at all. On the contrary – it is one of the basic assumptions in cognitive psychology that participants can solve problems precisely because they have solved problems of some kind before. One of the goals in research on problem solving, then, is to identify *common principles*. Consider the following riddle (found at www.riddles.com):

Example 2.4   All the electricity was out in town and none of the street lights or traffic signals had power. A dark limousine was cruising down the newly paved blacktop, with its headlights off. A young boy dressed totally in black (with no reflectors) stepped out to cross the street. The moon wasn't out and the boy had no flashlight, yet the driver stopped to let the boy cross the street. How did the driver see the boy?

Confronted with this riddle, you might start thinking about what the solution might be: did the driver have supernatural powers, did they perhaps sense the boy in some other way – or did the description fail to mention another type of artificial light source? Then, you might remember how riddles normally work: perhaps there is some trick involved, some obvious aspect that you're somehow expected to forget? And this memory of previous riddles might lead you to the solution: the driver saw the boy because it all happened in broad daylight.

In this example, a common underlying principle is the idea of a trick, or the expectation of a typical inference of the kind that humans make during reading. Inferences happen all the time, as language never conveys all the information about the situation described to the last detail. Crucially, we assume that the things that are mentioned in a text are there because they are relevant (Sperber & Wilson, 1986 – see also Chapter 3). In Example 2.4, there are lots of references to the lack of artificial light sources; a very natural assumption is that these light sources would be required in order to see properly. Therefore, we automatically assume that the story must be set during night-time. We might not even remember having made this assumption – it simply happens as we read.

The riddle draws on this very basic and common reading principle; it encourages the assumption that the artificial light sources are relevant – but in fact they're not. It also fails to mention that it was actually daytime. As a consequence, it is safe to assume that most readers will be led towards believing that it was dark. The riddle solver's cognitive task is to break this principle, or to realise consciously that there might have been a trick there, an unspoken obvious inference that they must resist in order to solve the riddle. Such a realisation is most likely to be possible if the riddle solver has seen similar principles at work before.

Once a riddle of this kind has been solved, the same person will be less likely to be tricked, and will find it easier to solve similar riddles. The feeling of satisfaction after having solved such a riddle comes from the subtle awareness that *normally* inferences are made automatically, but the successful problem solver was clever enough to resist this principle. If inferences weren't normally at work, there would be no challenge and no satisfaction. A reader of the above riddle would not even see a problem to solve – we don't normally (during daytime) have problems seeing people cross the street, even without artificial light sources.

Generally, in cognitive psychology researchers are not simply interested in how participants solve the *specific* problem at hand. It is far more interesting to try to find common underlying principles. So when observing how people solve a specific problem, researchers will aim to relate it to something more general. In this example, this concerns both the underlying reading principle (as a feature of the riddle), and the processes through which this is detected.

Some riddle solvers might refer to previously solved riddles, and some might be consciously aware of inference processes. Others might actually think of the sun as a possible light source directly, and not make the night-time inference in the first place. This leads to different problem-solving procedures, which again might be similar to problem-solving procedures in other domains.

So this is another requirement: beyond being *manageable* and *bounded*, problems that are targeted in cognitive psychology should also be *generalisable* in some sense. The aim is to study cognitive processes on a general scale, with specific problems as examples. By combining and comparing solution paths to different kinds of specific problems, researchers can distil the cognitive processes involved in problem solving in a more abstract way, that is, on a more general scale. Accordingly, the specific problems used in an experimental setting in cognitive psychology are not picked randomly. Instead, they are often chosen in order to support or falsify a certain existing theory about problem solving, and involve specific hypotheses about the underlying cognitive processes and strategies. Newell and Simon (1972) provided a thorough overview of basic problem-solving principles identified at that time; most current research on the details of such principles ultimately relates back to their seminal work.

Importantly, the thought process at hand also needs to be *measurable* in some way. There are many ways of accessing cognitive processes; these include reaction times, behavioural results, task responses, brain measures, and so on. The crucial point is that the researcher needs to identify a measure that adequately reflects the cognitive process at hand. Or in other words, the kind of cognitive process that is being targeted needs to be accessible by the measure that the researcher is using. Here, we are concerned with verbal data analysis for purposes of accessing cognitive processes. Accordingly, we are only concerned with those kinds of thought processes that are actually *verbalisable* in some way or other.

As we have already seen, there are limitations to the kinds of information that can be derived on the basis of language. Generally, only processes that require a minimum of conscious thought are verbalisable; this excludes memory retrieval, activation and recognition, automated procedures, sudden insights or realisations, and the like. Some of these can be reported after the fact, if people remember them (Ericsson & Simon, 1993). Higher-level cognitive processes and strategies may be either unconscious or conscious, or we may first be unaware of them before they reach our consciousness sufficiently that we can report them (Siegler & Stern, 1998).

As a simple example, assume that John has decided to search for a particular object, say, his keys. Then he could verbalise things like 'I have decided to look for the keys now,' and 'I am still searching for the keys,' and so on. These verbalisations aptly reflect the conscious decision and the action of searching.

However, in terms of cognitive processes, there's much more going on. John's decision to start the search process activated a range of perception processes, including visual search patterns (eye movements) that John will not normally be aware of. Likewise, when John finds his keys, he'll be able to shout, 'Found them!' – but he will not be able to say how exactly he managed to recognise the keys. Both perceptual processes and recognition are low-level, largely automatic cognitive processes. They are *associated* to the verbalisable cognitive processes of deciding and acting, as well as to the realisation that the keys have been found – but as such, they will not enter any verbal protocol.

That said, CODA as a tool is nonetheless suitable for – and indeed developed for – detecting a range of things in language that the speaker might not actually be aware of. The structure of language represents some aspects of the speaker's thought that will enter the verbalisation, independent of whether or not the speaker intends them to come through. For instance, if John exclaims, 'Found them!', this particular choice of words and intonation signals some element of surprise and delight, even though he doesn't actually *say* that he's surprised and delighted. Other aspects conveyed implicitly and subtly through linguistic choices include the perspective used, the level of granularity, the kinds of things that the speaker takes for granted or represents as new, and so on. However, looking for such aspects will still depend on verbal data being available. If John hadn't said anything when finding his keys, only the behavioural action of holding the keys in his hand would be available for the researcher to analyse and to conclude that John had found them. In such a situation, if the researcher wants to address subconscious cognitive processes that do not get reflected in any kind of verbalisation, CODA will not provide any insights – there simply won't be any relevant verbal data to analyse.

In sum, complex thought processes can meaningfully be analysed within cognitive science – and using CODA – to the extent that they are not random, but instead represent generalisable processes that relate to previous research in some way. Analysis of language data will be most successful if the task at hand is manageable, bounded, specific, measurable, and verbalisable; the clearer the task can be represented along these lines, the more meaningful conclusions can be drawn from the resulting patterns in the linguistic data.

2.3.2   *How Are Verbal Data Collected to Address Complex Thought Processes in Cognitive Psychology?*

In the history of cognitive psychology, one of the earliest methods of investigating problem-solving processes was introspection. The analysts simply reported the various problem-solving steps from their own memory. That is, they put into words what they remembered doing themselves as they were solving the problem at hand. Although these researchers did not actually analyse language as a representation of thought, they certainly *used* language to represent their thought processes. Systematic and detailed representations of this kind were regarded as good analyses of the problem-solving process. This methodology has not completely died out, although it is now primarily used for illustration of some well-known and easily communicated phenomena, rather than being regarded as analysis in itself.

Later, researchers started asking other people about their problem-solving processes, and this led to increased recognition of the fact that different individuals may well solve the same problem in very different ways. Again, verbal representations of thought were taken as evidence for actual thought processes. Both of these approaches – introspection and asking participants about their problem-solving steps – came to be attacked; they were widely criticised as being too subjective and biased to the analyst's own views. Indeed, there is little control in such approaches, as the analyst may very easily influence what they report from their own thoughts, or how they ask the questions to the participants, guiding them towards the kinds of answers that they'd like to hear.

Nevertheless, the idea that complex thought processes can be expressed by talking about them has not been dropped from cognitive science, and in fact there is little choice: language simply is the most preferred medium of communication; this is the way in which we are used to telling others what we think. The challenge, then, is to make this 'window' to the human mind more systematic, more reliable as evidence, and less susceptible to the analyst's preferences and biases.

One way to do this is to ask more than one person: to collect data from a larger group of participants who individually verbalise their thoughts in a given task, under controlled circumstances. This tradition was developed in the second half of the twentieth century, including a range of very clearly motivated design considerations for experimental studies. The methodology was laid out in much detail by Ericsson and Simon (1993), who demonstrated that controlled verbal data elicitation can take various different forms, serving diverse purposes. The most prominent forms are *think-aloud* protocols produced during task performance, *retrospective reports* that are collected subsequently, and *post-performance interviews*, which can involve a range of further questions asked of the participants once they have found a solution.

All of these different verbalisations can highlight cognitive strategies that the participants use, but they do so in different ways. This has to do with memory constraints. When people remember solving a problem, they might access information from different sources: directly from short-term memory, or from long-term memory, depending on what kinds of information were stored in what stages of the problem-solving process. Accessing long-term memory in particular involves the danger of integrating information that stems from other sources than the task just solved. For instance, people easily confuse the memory of what they just did with what they usually do. Therefore, it is useful to employ different methods for different purposes, and it is necessary to be aware of the various implications of accessing memory.

Ericsson and Simon (1993) proposed that the most effective way of obtaining verbal data that directly concerns the task at hand, rather than information from long-term memory, is to ask participants to *think aloud* during the task. If participants simply say aloud what they are thinking as they are solving the task, they will neither have time nor any need to access information from long-term memory, except for the type of information that they do actually need to solve the task (if any). Therefore, think-aloud verbalisations are likely to reflect what participants really attend to for the problem-solving or decision-making process.

However, importantly, this is only the case if participants are conscientiously encouraged to say out loud what they are thinking, nothing else. Researchers who are keen to find reasons for thoughts, or to find out further details about a particular aspect of the problem-solving process, might be tempted to ask questions that go beyond simply thinking aloud – and then the participants will provide verbalisations that might not actually represent their own thought processes closely. Instead, they would be guided and influenced by the researcher. Therefore, the instruction for a think-aloud protocol needs to be as neutral as possible.

More recent articles (e.g. Clark, Li, & Shepherd, 2018; Leow et al., 2014) demonstrate that the general procedure advocated by Ericsson and Simon (1993) is still regarded as valid and useful. Van Someren, Barnard, and Sandberg (1994) offered a complementary, more pragmatically oriented account of think-aloud data elicitation practices. And there are a number of related methods. Spiers and Maguire (2008) recorded participants' behavioural decisions during a virtual-reality wayfinding task. Following task completion, the participants were shown the recording and asked what they were thinking at particular places. While one might suspect that participants may have been reporting ideas that they did not actually consider during task performance, results turned out to be fairly systematic, consistent with the behavioural data, and extremely informative with respect to the research questions at hand. Thus, this type of data provides yet another perspective on the cognitive processes that may be relevant for problem-solving tasks.

For research on the usability of software applications, Boren and Ramey (2000) suggested extending Ericsson and Simon's approach to a communication-based one. In their approach, the experimenter is allowed to communicate in a fairly natural way with the participant in order to elicit more information, and to support the user in exploring the usability of the application being tested. Krahmer and Ummelen (2004) compared this approach directly with Ericsson and Simon's. They found that dialogic interaction during performance appeared to have an influence on task success but not necessarily on the contents of the comments being produced (think-aloud vs. dialogue).

Generally, we can conclude that verbal data can be (and have been) collected in a range of different ways in cognitive science. The more systematic methods are more likely to lead to meaningful results than randomly remembered thoughts or informal interviews. Chapter 8 will provide a more general outline of suitable methods to elicit verbalisations of complex cognitive processes for CODA purposes.

2.3.3   How Directly Are Thoughts Expressed in Verbal Protocols?

Some thought processes are straightforward enough that the procedural steps are clear and can easily be verbalised. Others may be a bit more complicated, and they might involve more subconscious processes or aspects that do not quite make it to conscious awareness. In such a case, it can become a rather challenging task to speak out loud what you're thinking, as you're not actually very clear about what you're thinking. In some cases, thinking aloud might not be feasible at all.

As a result, think-aloud protocols can, under certain circumstances, be somewhat cryptic. Consider the following extract from a study that involved participants travelling through a kind of virtual tunnel, shown on the computer screen (Tenbrink & Salwiczek, 2016). The numbers denote hours:minutes: seconds–tens of seconds in the recording.

Example 2.5

> uh 00:08:32–3
> so – left. 00:08:33–9
> alright now – left turn 00:08:42–3
> um 00:08:44–3
> pretty sharp left turn 00:08:48–6
> uh 00:08:50–0
> yeah. 00:08:53–3

This participant did not say much, although they clearly adhered to the instruction – they did verbalise what they experienced during the tunnel travel. The information given in this think-aloud protocol is very sparse. It is basically a verbalisation of the tunnel's turns as shown on the screen, supplemented by a few discourse markers such as *uh*, *so*, *alright*, and the like which are typical in spoken language. Analysing verbal material of this kind can be very challenging, and the researcher definitely needs a clear analysis perspective to derive meaningful insights.

For these reasons, in order to avoid any influence of verbal data collection on the actual thought processes, and in order to avoid the unintelligibility of think-aloud protocols in some settings, it is sometimes worth considering other methods of data collection. Ericsson and Simon (1993) suggested that under certain circumstances retrospective reports can be nearly as adequate in representing thoughts as think-aloud protocols. If participants are asked directly after the task what they remember thinking about during the task, there is a high chance that the actual thought processes are still available in short-term memory. Only if this is the case can participants be expected to actually report their thoughts? Otherwise, they would inevitably resort to thinking about and reporting some selected thoughts from long-term memory – such as how they would usually solve a task like this, or what they think is the best way of doing it, or what the reasons are for doing things in a particular way.

In one case study (Tenbrink, 2008), I compared individual verbal protocols of cognitive processes related to a problem-solving process: think-aloud data, a written retrospective report, and a more common or familiar text type: writing an instruction for a friend. While Ericsson and Simon (1993) were primarily concerned with the veridicality of verbal protocol data – that is, how accurately they could be assumed to reflect thoughts – I was interested in the different kinds of information and textual features of the three types of data. One goal was to identify to what extent moving away from the immediate, on-line production of a verbal protocol distorted the data. Would information be added that did not seem to be directly relevant to the actual problem-solving process? Would participants be led into further thoughts that they did not really employ while doing the task? Along with this, another goal was to identify to what extent the verbalisations were useful for the researcher in terms of intelligibility.

Just like in Tenbrink and Salwiczek (2016) (see our earlier Example 2.5) and in many studies reported in Ericsson and Simon (1993) and elsewhere, the think-aloud protocol analysed in Tenbrink (2008) was rather sparse and required a fair amount of interpretation and inferencing on the part of the analyst. In contrast, the written reports were coherent and more like normal texts; accordingly, their content was clearer, more explicit, and easier to analyse.

In terms of content, there were indeed fundamental differences – each of the verbalisations provided a different perspective on the same thought process. Although sparse, the think-aloud data provided insights about incremental learning processes over a period of time. Also, they reflected more direct, lower-level cognitive processes that would not make their way into a retrospective report, which requires more conscious reflection. In contrast, the retrospective report focused more on general processes, and provided an adequate, concise, coherent summary of what was going on. Finally, the instruction written for a friend included further information – added thoughts that might be useful for a person confronted with the same task in the future. Just as Ericsson and Simon (1993) suggested, such additional thoughts were not necessarily part of the participant's own cognitive processes during the problem-solving task. They must therefore be analysed at a different level, taking into account the more fictitious nature of this kind of verbalisation.

Altogether, different kinds of verbalisations can lead to different kinds of insights. The researcher collecting data in this way needs to be aware of the variability of cognitive perspectives, and should keep in mind how important it is to use a method of collecting data that adequately suits the research goals in this light.

2.3.4   What about Metacognition?

One problem that has often been pointed out by critics of verbal data analysis in cognitive psychology is that the participants might not report their thoughts directly, but rather report what they *think* about their own thoughts. That's called metacognition, and the critics are right: it is not the same as reporting one's thoughts. In fact, it is quite similar to the following common mistake made (for instance) by inexperienced researchers, or by non-experts who are simply interested in something. Imagine you want to find out how frequently people use swear words in different everyday contexts: in the family, at school, with friends, during work. The easiest way, it seems, is to simply ask them. You could use one of the many questionnaire or survey tools that are now available on the web for free, and collect data without any effort whatsoever. So you design your questionnaire, and just ask all the questions you're interested in: how often do you use swear words in the family? How often at school? How often with friends? And so on. People can then choose and click their answers: Never. Once a day. Once every 100 words. Every five minutes.

However, there is a problem with this. How can they be sure? How accurate is the information they provide? Quite certainly, people won't record their everyday language use for you and do an exact frequency count before they participate in your survey. They will just make a guess. Perhaps it's a very informed guess, or perhaps it is a wild one – you have no way of knowing! It would probably make no difference if you asked them explicitly: how often *do you think* you use swear words in the family? at school? And so on. People's answers will be the same – they will reflect what they *think* they do, rather than what they actually do.

That is, unless you explicitly get them to verify their intuitions. In order to find out how often they really use swear words, you could, for instance, ask them to note down every single instance of a swear word, whenever they use them, along with the context: in the family, at school, and so on. This should get you a bit closer to the truth, in terms of actual usage. However, these results would reflect how often people *remembered to note down* their use of a swear word – and that's still different from their actual usage.

But – does this make the use of questionnaires entirely worthless? That would be going too far. In fact, questionnaires and surveys are frequently used in research across many disciplines; they are generally regarded as a very valuable (and valid) research tool (see, e.g., Rasinger, 2010, for linguistics). However, the question is what exactly is taken from them. If you ask people how often they use swear words, the answer will definitely show you something: namely, how often people *think* they use swear words. And this can be a quite interesting kind of result, particularly in relation to other results – such as actual usage, identified in other ways. Then, it could be a target of research to find out how aware people are of their use of swear words. The degree of correspondence between people's guesses and their actual use of swear words could depend on certain factors. Perhaps they have a strategy for using language, or they have been told explicitly to avoid swear words at home. Whether this affects the accuracy of guesses about actual habits could be quite interesting to investigate.

So, back to our question about metacognition. If we ask people what they're thinking, won't they just tell us what they *think* they are thinking? Experimental participants will not want to mislead us – in fact, they'll be doing their best to find out what they're thinking, so that they can report it to us. Simply asking somebody to report their thoughts can make them aware of their own thought processes, and this can change them: it can bring things to consciousness that weren't there before – and it can mean that they *think* they have been thinking in a particular way, when in fact they haven't.

For instance, you might be caught dreaming or intensely thinking about something, and absent-mindedly doing something that was fully unintended: let's say you have been scribbling drawings or words onto a piece of paper in front of you, which might happen to be an important document. Your friend's exclamation of 'What do you think you're doing?!' makes you 'wake up', and you realise, with a start, what you are doing. Perhaps your answer to the friend's question will be something like 'Oh – oops – nothing, sorry!' However, it's also entirely possible that you instead come up with an explanation of your thoughts and actions – you would rationalise your actions post hoc, so to speak, and you might even believe that you're telling the truth. Saving face is a natural human aim, which might lead to some confusion of thought where face is felt to be threatened.

Similarly, people who are asked to verbalise their thoughts in an experimental task such as problem solving might start thinking about (and verbalising) how they think about their task, related to what they think is expected of them. This might change how they actually or naturally think about it, or it may trigger new kinds of conscious thoughts (Smagorinsky, 1998). To address this problem, Ericsson and Simon (1998) specified the methodological circumstances under which cognitive processes can fairly safely be assumed to be simply *externalised* without alteration.

Most crucially, it clearly matters in what way procedural instructions are given to the participants (see Chapter 8 for concrete procedural suggestions). Participants should be clear about the expectation to simply say out loud what they're thinking anyway, no matter what it is, without any specific value attached to any particular direction of thought. Ideally, they should be trained to do this in a warm-up task. In contrast, Ericsson and Simon (1998) proposed that *explaining* or *describing* thoughts (as in social speech) represent different types of discourse that involve further considerations with respect to the communicative situation.

As long as appropriate care is taken in the procedural design, there are good indications that, under the right circumstances, verbalisations will indeed express thought fairly directly. Problem-solving tasks concern high-level cognitive operations, such as decisions and plans for future actions. These are the kinds of thoughts that typically involve conscious awareness anyway, independent of being asked to think aloud. In Ericsson and Simon's (1993) terms, expertly collected think-aloud protocols (and, under adequate circumstances, retrospective reports) elicit just those aspects that are attended to (or 'heeded') by participants anyway.

If *performance* is not affected by the requirement to think aloud, then it is likely that the *thought* processes are not affected either. However, it is not easy to predict whether or not this will be the case in any specific study. Having to formulate thoughts out loud might either hamper the subconscious problem-solving processes, or it might help them, as the need to think aloud can favour some kinds of processes that are beneficial to the task at hand. Since there is no way of eliminating all potential issues coming up along these lines, a control group without the requirement to think aloud may be the only way to ensure that there is no direct effect of thinking aloud on the actual problem-solving process and performance. Russo, Johnson, and Stephens (1989) came to this conclusion nearly thirty years ago, and a host of subsequent research has not changed this: there are probably as many studies showing some effects of thinking aloud during the task as there are studies showing no effects whatsoever (Gralla, 2013). This depends on the nature of the task and many other factors playing together.

2.3.5   What Can Linguistic Analysis (CODA) Add to Traditional Verbal Protocol Analysis in Cognitive Psychology?

The main contribution of CODA to verbal protocol analysis lies in the systematic analysis of linguistic structures, based on insights from cognitive linguistics and other resources that will be explored in subsequent chapters. In contrast, Ericsson and Simon (1993) suggested identifying aspects of interest and extracting them from the original data set for further exploration. Typically, this would be conceptual aspects that the speakers are themselves aware of, such as particular thought processes or strategies. To achieve this, the *content* of verbal data is in focus, ignoring to a large extent the linguistic structures used to express this content. In fact, Ericsson and Simon (1993) explicitly recommended that the analyst should transform the original input into a categorisation scheme that is directly related to the theoretical motivation for the study at hand – moving away from the actual words used. With this kind of analysis, the linguistic structures used by participants get lost in the process and then cannot be accounted for in subsequent analysis steps.

Another suggestion by Ericsson and Simon (1993) was that annotation and analysis should be as context-free as possible, and therefore the analyst should not be biased by the preceding or subsequent discourse. But language use is heavily influenced by context – it is sometimes nearly impossible to interpret the speaker's meaning correctly if the preceding discourse is entirely ignored. At the very least, a range of potential implications and concepts will get lost in this way. Accordingly, this recommendation has subsequently been criticised and questioned, for example, by Yang (2003).

Despite these suggestions, linguistic structure hasn't been entirely ignored in this research tradition. Ericsson and Simon (1993) themselves give some examples for linguistic patterns that turned out to be meaningful in their data. And other researchers have explored the potential contribution of linguistic features in various ways. Bartl and Dörner (1998) and Roth (1985) both went beyond established content-based protocol analysis by looking at the linguistic structure of think-aloud protocols. They were particularly interested in the difference in thought processes between successful and unsuccessful problem solvers. Success could be reflected in the way hypotheses were formed and expressed, or in differences in the discourse structure or other features detected by systematic analysis.

Roth (1985) focused on possible differences in 'thinking style' that were detectable on the linguistic surface, drawing upon a wide range of linguistic features motivated by the earlier literature. For instance, according to his analysis, unsuccessful problem solvers produced more words of a sort that Roth associated with dogmatic writing and thinking, such as *all, always, without any doubt*. Also, they used adversative conjunctions (*but, besides, either/*

or) and negations (*none, no, never, nothing*) more frequently than successful problem solvers; this could be traced back to a reduced clarity of understanding during the task. Such linguistic markers may be indicative of relevant individual differences in how people deal with challenges, such as when important information is missing at the beginning of a task.

Linguistic analysis can also enhance the understanding of content. Content-based categories tend to depend heavily on the analyst's intuitions, in spite of genuine attempts to do this systematically, for example, following the very detailed procedures suggested by Krippendorff (2012). Content analysis generally means that the analyst needs to do a lot of interpretation and abduction – inferences based on what they know about the discourse context. Content analysts use their ability to comprehend a text intuitively, based on their knowledge of language together with context information, typically related to an analytic framework (Krippendorff, 2012).

Instead of ignoring linguistic structures in this process, a closer look at the linguistic features of the text can decisively support this analysis step, based on insights about meaningful linguistic categories – for instance by providing criteria for content categories. For example, the analyst might find that a specific aspect of a problem-solving procedure is regularly expressed using specific types of expressions or grammatical constructions. Such an association between a particular cognitive aspect and a linguistic feature can be very interesting, particularly if it can be quantified. It might be interesting to point out that one participant said 'Heureka!' upon finding a solution to a problem – but it would be more interesting to see if there are some kinds of exclamations that are regularly and systematically associated with finding a solution to a problem, for instance '*ah!*' If the exclamation *ah!* is recognised as a marker indicating (sudden) insight in one study, this finding can guide subsequent studies in specifying its role (and that of further linguistic indicators) within the problem-solving procedure. In Chapters 4–7, and in the Register of Linguistic Features, we will take a closer look at various linguistic markers that have been identified as being associated with particular cognitive phenomena.

Some indicators will be specific for a certain kind of task and will need to be identified directly for the study at hand. However, others are fairly generic and informative across scenarios. For instance, an ongoing search process may typically be accompanied in think-aloud data by verbs that directly express search or perception more generally, such as *look (for)*, *search*, *see*, *find*, perhaps along with locative questions or statements using *where*.

While such expressions represent the general cognitive process itself, other indicators externalise thought in other (conventional) ways. The exclamation *ah!* is an example of this: it expresses the problem solver's insight indirectly, not by talking about the insight, but by a spontaneous reaction that signals it. Similarly, the discourse marker *okay* is often used to mark the beginning of a new step in a problem-solving process. Verbalisations of this type would typically reflect cognitive processes that the speakers themselves are (or can be made) aware of. If asked why they exclaimed *ah!*, the speaker will be likely to say something along the lines of 'Oh, I just realised/understood that … ,' explaining the nature of the insight.

Linguistic analysis often also highlights systematic patterns that the participants themselves take for granted, and that are not directly visible just by reading the words carefully. Any sentence, uttered in a specific context, carries a host of features that reflect certain cognitive structures. This includes the underlying perspective of the speaker, the level of granularity chosen, the kinds of things they take as given information, what they currently attend to, and the like: all of these specific conceptual aspects are reflected in language systematically – without necessarily requiring the speaker's conscious awareness. We will take a closer look at these aspects in Chapters 4–6.

One previous systematic approach that used linguistic methods for the investigation of verbal protocols was reported in a collection by Caron-Pargue and Gillis (1996). They described the initiation of a project called PROVERB, following related studies (Caron-Pargue & Caron, 1989). The project leaders proposed that 'a careful study of the linguistic form of subjects' verbal reports during a cognitive task enables a characterization of the cognitive processes involved … [L]inguistic markers and their organization in the developing discourse play a crucial role in discovering the intricacies of the underlying cognitive processes' (Caron-Pargue & Gillis, 1996:6).

The various articles in the collection showcased diverse applications of this approach. For instance, certain modal particles and other lexical choices were shown to indicate central elements, hierarchical structures, and particular operations in a problem-solving process. Also, certain changes of reference types systematically reflected a cognitive change, rather than serving any communicative purposes. These ideas and initial findings are well within the scope of CODA. Unfortunately, PROVERB had to be terminated shortly after the publication (for reasons unrelated to the project itself). Only specific aspects of the original project were pursued further, such as the interpretation of discourse markers with respect to their relation to cognitive functions and decision processes (Bégoin-Augereau & Caron-Pargue, 2009; Caron-Pargue & Caron, 2000).

There is one further important layer that a linguistic perspective adds to traditional protocol analysis in cognitive psychology. As noted above, verbal protocols of cognitive processes can take various different forms, such as think-aloud protocols, retrospective reports, post-performance interviews, and a range of further methods such as task dialogues or instructions to future problem solvers. From a CODA perspective, these considerations are relevant in terms of *text types*. Different forms of text have long been known in linguistic research as being systematically different in decisive respects, since they serve different kinds of purposes.

Relevant insights come from areas of discourse analysis and text linguistics (an earlier research field aiming at identifying different types of text, now mostly covered by discourse analytic approaches), and they will be taken up in more detail in Chapter 3. For instance, an interview situation differs from a think-aloud situation in that a direct addressee is involved; the speaker will formulate their thoughts in a way they think is suitable for the interviewer. In this respect, an interview is similar to a task dialogue in joint action, or to an instruction to a future problem solver. In all these cases, speakers will think about their partner's knowledge and expertise, and adjust the way they talk accordingly.

Additionally, in dialogue, speakers often take up some formulations that they have used or heard before – we discussed this in Section 2.2 in terms of priming and interactive alignment. All of these aspects are more related to communication than to cognition, but they influence the features of verbal protocols considerably. Again, conforming to the conclusions of Ericsson and Simon (1993), think-aloud protocols are the most neutral version, as the influence of the addressee is kept to a minimum. Nevertheless, a present experimenter may well be the 'addressee' for a think-aloud protocol in the participant's mind – even if they tell them *not* to explain anything to them but simply express their spontaneous thoughts. This effect cannot be ruled out entirely, and a linguistically aware analyst should keep an eye out for indications and effects of communicative considerations in verbal protocols.

In summary, CODA adds a layer of linguistic insights to the traditional analysis of verbal protocols of complex cognitive processes. This additional layer does not have to be based on in-depth linguistic expertise; it simply means looking at the *medium* of the message conveyed. Beyond categorising content as is typically done in cognitive psychology, the analyst examines patterns in the way people express their thoughts in language. This can lead to a range of insights about cognition that go beyond content, as discussed extensively in Chapters 4–7.

3   Resources

When doing CODA, researchers can draw from a wide range of insights across approaches and disciplines – we have already seen some of this in previous chapters, and we will explore the idea further here. The range of findings in the literature that can highlight the significance of systematic patterns in language data is vast; your creativity for bringing in relevant insights when using CODA is as valuable as anyone's. CODA itself is theory neutral; the goal when doing CODA is to investigate thoughts and thought processes on the basis of language data. This goal will guide the analyst when selecting resources to interpret language data meaningfully in relation to a specific research question.

This chapter will highlight three main research areas that have previously informed CODA projects, so as to exemplify a range of relevant resources, and hopefully inspire you to explore more of the available rich resources in linguistics and beyond. The three areas that we will outline here are cognitive linguistics, discourse analysis, and functional grammar – each of them far too wide and diverse to be represented adequately. Nevertheless, the relevance of established insights and methods in these fields should become clear in this chapter, and there will be plenty of pointers to the literature to follow up.

3.1   Cognitive Linguistics

Cognitive linguistics is the study of language in relation to the mind. Typically, in this field, this concerns structures in the linguistic system: cognitive linguists are interested in how linguistic systems reflect structures in the mind. They look at syntactic as well as semantic structures in many different ways, develop theoretical accounts of how structures in language relate to thought, discuss how the physical world and the human body relate to thought and language, compare different languages with respect to how they represent the world and their speakers' thoughts, and much else. The field is very varied and consists of more than a single homogeneous approach, where the term *cognitive linguistics* serves as an umbrella term for research that addresses the relationship between language and thought.

Historically, cognitive linguistics developed out of a need to counteract a prominent belief commonly held early in the second half of the twentieth century, namely that the concepts expressed in language can be adequately described by abstract formalisms and definitions. Formal approaches to linguistic structure were mainly inspired by Chomsky's generative grammar theories (e.g. Chomsky, 1972), which reinforced and developed earlier approaches (e.g. Montague, 1970). In cognitive linguistics, there is general agreement that such formal approaches are not sufficient to capture linguistic concepts, relations, or structures in a cognitively adequate way; there is more to the relationship between language and thought, and this must be addressed in different ways. Cognitive linguists aim at accounting for the structures in natural language by focusing on *meaning*, and they consider how fundamental aspects of cognition are reflected in language. The following sections will take a closer look at a range of central insights.

3.1.1   Theoretical Basis: Conceptual Meaning Does Not Directly Reside in Words

How do words relate to meanings? Can a word really express what we have in our minds? What is there in a word such as *car* that evokes a mental image in our head? Does the word itself somehow carry this image, or what else is happening? Common sense tells us that it can't really be the word itself – the sound of the word *car* does not sound like a car, the written version does not look like a car, and other languages have quite different words for the same thing anyway. Is a *car* more like a car than an *Auto* (German) or a *bil* (Norwegian) or a سيارة ('sayyāra', Arabic)? There is no reason to believe that this is the case. The words are recognised as direct translations; as such, the form of the word is irrelevant, both in terms of its sound and in terms of its written shape.

There are some interesting exceptions. In languages with a character-based writing system like Chinese, one may often find that a character represents part of its meaning – see examples in Table 3.1. In Chinese, some numbers or quantities are represented in a transparent analogical manner. The character for *person* looks like a simplified drawing of a person, the character for *big* resembles a person opening their arms to show something big, and the character for *door* looks like a door. However, these correspondences are limited and fairly abstract. Without prior knowledge, it is not easy to infer the meaning from the characters even in these cases, and many characters in modern Chinese do not have any obvious relation to their meaning at all.

Alphabet-based writing systems like the one used in English do not provide any such clues at all. Systematic correspondences exist between sounds and letters, but not between letters and meanings. Correspondences between sounds

Table 3.1 *Examples of Chinese characters that represent their meaning to a degree*

1	一
2	二
3	三
tree	木
many trees	林
forest	森
fire	火
burn	炎
flame / spark	焱
person	人
big	大
door	门

and meanings do exist, but they are rare and exceptional – as when we pretend that the cat says *miaow* and the dog says *bow-wow* or *woof-woof*. However, this idea is limited by the fact that several versions of this kind of onomatopoetic language exist even within English, and that other languages have their own versions of it. So in general, we may conclude that words aren't the same as meanings. But nevertheless words *mean*, without a doubt. How do they do this?

Many theories and approaches are available that aim to solve this puzzle. Here, we will look at Evans' (2009a) LCCM theory as one example that represents a well-developed framework which is based on widely shared assumptions in cognitive linguistics. LCCM distinguishes linguistic content (LC) from conceptual models (CM). The idea is that concepts, as such, are too rich and complex to be encoded directly in language. The linguistic level expresses a limited amount of content, but the more crucial meaning aspect is represented by something much more complex: the conceptual model that the lexical item provides access to. This view is also sometimes referred to, quite aptly, as 'access semantics'. So instead of representing concepts with their full meaning, language provides a more abstract and schematic access point to conceptual knowledge.

For instance, imagine you hear the word *red*. This word evokes a certain colour in your mind; it provides access to visualisations of this colour. Your mind draws on rich and varied experiences for this, which you can use flexibly. Which shade or quality of the colour will you think of when hearing the word? Without context, this is really hard to predict, even though there are some prominent structures in our minds (as we will see in Section 3.1.2). But if you add a noun to the adjective, you will immediately get a more specific, more restricted idea of the colour. Think of *red ink* – that's more concrete than simply hearing the word *red*. The work *ink* narrows down the colour range to include only those shades of red that you would expect to see in ink. In contrast, think of *red hair* – now the visualisation in your mind will probably be quite different from the mental image you had when considering *red ink* (Evans, 2009b). It will be a different *red*.

Thus, adjectives of colour allow for a wide range of possible associations. But this is not only true for adjectives. Nouns such as *ink* and *hair* also both provide access to complex concepts of particular types of entities, which are schematically represented. Ink can be black or blue or red, and so on, and also vary in other respects; hair also comes in different styles and colours. On hearing the nouns, you may have a vague idea of this variability, or you may not be entirely aware of it. As soon as context comes into play, the variability becomes less flexible. A combination with the adjective *red* allows you to narrow down the range of meanings associated with *ink* and *hair* – just as *ink* and *hair* narrow down the range of possible visualisations of the colour *red*.

As shown in this example, words can provide access to a wide range of ideas. These are referred to in cognitive linguistics as *encyclopaedic knowledge*. It is almost as though we had an encyclopaedia in our heads, which we open as soon as we come across a word. Our minds instantly provide the knowledge that we need as we're processing the word. This is not to say that the whole encyclo-paedic entry is activated, with all its subtleties. Since we almost always get the context immediately along with the words, we can safely ignore other kinds of knowledge that we might have access to in our minds – everything that isn't relevant in this particular context of usage.

When we produce language, the principle is the same: we use words as access points to our minds, referring to the vast resource of encyclopaedic knowledge that resides there. Words may not adequately express what we mean, but they can certainly serve as pointers. We use words in context to mean much more than what we can actually say, as the words themselves are rather limited. And then we tend to take it for granted that our listeners will have similar encyclopaedic knowledge, activated by those same access points. More often than not, this is not exactly the case – and this explains why people often misunderstand each other. Even if they use the same words in the same context, they may not share precisely the same ideas.

With respect to CODA, the lesson is that words *mean* in a complicated way, that they may mean different things to different people, and also that they are highly relevant access points to the speakers' minds when representing con-cepts. When analysing linguistic data, we need to be aware of the flexibility of these access points, and of the crucial importance of context when interpreting them. To understand more systematically what can be conveyed, by the use of words in context, we need a clearer idea of how meanings are structured in words – and in our minds. To this we turn next.

3.1.2   Semantic Structure Reflects Conceptual Structures

Some of the most well-known and valuable insights in cognitive linguistics concern how conceptual meanings are organised in the mind. Humans have for a long time been interested in the categories that are expressed by words. For instance, what is a *chair*? Intuitively, when asked about the nature of the category *chair*, most people would explain what kinds of features a chair has – typically four legs, a surface, a backrest, and so on – and possibly also what it is used for – a chair is something to sit on.

Digging deeper along these lines points the hobby linguist in the same direction as earlier approaches, going back all the way to Aristotle (Taylor, 1989): namely the challenge of finding the precise set of necessary and sufficient features that correspond to our intuitive understanding of the category *chair*. In Aristotelian terms, a category is defined by whatever features constitute its *essence*. The essence of a *man* would be something like *male two-legged animal*; other features that are associated with specific men would be *accidental* – such as being tall and slim (or not). This kind of view has dominated many disciplines (including linguistics) for a long time. It is represented in dictionaries and encyclopaedias that provide definitions for technical terminology, and it continues to serve a range of very useful and legitimate purposes – such as providing scientific definitions for categories that need a precise treatment.

However, while expert definitions have their rightful place, this way of handling categories might not correspond to what people normally have in mind, or how they conceptualise a category. Sometimes expert definitions clash with folk concepts. A well-known example is the treatment of mammals such as whales as *fish*, even though most people are aware that this is not 'really' (scientifically) the case, as the definition of *fish* excludes mammals. Most clashes between expert and everyday categorisation are probably more subtle, and less fundamental. But above all, the classical feature-based approach simply does not do justice to the categorisation processes in people's minds. There is more to human categorisation than degree of expertise. Human categories are highly structured and meaningful, not just limited by lack of knowledge about specific facts.

Wittgenstein (1953) was one of the first, and the most widely heard, to challenge the classical feature-based view. He pointed out that it is perfectly possible for a category to have members that do not share a single feature. Such categories might get multiple entries in an encyclopaedia, or a complex definition with many alternatives. For instance, consider the word *game*. What do all games have in common? In Wittgenstein's argumentation, there is a counterexample for any feature that one might think of: games might be played alone or with others, they might be competitive or not, they might be for fun or serious (as with the Olympic Games), and so on. Nevertheless, the mere existence of the umbrella term *game* seems to suggest some commonality, some joint basis that warrants placing all of those different items into a single category.

Wittgenstein's solution for this apparent dilemma was to suggest a different approach altogether: he introduced the notion of *family resemblance*. In a family, not all members need to have anything in particular in common – yet they might still be recognised by others as belonging to a single family. Some share red hair, others share a particular form of nose, some might have both features, and yet others might share something else entirely. As long as there are some connections throughout, the family resemblance is recognisable, providing a conceptual motivation for the overarching category. Families, as such, are of course genetically related, so this is only a metaphor for explaining what might be going on in other categories. Not all games have something specific in common, but games around the world share some out of a wide range of possible features that games might have. Most games will be for fun, but those that aren't share other features also found in other games.

These ideas triggered an astonishing range of empirical studies concerned with the nature of categories in the human mind. Eleanor Rosch (e.g. 1978), for instance, carried out a battery of studies that identified crucial structures of categories, well beyond the earlier assumption that categories can be exhaustively understood based on features defined by experts. From this line of work, two main findings stand out that complement Wittgenstein's ideas: first, that categories normally exhibit a *prototype* structure, and second, that some categories are more *basic* than others.

Prototype structure means that some members of a category are regarded as more representative than others. Consider the category *bird*. What kind of bird comes to your mind first when you hear the word? Most likely, it will be one of the most common birds encountered in your spatial environment: a robin perhaps, or a blackbird. While the bird type seen as prototypical is culturally dependent, the phenomenon as such is not: all cultures would regard some birds as more typical members of the category *bird* than others. A rarely encountered bird which exhibits unusual features (or lacks the usual ones), such as a *penguin*, would seldom be regarded as a very good example of the category.

The other, equally important insight that came into focus in the 1970s concerns a deeper understanding of the hierarchical structures of categories. We all know that some categories are subtypes of other categories – for instance, an armchair is a type of chair, and a chair is a type of furniture. Not all of these category types are conceptually equal, or play the same role in linguistic communication. Brown (1958) suggested that there is a level of maximum utility, a word that is most frequently used rather than other options – and this is what parents use when speaking to their children, and accordingly it will be the word they learn. Thus, children will learn to use the word *fish* to refer to a broad range of animals in the water, and differentiate on land between *dogs* and *cats*.

Rosch et al. (1976) took these ideas further by examining in detail what in particular characterises such a *basic level* of category usage. They found that basic-level categories tend to share the highest number of features, while being most discriminative from other categories. For instance, *chairs* are structurally and functionally relatively similar, but clearly distinguished from other types of *furniture* such as *tables*. The more specific notion of *armchair* adds some specific features, but *armchairs* are still similar to other kinds of *chairs*.

Both aspects of categorisation, prototypes and basic-level categories, are cognitively very central and play a major role in the use of words. The understanding of conceptual semantics has benefited vastly from the discovery of these structures in the way humans categorise. With respect to CODA, these insights can be very useful for interpreting language data in the context of a particular situation. For instance, if an experimental task triggered an unusually high number of references to *quadrupeds* rather than *dogs*, *cats*, *horses*, and the like, this would point to a major shift in categorisation (away from the basic level) that is likely to be significant in the empirical context.

Also, it can normally be assumed that people refer to prototypical members of a category when using a word; deviating from this will often trigger the usage of a more specific term. Thus, when encountering a robin (in an environment where this bird is common), people might stick to the basic-level term *bird*, but they might refer to a penguin as *penguin* because of its non-prototypicality within the *bird* category. Such choices of words are meaningful, and need to be interpreted in light of what is known about human categorisation.

Categorisation is central for understanding the nature and structure of meaning in the human mind, but it is not the only cognitive principle at work. The most thorough and systematic approach to cognitive semantics to date was provided by Talmy (2000). Talmy identified a range of organising principles that explain how meaning is structured and expressed in language. First of all, linguistic meaning is schematic rather than highly specific. This concerns all sorts of words. To return to our example of a *chair*, the concept would invoke in speakers' minds a schematic image of a chair, rather than a specific one. Speakers are usually able to sketch such schemas on paper from an early age, demonstrating that they know how to abstract from specific features of particular examples of objects. But not only objects are schematically conceptualised in this sense – other words are, too: even a (small and seemingly insignificant) preposition like *on* exhibits a regular schematic conceptual structure.

Another organising principle discussed by Talmy (2000) relates to the flexibility of language use. There is always more than one way of expressing thoughts and facts. Very often, how people choose to say things depends on what is important or in the foreground for the speaker, and which kinds of things are seen in contrast to this. Talmy's notions of Figure and Ground are a central case in point. In the sentence *The bike is next to the church*, the word *bike* is the Figure, and *church* is the Ground. To some extent, the notion of Ground is similar to 'background'. The Figure is in focus, it is what is being talked about, against the background of something that is (typically) already known. The church, in the example, would be a prominent landmark that people know about, and which can be used to describe the current position of the object in question (the bike). Turning the sentence around would therefore be very odd – *The church is next to the bike*. From an objective, spatial point of view, there would be no reason why this shouldn't be exactly the same spatial relationship. Speakers, however, make their linguistic choices on the basis of underlying principles such as foregrounding and backgrounding. Talmy (2000) suggests a wide range of further principles in this regard. Many of these can be extremely helpful for interpreting linguistic choices when doing CODA.

Altogether, cognitive linguistic research recognises a range of ways in which meanings are organised in the human mind. These structures highlight the close relationship between language and thought *in general*, representing a rich resource for the interpretation of language used in *specific* situations.

3.1.3   Syntactic Structure Reflects Conceptual Structures

Similar to insights in semantics and in part overlapping in scope, cognitive linguists have also looked at *syntax* from a conceptual perspective, and suggested that structural aspects in grammar relate systematically to structural aspects of conceptualisation. This view departs fundamentally from approaches that address syntactic structures primarily to identify systematic rules of representation (e.g. Chomsky, 1980), or to relate them to functions of language use (as addressed in Section 3.2). One of the most prominent proponents of cognitive grammar is Langacker (1986). Langacker's approach is parallel to Talmy's approach to cognitive semantics in many ways. Like Talmy, Langacker points to systematic abstract meaning structures across domains in both semantics and syntax.

Langacker's cognitive grammar is unconventional in many ways. For instance, it makes heavy use of drawings to describe schematic meanings in syntactic structures, such as Figure 3.1. This kind of metalanguage expresses the view that grammatical structures, including word categories such as nouns and verbs, are symbolic in nature, and not merely autonomous and arbitrary

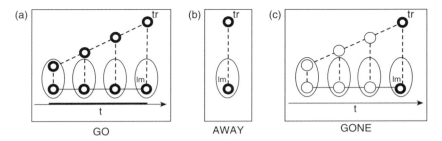

Figure 3.1 Profiled meanings in Langacker (2002:6).
In (a), *go* refers to the interconnections between entities where a trajectory (tr) moves away from a landmark (lm). In (b), the relationship of being *away* is demonstrated by the distance between trajectory and landmark. In (c), *gone* indicates a trace of the movement leading up to the state of being away.

structures of language. In other words, grammatical units express conceptual meaning just as lexical items do, as discussed in the previous section.

Langacker (1986) spells out how schematic meanings that are associated with individual lexical items combine with other schematic meanings in a sentence structure. For instance, in *drop the cup*, the lexical item *drop* schematically assumes two participants – one that drops and the other that is dropped. Langacker calls these *trajector* and *landmark* (similar to *Figure* and *Ground* in Talmy, 2000). Trajectors and landmarks combine in sentences by profiling particular aspects of the described situation, that is, making them more prominent than other aspects. In *drop the cup*, only *cup* (the *landmark*) is explicit – but not who or what is doing the dropping (the *trajector*). This activates a specific substructure of *drop* by providing information about one of its participants. In a similar vein, Figure 3.1 contrasts the profiled meanings of *go*, *away*, and *gone*.

The notion of profiling highlights that the same situation can be expressed from different perspectives: compare *The hill falls gently to the bank of the river* to *The hill rises gently from the bank of the river.* The distinct perspectives induce a sense of directionality even though the described situation is static – there is no motion involved in a landscape description. Langacker explains such phenomena by introducing a distinction between *sequential* and *summary scanning*. In sequential scanning, we experience events or situations as temporally extended, as when we follow a ball's trajectory flying through the air. In summary scanning, our experience is accessed as a whole; the ball's trajectory can be described as a *curve*, a single schema rather than a sequence of successive states. Speakers' choices when using language highlight the way they conceive of the situations, and how they wish to profile them. The choices are not inevitable, there are always different ways of profiling the same state of affairs.

Altogether, much like the structures in meaning, language also reflects structures on a grammatical level that systematically relate to structures of thought. Analysing the syntactic structures in discourse data can therefore highlight interesting aspects of thought, reflected in the constructions chosen by speakers.

3.1.4   Usage Patterns Reflect Conceptual Structures

While much research in cognitive linguistics focuses on the structures of language and what they are capable of expressing, some strands more directly address the use of language. Apart from CODA, there are two main ways in which language use is prominent in cognitive linguistics. On the one hand, examining how language is used allows for the identification of generalised patterns across contexts. This highlights how speakers tend to conceptualise certain phenomena. On the other hand, generalised language usage patterns explain decisive aspects of language acquisition.

Concerning the first idea, Levinson (2003) showed how speakers in different cultures use their languages differently to describe spatial relationships. First of all, he developed a theoretical account of spatial reference systems, and identified a limited number of options which he called *intrinsic, relative,* and *absolute*. All reference systems involve a *locatum* and a *relatum*. The locatum is an object whose location is to be described (e.g. where is the *ball?*) The relatum is another object (or person) that speakers refer to in order to describe where the locatum is. For instance, in *The ball is in front of Anita*, Anita plays the role of relatum. In an intrinsic reference system, only the locatum and relatum are needed, but the relatum must have some kind of intrinsic directionality. The ball can't be *in front of the balloon* because balloons don't (normally!) have front sides. But it can certainly be *in front of the car* – a car is a suitable relatum for an intrinsic reference system, as it has a clear front (just like *Anita*).

If a relatum is used that doesn't have any clear sides of its own (like a balloon), speakers will normally need something else in addition – some kind of perspective, or point of view. This is what Levinson (2003) calls a relative reference system. *The ball is in front of the balloon* makes sense if you use your own perspective on the scene, or your partner's – you could say, *From your point of view, the ball is in front of the balloon*.

The third type of reference systems in Levinson's classification is called absolute: a system for directions that is always present in a culture, independent of perspectives or intrinsic sides. In Western cultures, compass directions are the most typical examples for this. Thus, using an absolute reference system, you could say, *The ball is north of the balloon*.

This sentence might sound a tiny bit unusual – and indeed it is, for many speakers. This was precisely the focus of Levinson's extensive research programme. He addressed the situations and contexts in which speakers regularly used spatial reference systems across different cultures. Absolute reference systems are widely known in Western cultures through the compass, but their use seems to be restricted to certain contexts: compass directions are primarily used to describe spatial relationships on a geographical scale. Whether people otherwise prefer intrinsic or relative reference systems is difficult to say – this seems to depend to a large extent on the usage context.

Across cultures, there are two remarkable patterns with regard to reference system usage. First, not all languages provide a set of options that corresponds to those found in English. While intrinsic reference systems seem to be pretty much universal, relative reference systems are not available in all cultures – and absolute reference systems can differ widely in their nature. Often, there are specific environmental features that cultures draw on to establish absolute reference systems. In the language of Tzeltal, for instance, people refer to objects as being *uphill* or *downhill* from each other – in a very similar way as one might refer to *north* or *south* in a Western society. This is because their landscape involves a prominent structure that appears to feature very prominently in the minds of Tzeltal speakers, even in situations where the hills themselves are not visible (Brown & Levinson, 1993).

And this is the second remarkable pattern: that speakers make use of the available reference systems in very different, culture-dependent ways. Absolute reference systems, for instance, may not be part of many people's everyday language when describing object locations in English, but other cultures use them all the time. They know at all times in what direction things and locations are, and how they are actually related to each other in space. Speakers of Yucatec Maya, for instance, typically show this actual relationship in gestures, rather than relating gestures to their own current or imagined perspective (Le Guen, 2011). Based on abundant empirical evidence, Levinson (2003) demonstrated that this is not just a matter of linguistic preferences, but instead reflects different patterns of thought. And this makes sense. To constantly be able to describe object locations in terms of their true relationship in space, equivalent to *The ball is north of the balloon*, people must think about space in a very specific way – a way that is unavailable to speakers in most Western cultures. Try it out: which compass direction are you currently facing? If you know the compass direction without having to look at the sun or calculate, you're a bit like the Yucatec Maya. Chances are, however, that you can't tell – not without clues to support your thinking.

Research of this kind investigates the use of certain aspects of a linguistic repertory to find out about patterns of thought, as with CODA; this includes studies that elicit unconstrained natural language data in controlled task settings (e.g. Senft, 1994). The account in Levinson (2003) focuses more on the general patterns within a culture, rather than addressing specific challenges for thought processes in empirical settings. The insights gained on that level are valuable resources for a deeper understanding of the significance of linguistic choices in more specific settings. For instance, if the general pattern in Western cultures is that speakers rarely make use of absolute reference systems in indoor settings, but a certain empirical scenario is found to trigger a preference for compass directions, this will be very meaningful for the analyst.

Apart from studies that directly target usage patterns along these lines, the overall use of language is understood as being the central foundation for findings in cognitive linguistics across the board. Patterns in linguistic structure such as those described in Section 3.1.3 are deeply motivated by the ways in which speakers use language (Langacker, 2000). The more frequently people use a specific linguistic structure, the more it will be entrenched in people's minds and in the linguistic system – and this tells us something about the importance of this structure for the specific language and cultural thought. Consider Langacker's distinction of trajectors and landmarks, described in Section 3.1.3. A great many verbs profile precisely two participants, mapping onto these roles. For instance:

Example 3.1   Anne is reading a book.
                Jake took the hint.
                Grandma is starting to cook dinner.

The grammatical *subjects* of these sentences are *trajectors* (Anne, Jake, Grandma), with the grammatical *objects* as their *landmarks* (a book, the hint, dinner). While trajectors and landmarks play out differently for other sentence structures and are therefore broader notions than the traditional subject and object categories, the simple structure demonstrated here is nevertheless one of the most cognitively salient, most frequent and entrenched, most central for human thinking as expressed in language. It comes as no surprise, then, that the same phenomenon – the ability of verbs to point to two (or less, or more) participants with different roles – has received much attention across various grammatical approaches. We will look at another one in Section 3.3. There we will see how central aspects in Systemic Functional Grammar are designed entirely around verbs and their decisive functional role in a clause.

Since frequency and usage are so central for explaining cognitively salient structures, they are also important factors for child language acquisition (Tomasello, 2003) – the second main idea mentioned in the beginning of this section. Children often do not acquire individual words but rather pick up frequently heard constructions, which they learn and first repeat as a whole, and then expand creatively. They might only be able to repeat single words to begin with, but a short word or phrase may stand for an entire utterance – which would be more complex in adult language. Thus, a young child might say *ball* to mean *Where's the ball?*, or *That!* to mean *I want that!* (Tomasello, 2003:65). Phrases like *Lemme see* or *Gimme that* are likely to be understood by the child, at first, as wholes, and only later parsed into their constituent elements. At some point, they learn to replace individual elements out of phrases such as *Where's the X?*, *I wanna X*, *More X*, *It's a X*, and so on. Such constructions are central and frequent in children's lives; they represent usage patterns that directly link up with the way they are starting to understand the world and interact with other human beings. In this way, a child's grammatical repertory gradually grows and becomes more complex, as a greater range of usage patterns become relevant.

This also explains why it is very different to learn a second language: usage patterns are already far developed and highly varied. It takes a long time to fill these pre-existing conceptual 'slots' in a new way, with a different language. This is even more challenging if the languages are built around different usage patterns, or patterns of thought. If you grew up using intrinsic and relative reference systems to describe where objects are, you won't find it very easy to learn a language in which absolute reference systems are the norm. Indeed, you might learn the words as such easily enough, but *using* them appropriately across a range of contexts might be quite a different matter.

Altogether, patterns of usage play a major role in cognitive linguistic research. Usage patterns explain certain structures in linguistic systems as well as in how they are acquired. As usage patterns differ in relevant ways between languages and cultures, research into how language is used across cultures, and in speakers of more than one language, sheds light on questions concerning the interrelationship between language and cognition.

3.1.5   *Conceptual Structures Start from Embodiment and Can Be Transferred*

Due to the fact that usage is central (as just outlined), language has developed in close relation to our lives, our ways of interacting with the world. This point leads us to the final central insight in cognitive linguistics that will be sketched here: meaning itself transfers from concrete physical action events towards more abstract settings. This insight is central for one of the most widespread and well-known areas in cognitive linguistics – the investigation of transferred meaning, often called metaphors. With their best-selling book *Metaphors We Live By*, Lakoff and Johnson (1980) triggered a keen interest in abstract uses of language, shared by a multitude of researchers throughout the world who aim to discover how and why metaphors characterise our thought and language.

For instance, much of our thinking has to do with *value*, either good or bad. Value, as such, is not physically accessible; it is more abstract than actions and things. But frequently *good* is related to *more* in the physical world, and *more* is related to *up*: more coins are good, and they add up to a higher pile! Such associations make the idea of value less abstract, more accessible in the real world. Over time, in English, *good* has become generally linked with *up*, as we can see in many expressions, as well as its counterpart, *bad*, being associated with *down*:

Example 3.2   Fran is in *high spirits* today.
Matt scored *lower* than his friends.
After a period of feeling *downhearted*, they now became *upbeat* about the plans.
The party was *highly* successful.

Lakoff and Johnson (1980) demonstrated that systematic patterns like these can be found in language in many ways that we aren't normally aware of. To take another example, *relationships* are frequently associated with *journeys*, as seen in expressions like the following:

Example 3.3   They *started* as a couple in 1982.
Anita and John had a fine friendship, without many hassles *along the way*.
Why did our love have to *end*?

The link is established through the joint notion of time: relationships develop over time, and journeys unfold in space as well as time. Space is physical, but time isn't – so space is brought into play in order to express the more abstract notion of a relationship. There are many metaphors that relate to space in some way. Indeed, time itself is very often expressed through the language of space:

Example 3.4   It was a *long* day.
Christmas is *around the corner*.
Good times are *ahead*.

In many of the expressions that invoke a transfer from a physical domain (such as space) to an abstract one (such as time), prepositions play a major role. By examining these prepositions in detail, Tyler and Evans (2003) spelled out how transfers of meaning can develop. For instance, the preposition *over* has a complex network of interrelated meanings, as demonstrated by the following:

Example 3.5   The cloth is over the table.
He jumped over the fence.
Like a bridge over troubled water . . .

The spatial relationships expressed in these examples are all somewhat different. The fact that various spatial meanings can be conveyed by the preposition *over* is the basis for the emergence of diverse non-spatial meanings, as in:

Example 3.6   She took a long time to get over the disappointment.
               Over time, things became better.
               I will think it over.

Tyler and Evans (2003) show how abstract meanings such as these relate to spatial meanings of *over* in a complex and interconnected system where spatial relationships are transferred to abstract domains. This is contrary to the widespread idea that prepositions express a random set of unrelated meanings.

Goldberg (1995) applied the idea of transferred meanings to the level of grammar (related to the ideas discussed in Section 3.1.3). For instance, consider verbs that involve three elements in a sentence. One of the most frequent examples of this type of verb is *give*. The grammatical pattern associated with the verb *give* reflects direct practical experience where things change hands: *somebody* gives *something* to *somebody else*. The three elements can be expressed in two different ways:

Example 3.7   Anna gave Paul a dog.

Example 3.8   Anna gave a dog to Paul.

Both constructions are common, but they are associated with somewhat different usage patterns – each construction can seem odd or just right, depending on various contextual factors that won't be explored further here (though the topic is interesting to pursue in its own right). There is also the possibility of leaving out the *giver*:

Example 3.9   Paul was given a dog.

Now, the same notion of transfer can be expressed without actually using the verb *give*:

Example 3.10   Joe painted Sally a picture. (Goldberg, 1995:143)

The use of this particular structure, which resembles the grammatical structure associated with *give*, automatically invokes the idea that Joe *gave* the picture to Sally when he was finished. Moreover, Goldberg (1995) points out that Joe must have intended for Sally to have that picture while he was painting it; it is not possible that he painted it for someone else and then later changed his mind. This is how strongly the *giving* notion is invoked by grammar – simply by the use of a construction that involves three elements and represents them in this particular way.

Altogether, many patterns in linguistic systems can be traced back to the fact that we live and talk in a physical world. Frequently experienced embodied patterns, such as transferring goods from one person to another, or stacking up things in a growing pile, are reflected in structures of meaning and grammar in language, allowing for a transfer into more abstract domains of thought.

This concludes my brief introduction to aspects of cognitive linguistics that may be useful when doing CODA. There is a lot more to be found in this wide field, and my selection of insights is not intended to be representative. However, I hope that my short introduction might provide a useful starting point for understanding the language people use to express their thoughts.

3.2   Discourse Analysis

We have already discussed diverse relevant methods and approaches, but undoubtedly the most common label typically associated with analysing the use of language is discourse analysis. This is because 'discourse' simply means language being put to use in actual situations, to communicate and to express thoughts and ideas, in spoken or written language. The label 'discourse analysis' encompasses a wide range of methods that generally aim to gain a better understanding of discourse. Not all of these methods are primarily linguistic. Typically, instances of discourse are analysed in relation to the communicative purposes they serve in a particular context. Especially in linguistics, the term 'discourse' is often seen in contrast to examples of individual sentences that are examined with respect to their structural and semantic features out of context. Discourse analysis means taking into account aspects on a larger scale than words or sentences – aspects that pertain to the wider context of language use.

Texts have structure just as sentences do, although the structures might be more varied. Many written texts start with some kind of introduction, followed by a main body (which may also have some internal structure) and a conclusion. Other discourse types have a very different structure; a phone call would begin and end with a greeting, and perhaps queries and wishes about well-being, rather than an introduction and a conclusion. Analysing common and systematic structures in different discourse types can lead to deeper insights about the nature of discourse in general. And specific aspects can be helpful in educational or professional training contexts. Knowing how a newspaper report is written to achieve the intended effects on the readership can be very useful when attempting a career in journalism.

Extending the scope on the level of language to include a piece of discourse that is larger than a sentence is one way in which context (or *co-text*) plays a role. Most approaches in discourse analysis go further than this, beyond the discourse as such. They also look at various factors of the context in which discourse takes place outside language. This would include situational factors such as the time and place of the discourse, who is speaking to whom, and the like. Many approaches focus on the significance of a specific instance of discourse within society – such as a public speech given by an influential political leader at a certain moment in history. This provides a perspective that motivates much work on discourse. Especially in the strand known as Critical Discourse Analysis (Fairclough, 1995; van Dijk, 2008), the main aim is to understand how language is used in society to influence, persuade, or manipulate other people.

CODA, with its focus on language used to express thought (rather than to manipulate), is not primarily *critical* in general. Nevertheless, the insight that society and situational context play a major role in the interpretation of language is certainly relevant. In fact, there are a number of connections between cognitive linguistics and Critical Discourse Analysis (Hart & Lukeš, 2009). For instance, the use of particular metaphors and construals in political or journalistic discourse not only reveals, to some extent, how the writer thinks about the matters at hand, but may also have certain effects on readers.

Teun van Dijk (2000), in a non-academic online article, offered a number of relevant thoughts concerning the notion of Cognitive Discourse Analysis; these included aspects of discourse processing as well as features of text that point to particular cognitive structures or operations, such as presuppositions and implications, lexical connotations, local coherence, and the like. Rather than developing this particular notion further in his work or applying it to specifically collected instances of language use in relation to thought processes, van Dijk has subsequently focused on the interplay between cognitive aspects (intentions, strategies, knowledge) and sociocultural context models (van Dijk, 2008). However, his ideas are indeed very relevant to what is presented in this book: for instance, we will take a closer look at the notion of presupposition in Section 3.2.2.

Apart from these general frameworks, there are many individual approaches and contributions that aim to identify systematic patterns in language usage – and many insights gained in this regard can be very relevant for CODA studies. In the following, we will first look at methodological aspects in discourse analysis (Section 3.2.1). Then we will outline a number of specific aspects that concern discourse rather than individual sentences, all of which may be relevant for CODA: information structure and presupposition (3.2.2), coherence devices and discourse markers (3.2.3), and lexical choices and specificity (3.2.4).

3.2.1 Methods in Discourse Analysis

As we have seen at the start of Section 3.2, different types of discourse analysis can be used to uncover various (social, cognitive, etc.) phenomena reflected in discourse. It is important to recognise that there is no way of analysing any instance of discourse completely neutrally, or in its entirety. Discourse analysis normally happens against the background of a research project or goal, and this determines the perspective adopted to analyse the data at hand. It affects the range of linguistic, social, cultural, or other phenomena that are taken into account in the analysis, and often also the type of data that are collected in the first place. Sometimes it is the data as such that drive the analysis, such as in corpus-driven discourse studies or conversation analysis; in such cases, researchers aim to avoid any preconceived expectations or frameworks.

We will look at specific procedures for CODA in Chapter 8. Here, the aim is to put the methodology into context and highlight the benefits of different, but related approaches. There is nothing self-evident or inevitable about a choice of data and analysis approach. Methodological choices of any kind are meaningful, and they affect what kinds of data are collected, what kinds of analysis procedures are used, and what kinds of insights are expected. Along the way, there is also the step of transcribing language data – and this, as well, constitutes a choice that can significantly affect the outcome.

A distinction is sometimes made between *Discourse* (with a capital D) and *discourse* (with a small d) (Gee, 2013). The first refers to the Discourse that happens in society at a larger scale, embedded in other social practices within a community (e.g. customs, traditions, shared concepts). The second refers to language in use, that is, specific instances of discourse that are part of a larger Discourse. Analysing discourse (instances) therefore necessitates taking into account the kinds of Discourses in society that are associated with this particular instance. It means understanding a particular interaction as an example or instantiation of what happens at a larger scale. This perspective will affect what aspects are looked at, and how they are interpreted.

The idea of experimental control is alien to this approach, because controlled experimentation seeks to eliminate the societal aspects that are the very target of discourse analysis of this type. Instead of collecting data under controlled conditions, therefore, samples of discourse are taken directly from the situations in which they happen, and analysed in light of the various contextual factors that come into play: the relationships between interactants, the social and spatiotemporal settings, and anything else that might be relevant for the unfolding of discourse. If a fully authentic sampling of data is impossible, semi-structured interviews may be a useful way to collect data. A flexible interview setting allows the participants to talk relatively freely, in a non-prescribed way, and this in turn allows the interviewer to gain insights from the analysis that are not directly influenced by any predetermined aspects of the interview itself.

Any instance of spoken language contains a wealth of information that may or may not end up in a transcript. The language data can be transcribed simply to represent content – and this is the normal level of transcription that one might find on the Internet, when looking for written versions of a public speech, court proceedings, and the like. Such content-based transcripts are typically regarded as sufficient to represent spoken discourse outside the realm of discourse analysis. Very often, the versions that are publicly available are edited; the rough edges of spoken discourse are smoothed out, certain formulations are improved, interruptions are ignored, and so on. Such editing makes the transcripts more readable and therefore serves their intended purpose: to make the content of a public event accessible in written format.

However, any deviation from the actual spoken event renders the transcript less reliable and therefore less suited for the purposes of discourse analysis. Researchers wishing to make use of existing transcripts should normally double-check the written version, in order to align it as closely as possible with the original discourse event.

Beyond deviation, editorial improvements, and inaccurate transcription, a transcript can be a true record but still inadequate for the purposes at hand. This is because transcribing always requires decisions as to what to include and what to ignore. It can be challenging to obtain all of the information that would be necessary for a complete analysis that addresses the current research goals. Contextual factors that pertain to the spatiotemporal, social, and cultural setting might be decisive. Gestures and mimics, body posture, and volume of voice may be recorded and added to the transcript, alongside language. The language itself may be transcribed at various levels of detail. At perhaps the most developed end of the scale of precision – opposite to publicly available non-academic general-purpose transcripts – one finds the well-established methodology of conversation analysis (Sacks, 1992). This method builds on the insight that an extremely detailed transcription of a speech event can highlight subtle mechanisms in conversation that one might otherwise miss. Compare the following (taken from an insightful tutorial[1] on conversation analysis provided by one of its proponents, Charles Antaki):

Example 3.11   Zoe: mum
                Lyn: hello I'm here
                Zoe: okay

Example 3.12   Zoe   Mum?
                Lyn   hello (pause)
                Lyn   I'm here (pause)
                Zoe   okay- (pause)
                Lyn   ((coughs/clears throat)) (pause)

Example 3.13   Lyn   ((at table with papers))
                      ((door?)) ((faintly, off camera))
                      (pause)

---

[1] http://ca-tutorials.lboro.ac.uk/transintro1.htm

Lyn [[looks up and over her shoulder towards door; holds gaze
while scratching cheek; looks down again]]
Zoe ((off camera)) Mum?
Lyn hello [[gaze stays down]]
(3 sec)
[[at end of which she
orientates upper body
towards door]]
Lyn I'm here
(brief pause)
Zoe okay
Lyn ((coughs/clears throat))
[[off camera: three ?
crockery bangs]]
(pause)
((door handle opening))

Example 3.14 Zoe   ((off camera)) Mum?
Lyn   .pt h↑ello
(3 sec)
Lyn   I'm here
(.8)
Zoe   (okay)-
(1.0)
Lyn   ((coughs/clears throat))
((clatter))
(3.0)

While Example 3.11 simply provides the words that were spoken in the
transcribed scene, Example 3.12 represents pauses and a non-linguistic human
noise (coughing) that might seem relevant. However, this is not very detailed.
Example 3.13 includes various non-linguistic aspects as well as body postures.
Example 3.14, finally, exemplifies a transcript that conversation analysts would
typically use. It does not include the non-speech details provided in Example 3.13,
but is instead very informative concerning the speech events themselves, including
length of pauses and aspects that pertain to speech volume and intonation contour.
These are represented by arrows, underlining, dashes, and the like.

As these examples demonstrate, transcripts can be veridical and accurate, but
still vary considerably in what they represent. The analyst decides which aspects to
include, which are relevant for their analysis goals. This may go well beyond the
aspects relevant to speech that are transcribed in conversation analysis, and also
beyond other non-speech events observed directly in the scene. Note that none of

the examples (3.11–3.14) reveal anything about the speakers' social background, the time of day, the previous and following discourse, and a variety of other factors that might explain what is happening in this short conversation. Discourse analysis means making decisions in this regard, but not random ones; they need to be well motivated in light of the research goals at hand.

Similarly, the methods undertaken when analysing the data can be rather varied, as they include systematic scrutiny of linguistic, metalinguistic, and contextual aspects as deemed appropriate by the analyst. This kind of choice also needs to be well motivated and appropriate for the purpose of analysis. Antaki et al. (2003) point to a number of things that one might confuse with discourse analysis or that may go wrong in attempts at doing discourse analysis – such as simply providing summaries, taking sides, picking out individual quotations, or spotting random individual features.

As I hope to have shown in this section, existing discourse analytic approaches have a lot to offer in terms of systematic methodology. Various excellent introductory accounts, such as Gee (2010) and Johnstone (2008), cover the field more deeply than can be achieved here. We will now look at a number of linguistic aspects that are frequently encountered in discourse analysis, and that may be useful to consider from a cognitive perspective as well.

3.2.2   Information Structure and Presupposition

Compare the following two sentences:

Example 3.15   Sam gave Rosie a book that was good to read.

Example 3.16   The book that Rosie was given by Sam was good to read.

Both sentences express the same information: that Sam gave Rosie a book and that the book was good to read. However, both sentences make different assumptions. In both cases, proper names are used to refer to people: Sam and Rosie. We either know them already, or we assume that we will soon learn more about them (unless they appear without context, as happens to be the case here!). In novels and stories, characters are very often introduced by name only, and the reader gradually becomes acquainted with them through further reading (or listening). In real life, upon hearing this kind of reference in a conversation, we might ask, 'who is Sam?' – unless we do already know who the speaker is referring to.

The two sentences are equivalent in this respect, but there is a third element in the event described, namely a book – and this element is not treated in the same way. Note, first, that Example 3.15 uses an indefinite article (*a book*), whereas Example 3.16 uses a definite one (*the book*). The definite construction signals to the reader or listener that the book should already be known. But in fact, the entire *event* of giving the book to Rosie is described as new or previously unknown in Example 3.15, along with the fact that the book was good to read. As a consequence, we could respond to Example 3.15 by either saying, 'Oh, did he?' or 'Oh, was it?' In contrast, in Example 3.16 the only information that is treated as new is the fact that the book was good to read. So a suitable reaction could be 'Oh, was it?' – but not 'Oh, did he?' If we don't remember that Sam gave a book to Rosie, responding to that part of the message becomes more complex: 'Oh, did he give a book to Rosie?'

Many insights can be gained by looking at the ways in which information is presented. The term *information structure* refers to the sequential order of information in a sentence, along with other ways in which information can be represented as new or already known across different languages (Steube, 2004). And the term *presupposition* refers to what is assumed to be already known, as signalled by definite articles and other linguistic devices (van Deemter & Kibble, 2002). Both work together in discourse, organising what is known and what is communicated as new. This contributes to the economy of language use and communication: new thoughts can be interpreted in the context of existing ones, finding their rightful place in the listener's mind, without having to build up an entirely new knowledge base from scratch.

Apart from definite articles, we find the following constructions that presuppose various facts (Spenader, 2002):

Example 3.17   That John stole the money matters.

Example 3,18   Trizia started sailing when she was eighteen.

Example 3.19   It was the bachelor who got madly drunk that night.

In Example 3.17, it is presupposed that John stole the money – there is no question of that. The only new information is that this fact actually *matters*. In Example 3.18, the presupposition triggered by the verb *start* is that Trizia did not sail before she was eighteen years old. In Example 3.19, it is already known that someone got madly drunk that night – the only question is who it was (namely, the bachelor). Note how the presupposition triggers relate to sentence structure. New information frequently comes at the end (as in Example 3.17), but not always (Halliday & Matthiessen, 2014). The specific structure in Example 3.19 (called *cleft* structure) enables the sentence to put a different element into focus (the bachelor), even though it is not presented at the end.

There is a lot more to discover about information structure and presupposition; it is a fascinating subject that has been taken up in many discourse analysis approaches. With its many implications for the ways in which knowledge is organised in our minds, this analysis perspective is undoubtedly relevant for CODA. We looked at some examples already in Chapter 1, and will return to these issues in Chapter 6 when considering how CODA can be used to examine inference phenomena.

3.2.3   Coherence Devices and Discourse Markers

How do sentences hang together, and how are utterances and ideas related to each other? How are such relationships expressed in language? Consider the following:

Example 3.20   Mary went to the bank. She needed to prepare dinner for fifteen people the next day.

When reading two sentences in direct succession, we expect that they relate to each other. In Example 3.20, there is only one direct indication that the two sentences are related: the reference to *Mary* through the pronoun *she* in the second sentence. One might also say that the word *next* implies a temporal relationship between the two sentences, where the event described in the second sentence takes place a day later than the event described in the first sentence. Such effects fall under the notion of *cohesion* as examined in Systemic Functional Grammar (Halliday & Matthiessen, 2014).

However, the most important aspect remains entirely implicit: namely the question of why the two events are mentioned together at all. This aspect is normally examined in terms of *coherence*. Coherence is somewhat more complicated than cohesion, as it concerns how we interpret sentences and how we understand their interrelationships on the level of (pragmatic) meaning. To understand how two sentences add up to a coherent whole, we need to make another inference – similar to the kinds of inferences that we discussed in the previous section, but on a different level. This particular kind of inference happens on the level of discourse relations. We assume that there is a reason for putting two sentences together, and therefore we infer a relationship between them.

In the above example, the inference will typically be causal: Mary went to the bank *because* she needed to prepare dinner for fifteen people the next day. There are a number of associations going on in our minds when we draw this conclusion, such as:

Example 3.21 Fifteen people is a large number – most people wouldn't do this every day. If it was normal for Mary to cook for fifteen people, it wouldn't have been mentioned.
If Mary does not cook for fifteen people every day, she might not have all the ingredients in the house that are needed to cook for such a large number.
If she doesn't have the ingredients in the house, she'll need to go shopping in advance before she can get started.
The dinner is only one day away. She needs to get started soon as this is a big task.
She will need to go shopping now. For this, she will need money.

> She is going to the bank because she needs money for the shopping.

The list of associations could be continued, spelled out in more detail, or made shorter. For some people, there may be more direct links between going to the bank and preparing dinner. Sperber and Wilson (1986) spelled out how such logical inference processes may take place in the mind, enabling us to determine how sentences can be understood as relevant to each other.

To avoid the effort of making these complicated inferences and assuming that the relationship is causal, the conceptual link between the two sentences in Example 3.20 could also have been made explicit by using discourse markers that signal coherence (Sanders, 1997; Schiffrin, 1987). Both of the following would contribute to this, in different ways:

Example 3.22   Mary went to the bank *because/as* she needed to prepare dinner for fifteen people the next day.

Example 3.23   Mary went to the bank. She needed to prepare dinner for fifteen people the next day, *you see*.

Example 3.22 directly states a causal relationship using a discourse connective (*because/as*). This is the most straightforward way of signalling a discourse relation. Example 3.23 remains implicit with respect to the actual discourse relation, but the discourse marker *you see* appears to invite the listener to establish a meaningful connection, supporting the inference of a causal relationship.

There is abundant literature on discourse relations and on the ways in which discourse markers contribute to them (and do other things in addition). Independent of the precise goals of discourse analysis, researchers frequently take these phenomena into account in order to gain a deeper understanding of the analysed discourse. Especially with implicit coherence, however, there is always an element of uncertainty as to whether the inferences made by the listener (or by the analyst) correspond to the intentions of the speaker.

3.2.4   Lexical Choices and Specificity

As a final example of the kinds of things that are frequently observed in discourse analysis, let's look at the level of words. Compare the following two possible utterances:

Example 3.24   There's a man and a dog on the beach.

Example 3.25   I can see a young athlete, perhaps twenty-five years old, and his pet, walking along the beach.

Obviously, Example 3.24 is much shorter than Example 3.25. Despite this, the speakers may both be describing the same situation; for instance, they may be looking at the same picture. One description is simply a bit more specific than the other. How exactly does this work? Clearly, Example 3.25 is not simply an expansion of the same – this would have been the case in a sentence like this:

Example 3.26   I can see that there's a young man, an athlete, perhaps twenty-five years old, and a dog, his pet, walking along on the beach.

This example combines both sentences – so now we have a true expansion, of both original sentences. To get a clearer idea of how Example 3.25 is more specific than Example 3.24, we need to do more detailed analysis.

While the reference to the beach is identical, the other two participants are referred to in different ways. In Example 3.24, both of them – the man and the dog – are referred to on the basic level of categorisation (see Section 3.1.2). This is the most neutral way of referring, which can be used for a relatively generic description. In Example 3.25, the case is different. Instead of a generic reference to *a man*, this time we learn that the man looks like an *athlete*, and that he is *young*; we even get an estimate of the age. In this context, *athlete* is subordinate to the basic-level category *man*: an *athlete* is a specific kind of man.

The reference to the *dog* is rather the opposite, as a dog is a specific kind of *pet*. This, as well, is a deviation from the generic basic level; it points to the specific relationship between the man and the dog in a way that is not accomplished in Example 3.24. This is reinforced by the personal pronoun *his*, which is missing in Example 3.24. We also get a sense of motion and action, expressed by the verb *walking* in Example 3.26; this is completely absent in Example 3.24, rendering the description far more static – which is supported by using the existential phrase *there is*.

Lexical choices are meaningful. They represent the way in which the speaker wishes to talk about what they see or think. A generic level of representation, using the basic level of categorisation, may not tell us much about the speaker beyond their desire to remain relatively neutral. Anything beyond this shows a bit more; in the above example, it reveals an eye for details such as the man looking athletic and young, as well as the relationship between man and dog. The interpretation of such choices is most successfully achieved through contrast and comparison of different samples or instances of discourse, analysed in light of theories about how lexical concepts are organised and accessed in the mind (see Section 3.1).

Since the same real-world objects and individuals can be described in many different ways, on different levels of specificity and with different associations, some lexical choices may sometimes seem to be more appropriate than others.

Indeed, speakers sometimes struggle to find a good way of describing things that is suitable for the context. In some situations, it may be possible to identify an ideal level of reference; this provides an opportunity for researchers to examine how good speakers are at identifying it. Consider the following random list of numbers:

Example 3.27   7, 5, 6, 3, 79, 288, 389, 230, 12, 35

Now, if a speaker wanted to refer to one of these numbers without actually mentioning it (this could be the rule of a game), they could say:

Example 3.28   It's the even one-digit number that is in third position in the sequence, from left to right.

Clearly, the speaker is referring to the number 6. But they could have done this in a simpler way: the information given in Example 3.28 is *overspecified*. It would have sufficed to just refer to the even one-digit number, since only number 6 falls into this category. And likewise, it would have sufficed to only refer to the third position of the sequence. Speakers do often include redundancy of this kind in their descriptions; overspecification is actually quite frequent in language use (Arts, 2004). In contrast, Example 3.29 would have been *underspecified* because there are several one-digit numbers:

Example 3.29   It's the one-digit number.

Further ways in which utterances can be ambiguous and underspecified can be found in a collection of papers edited by van Deemter and Peters (1996), which provides a valuable resource for discourse analysis. Relatedly, Bierwisch and Schreuder (1992) made the point that single lexical items can serve various purposes, depending on the syntactic and discourse context. The associated concepts can normally be disambiguated and identified, as in the following (Bierwisch & Schreuder, 1992:31):

Example 3.30   He left the institute an hour ago.

Example 3.31   He left the institute a year ago.

The same word *institute* denotes a building in Example 3.30, and in Example 3.31 an institution or affiliation. It is interesting to see how the time frame suggested at the end of the sentences – an hour as opposed to a year – gives not only the word *institute* a different interpretation, but also the word *left*. Within a short time frame, one might automatically assume that the described event is on a small temporal scale, as in the physical event of leaving a building. Within a long time frame such as a year, such an interpretation would normally seem inadequate; therefore, the assumption is that the leaving event is much more consequential and concerns the entire life situation. All of these assumptions are (again!) inferences that the reader or listener derives from world knowledge that is filled in upon the mention of individual lexical items, such as temporal references. Discourse analysis often aims at revealing insights of this kind, and the interpretation of linguistic choices in relation to cognition is no exception.

Generally, it often makes sense to look closely at the lexical choices a speaker makes, for any number of reasons. This is a frequent method across discourse linguistic approaches. With CODA, an analysis focus on lexical choices means identifying lexical items that reveal certain relevant aspects of cognition (such as focus of attention, see Chapter 4, or level of granularity, Chapter 5). In other approaches in discourse analysis, lexical choices may reveal further interesting patterns, depending on the specific type of discourse at hand. Altogether, as we have seen in this section as a whole, many of the principles used in traditional discourse analysis are equally valid for CODA.

3.3   Functional Grammar

Systemic Functional Grammar (SFG) (Halliday & Matthiessen, 2014) is a widely recognised grammatical framework that has a lot to offer for CODA research, both from a theoretical point of view and with respect to a number of specific analysis perspectives. We have already come across this framework several times in this book, and will encounter further details later on; this section offers a concise introduction for reference. We will start with an overview of the theoretical basis (3.3.1), which enables us to look at the three main levels of analysis that are central to SFG: the interpersonal level (3.3.2), the ideational level (3.3.3), and the textual level (3.3.4).

3.3.1   Theoretical Foundations of Functional Grammar

Doing CODA means looking at linguistic choices: identifying what speakers do with language, out of the many things that they could have done. Understanding the significance of what speakers choose to do, therefore, has a lot to do with understanding what else they could have done. SFG provides a framework for this kind of understanding. It accounts for the various functions of language by showing what the overall system of linguistic choices looks like and what it offers to speakers. In fact, every aspect of grammar can be explained using the notion of choice, as part of the overall system. Take, for instance, the grammatical notion of *mood*. The same content can be expressed in various ways depending on mood:

Example 3.32   Luke will travel on Thursday.

Example 3.33   Will Luke travel on Thursday?

Example 3.34   Luke, travel on Thursday!

The choices that are available to express this same content represent the mood system in English: namely, declarative (Example 3.32), interrogative (Example 3.33), and imperative (Example 3.34) mood. These are the options on a grammatical level that a speaker has at their disposal. The speaker's choice in a situation expresses their relation to it: they either express the content as a fact, or they question whether this same content is a fact, or they command it to become a fact.

Mood therefore has to do with what goes on at the *interpersonal* level – the level where grammar shows the relationship between speaker and hearer (or writer and reader), which we will explore in Section 3.3.2. The content, as such, is expressed by grammatical choices on the *ideational* level, as we will see in Section 3.3.3. In addition, the information in the text is organised by a number of devices that show what a speaker takes as relevant and wishes to point out. This relates to the notion of information structure that we briefly looked at from a theory-neutral point of view in Section 3.2.2. In SFG, this is addressed in terms of the *textual* level of analysis (Section 3.3.4). At all three levels, speakers always make a choice whenever they use language. The grammatical system of the language they use provides them with options in many different ways, and all of these choices are meaningful: after all, it is a big difference whether somebody simply notes that Luke will travel on Thursday, or wonders if that's the case, or commands him to do it.

With this notion of choice as a central concept, SFG provides a thorough toolbox for interpreting every instance of discourse in relation to its occurrence. Awareness of the overall repertory, and of the distinctions between the options, enables a valid assessment and interpretation of specific linguistic choices in relation to the situational context. While any account of grammar in linguistics provides relevant insights with respect to a language at hand, SFG provides a particularly useful resource as it is designed up front in terms of a *network of options*. This network allows for identifying the meaning relationships and metafunctions that constitute the structure of lexicogrammar.

Knowing how the network operates *in general* helps in identifying aspects of language that are *specifically* meaningful for a certain analysis perspective. For CODA purposes, the distinction between different levels of meaning and functions of language highlights those linguistic features of a text that relate to cognitive aspects, alongside other features that pertain to interpersonal or textual functions, or simply represent what's happening in the real world. Here, knowing how the network works in general helps to understand what a particular choice shows us about the way the speaker represents their thoughts.

Other approaches use SFG for a range of other purposes and are less focused on cognitive aspects. In fact, the main founders and current proponents of SFG are primarily oriented towards understanding language in relation to society. Text and discourse are seen as meaning-making instances of language; they are best interpreted in relation to the overall system, taking into account the context of where they are produced. Moreover, structures of linguistic features in texts are explained by reference to the purposes for which the texts are produced. Different kinds of situational contexts call for different ways of using the network of options, and SFG provides a precise basis for explaining how this is done.

SFG was developed for the English language (Halliday & Matthiessen, 2014), but its approach and framework are not limited to it, and have in fact been transferred to a broad range of other languages (Butler & Gonzálvez-García, 2014). Halliday himself has worked extensively on Chinese and has included various discussions of it in his work. Schlobinski (1996) used insights from functional grammar as a basis for empirical linguistic analysis methods for German. The list could be continued. Altogether, a large and vibrant community works with and expands SFG today, both as part of and beyond the International Systemic Functional Linguistics Association.

After these general observations, we will now turn to the specific analysis levels that are prominent in SFG, starting with the interpersonal level in the next section.

3.3.2   The Interpersonal Level of Analysis in Functional Grammar

At the interpersonal level of language, grammatical choices tell us how a speaker relates to a certain idea, and how they wish to convey that idea to the listener. One might say that, at this level, the relationship between speaker and hearer is represented in grammar. We have already encountered the notion of *mood*, which tells us whether the speaker represents something as a fact (using the declarative mood), or questions it (using the interrogative mood), or commands it to become a fact (using the imperative mood). This aspect belongs to the interpersonal level of analysis.

There is an interesting grammatical observation here. In English, mood choice affects only two elements of a clause – the Subject and the Finite. Returning to Examples 3.32–3.34, if we say *Luke will [travel on Thursday]*, the Finite *will* follows the Subject *Luke*, and this indicates a declarative clause. If we turn the two around, we get *Will Luke [travel on Thursday]* – and as a speaker of English we immediately recognise the interrogative. That's all it takes. The imperative is special in that the Subject can be left out – though it may be included for clarity: *(Luke), travel [on Thursday]!* Therefore, analysis on the interpersonal level in English strongly focuses on Subjects and Finites –

which are not always easy to identify, and I will leave discussion of this to the grammar books (e.g. Halliday & Matthiessen, 2014).

But there's more to observe. For one thing, speakers aren't always sure about facts, or there may be other ways in which the message is less than straightforward. For another, it is not very polite to express direct commands, and sometimes speakers may want to avoid asking direct questions using the interrogative mood. As a result, the function of an utterance is not always directly reflected in its grammatical form. Nevertheless, the grammatical system does reflect the underlying interpersonal relationships in a range of ways.

Let's look at modality first. Modality means that the message is somehow modified with respect to the speaker's stance towards it, or the extent to which something can be argued. Not every declarative message directly reflects a clear and indisputable element of truth; facts can be represented as true or not true, or somewhere in between these two poles. For instance, the speaker might want to modify the definiteness of Luke's travel plans (in Example 3.32) a little, and change various aspects around – all related to the Finite:

Example 3.35   Luke may/might/could travel on Thursday.

Example 3.36   Luke must/should travel on Thursday.

Example 3.37   Luke will certainly/definitely travel on Thursday.

In Example 3.35 and 3.36, the Finite itself is changed from *will* (expressing a high degree of determination) to something other, indicating levels of certainty, possibility, or obligation. In Example 3.37, similar modulation is expressed outside the Finite, namely by a modal Adjunct (*certainly* or *definitely*) that is associated with the Finite. The Adjunct fulfils very similar purposes to the modal Finite, but it does so in a different way – and there are many of them. SFG provides the entire network of options in English, which can be accessed in Halliday and Matthiessen (2014).

Second, consider the relation between function and form. Instead of using a direct command in the imperative form, an English speaker is more likely to express a wish by using modality, for instance a version of Example 3.35 or 3.36. In such a case, we might still understand the utterance to be some kind of command or order, but it is expressed in a socially acceptable way: as a declarative with appropriate modality, rather than in imperative form. Although the imperative is socially less acceptable in English in many situations, it does occur in certain social contexts, such as in emergencies: *HELP!!*, towards children: *Sit down now and be quiet!*, and in recipes: *Heat oil in a pan. Add the garlic ...* etc. This is an example where the choice of grammatical patterns reflects social contexts in which they are appropriate.

Following this brief introduction to the interpersonal level of analysis in SFG, we will now turn to the analysis of how the world is represented – the ideational level.

3.3.3 The Ideational Level of Analysis in Functional Grammar

The ideational level concerns how ideas are expressed in language. At this level, perhaps a little surprisingly, the analyst looks first to the main verb. As we have already noted above, verbs come with different kinds of expectations, so to speak: they demand either one or more elements (called 'participants' in SFG) to go with them. Importantly, these participants frequently need to be of a particular nature. Consider our previous example, repeated here:

Example 3.38   Luke will travel on Thursday.

The main verb in this example is *travel*. If you think about travelling as an activity, it is sufficient to have just one participant that does this activity: the *Actor*, in this case Luke. Therefore, it is possible to end the sentence after the word *travel* – the bit about Thursday is merely a *circumstance*; it is not essential to the sentence. You can't add another participant such as **Luke will travel Joanne* . . . If we want to include Joanne, we can either add her to the Actor bit, as in *Luke and Joanne will travel* – or we can add her in a similar way to how we have added the information about Thursday: in a prepositional phrase, as a circumstance, as in *Luke will travel with Joanne / to Joanne / without Joanne* . . . etc.

Many verbs are like *travel* in this respect, in that they require only an Actor: *jump*, *walk*, *read* – there is no limit to the lexicon here. However, there are also plenty of verbs that do not work that way. For instance, we can't just say *Mary gives*. To make a clause with a verb like *give* complete, we need as many as three participants: an Actor (e.g. *Mary*), a Goal (*the book*), and a Recipient (*Paul*).

Example 3.39   Mary gives Paul the book.

This is not to say that every clause needs to express all three participants explicitly – languages are rather too flexible for that. Passive constructions are excellent resources to 'hide' the Actor:

Example 3.40   Paul was given the book.

Nevertheless, the third participant is understood as somehow present, although we don't learn who (or what) it is in a passive construction like Example 3.40. The verb *give* normally demands three participants, and therefore the implication can be readily inferred that there must be a third participant, even though it is not expressed.

Importantly, not all participants are persons – as we have seen by calling the *book* a participant. The notion of *participant* is one of function, not form, and therefore there can also be other kinds of participants. In fact, some verbs regularly call for participants that are often as complex as a whole clause:

Example 3.41   Timothy said that we should go home immediately.

In Example 3.41, we can't simply end the sentence after *said* – we would immediately wonder *what* Timothy said. This is called the *Verbiage*. Verbs like *say* expect a Verbiage as one of their participants, along with another participant called the *Sayer* (Timothy). Instead of *that we should go home immediately* we might, however, hear any of the following:

Example 3.42   Timothy said *a word*.

Example 3.43   Timothy said *nothing*.

Example 3.44   Timothy said more than anybody else in the room.

All of these different linguistic forms can serve the function of Verbiage. We can't do without a Verbiage with a verb like *say*, but we can express it in many different forms.

Because verbs behave very differently with respect to the kinds of participants that they require, they are categorised into various different classes. Verbs requiring an Actor (and potentially other participants) fall into the *material* category, and verbs requiring a Sayer and Verbiage into the *verbal* one. A further category that is particularly interesting from a CODA perspective is the *mental* one, which comprises verbs that have to do with thinking and feeling:

Example 3.45   Jean wondered about the question.

Example 3.46   The grandparents felt that the children were safe.

Verbs such as *wonder* and *felt* expect a Senser and a Phenomenon – someone who senses, namely *Jean* in Example 3.45 and *The grandparents* in Example 3.46, and something that is sensed, namely *the question* and *that the children were safe*, respectively. Halliday and Matthiessen (2014) pointed out that while the range of possible participants that can be Sensers is fairly restricted (only someone or something with sensorial ability can sense!), the range of things that can serve as Phenomenon is very wide – we can think and feel quite a lot of different kinds of phenomena, and we can express them in many different grammatical ways.

The category of *relational* processes concerns clauses that are constructed around the verb *be* (and some related options), as in:

Example 3.47   The world is your oyster.

Example 3.48   The statue was extremely tall.

Example 3.47 relates the *world* to a different concept, *your oyster* – and thus *identifies* the world as something that can be expressed in these terms also. Example 3.48, in contrast, relates the *statue* to an *attribute* (*tall*). Again, the second participant in these kinds of clauses can take on many different forms, any of which serves the function of a participant in this kind of clause.

Altogether, Halliday and Matthiessen (2014) highlighted the importance of verbs in the organisation of clauses. Suggesting that verbs are used to express different kinds of 'worlds', they differentiated the *world of abstract relations* (as expressed by relational processes) from the *world of consciousness* (thinking and feeling) and the *physical world* (acting and behaving). This kind of fundamental distinction provides a useful resource for analysing verbalisations of mental representations. Identifying types of verbs can be a very useful starting point for identifying systematic patterns in the speakers' thoughts, looking at whether relations or physical actions are expressed, and to what extent the speaker refers to thought processes and feelings directly.

The next section will conclude our brief introduction to SFG analysis levels by looking at the third level, which concerns textual structure.

3.3.4   The Textual Level of Analysis in Functional Grammar

The third level of analysis in SFG concerns the organisation of text *as text*: for example, what kinds of ideas are presented first or last, and how they are structured in relation to each other. In SFG terminology, the *Theme* is the part of a clause that concerns what the text is about, whereas the remainder (called the *Rheme*) is used to say whatever there is to say about it. In English, the Theme is represented as the first element in the clause. So in the previous Example 3.47, *the world* is what we're talking about, and what we're saying about it is that it *is your oyster*. Themes are typically connected in some way to the context: there is generally a reason for why the Theme is chosen the way it is, that is, why we choose to talk about this particular Theme. This becomes particularly interesting when talking about Theme development across clauses. For instance, consider the following short text:

Example 3.49   John went to the store. It was closed. Opening hours seemed to have changed.

The text starts with *John*, which is a reference to a person that we might or might not know – in any case, it is clear right away that the text is about John. Within the remainder of the first clause, in the Rheme, we find a reference to *the store*. This is picked up as the Theme in the second clause – namely by the use of the pronoun *it*. In the Rheme of the second clause, we find the information that it was *closed*. This topic is picked up as the Theme in the third clause, through the reference to *Opening hours*. Thus, we can see that, twice, the Theme of a new clause relates to the Rheme of the previous clause. Sometimes such a relation is established by pronoun reference (such as *the store – it*), and sometimes by semantic links (such as *closed – opening hours*) that the reader or listener can identify easily.

Going from Rheme to Theme, as in the previous example, is a relatively typical thematic development in coherent texts. Another frequent option is to simply go from Theme to Theme. In Example 3.50, the Theme *John* in the first clause is picked up by the pronoun *He* in the two subsequent clauses.

Example 3.50   John went to the store. He felt tired today. He hadn't slept well . . .

Looking at thematic developments across clauses and establishing the relationships between Themes helps to identify the ways in which speakers relate topics to each other in discourse. This varies considerably across types of discourse, but the general fact remains that how sentences are structured is important – it matters how they begin or end. This is closely related, but not identical to the notion of information structure discussed in Section 3.2.2. Information structure refers to what is presented as *given* and what is *new* – and this is not quite the same as what a clause is *about*. The given part of a sentence is very often in Theme position, making the new part equivalent to the Rheme. But this need not be the case. Especially in spoken language, speakers have other means of making the new part prominent in discourse, namely by contrastive stress:

Example 3.51   My *brother* went to jail, not my sister!

To conclude, discourse shows systematic patterns and features on three levels. A focus on the interpersonal level highlights how the relationship between speaker (or writer) and hearer (or reader) is represented in the discourse. A focus on the ideational level reveals the representation of the (real or imagined) world, and a focus on the textual level draws attention to the way discourse is structured, related to the medium in which it occurs.

At all three levels, analysis becomes most revealing when looking beyond the elements and features of a single clause, towards the patterns and structures of entire texts and instances of discourse. This is, in fact, what SFG is designed and used for: the interpretation of text beyond single clause structures, in light of the various functions fulfilled by linguistic choices. We have seen this most clearly at the textual level, because thematic development is best understood across clauses. However, discourse analysis based on SFG works similarly at the other levels as well. Looking at the interpersonal level is most interesting when tracking in detail throughout a text how speakers put ideas across to recipients, using various forms of modality. And looking at the ideational level can be highly revealing when identifying patterns of verbs and participants, which may vary at different places in a text.

Throughout this chapter, we have identified a range of linguistic phenomena that cross over theoretical approaches in cognitive linguistics, discourse analysis, and functional grammar, all of which are relevant for analysing the language speakers use to express their thoughts. The fact that similar notions and insights appear as part of different approaches underscores the idea that CODA, as such, is theory neutral. Indeed, some of the notions or tenets in different approaches (such as functional grammar and cognitive linguistics) may be felt as incompatible, or at least not easily reconcilable. Rather than aiming to combine or contrastively review theories, my goal in this chapter was to point to relevant insights within and across theories that can be drawn upon to understand speakers' use of language in collected data in relation to cognition.

In this vein, linguistic resources of any kind can be helpful for identifying the significance of linguistic choices. It may be more important to recognise that linguistic choices are significant – relative to the situation of language production in light of the overall network of options – than to subscribe to a specific theoretical approach in linguistics.

4   Identifying Cognitive Orientation

Now that we have covered the general resources and theories underlying CODA, it is time to get more specific: what kinds of conceptual aspects can be explored using CODA? Let me stress again that there is no actual limit here. The language we use is rich with phenomena and conceptually interesting structures, many of which may yet be detected in the future. Some insights stand out as points of connection between linguistics and cognitive science – where linguistic research highlights conceptual aspects that the linguistic system makes prominent, precisely in areas that are frequently targeted in cognitive science research. The next four chapters will explore a selection of these. Chapters 4 and 5 deal with conceptual aspects that are represented in every instance of language use, and Chapters 6 and 7 concern further phenomena of relevance for many settings targeted in linguistic and cognitive science research. Each phenomenon will be discussed along with an example from CODA research.

In this chapter, we will look at two conceptual aspects that both pertain to cognitive orientation – the way we perceive the world and think about it: attention (Section 4.1) and perspective (Section 4.2). Attention concerns *what* we orient to, in terms of cognitive focus, and perspective concerns *how* we orient to it, that is, from which point of view.

4.1   Attention

The role of attention for cognitive processes can hardly be overestimated. We can't think consciously without paying attention – this would be a contradiction in terms. Conscious thinking about something means (among other things) that we are attending to it. Therefore, knowing where someone's attention is focused at any given time is central to understanding the cognitive processes involved in a given task. This is true for any type of cognitive activity: attention is just as central for viewing a picture as it is for solving a tricky problem. In both cases, we might pay attention to some things but completely miss others.

In addition to our conscious attention focus, thinking involves some aspects that we aren't aware of, and aren't paying attention to. Our subconscious might guide our attention in ways we don't notice. It might lead us to sudden insights or solutions to a problem that we have been trying hard to solve (e.g. Schooler, Ohlsson, & Brooks, 1993). We might be unaware of something we see from the corner of our eye. All these things are possible, and they are exciting areas in cognitive science research. However, the things that we are paying attention to are the things that are most prominent in our minds. Much research in cognitive science therefore aims at gaining insights about this central factor (see, e.g., Anderson, 2009), and about the interplay of conscious attention focus with other, less prominent processes that guide thinking.

Not surprisingly, attention likewise guides the use of language. Focus of attention constrains what is said, as well as how it is said. In a sense, everything we say reveals where attention is currently focused. Remember when you were a child, at school, and were daydreaming – just not paying attention to what the teacher said? You wouldn't have been able to answer a direct question, leading to embarrassing silence or making something up instead of a meaningful response. And perhaps you have been caught asking a question concerning something that you should already know – had you only been paying attention . . .

Spouses tend to know exactly when their partner pays attention to what they're saying and when they don't; they can identify the little signs in the loved one's reactions that reveal whether they're actually with them – or rather far away in their thoughts. And sometimes there is something in a formulation that strikes you as odd, as not quite in sync with what you've just said. Perhaps you couldn't quite put your finger on it, but you do get the feeling that your conversation partner isn't entirely on the same page. And this may well be the case because they weren't paying attention – or because their focus of attention was on something slightly different. Your attention focus differs from theirs, and this directly affects communication, or how well you feel understood.

Based on these everyday experiences, we all have intuitions about the close relationships between attention, thought, and language use. Such intuitions can be important when doing CODA, as they can provide a suitable starting point for deeper scrutiny. Doing analysis may mean turning intuitive observations into something far more systematic, something that can be used as evidence for a particular phenomenon that the analyst is pursuing. In the following, we will explore the conceptual factor of attention in more detail first from a cognitive science perspective (Section 4.1.1), second from a linguistic one (4.1.2), and then look at connections between the two in previous research (4.1.3). An example from CODA research will conclude this section (4.1.4).

4.1.1   Attention from a Cognitive Science Perspective

Nearly half a century ago, Neisser and Becklen (1975) conducted an ingenious experiment in which participants were shown short video films that were overlaid visually, such that they were watching two films at once. They were asked to pay attention to only one of these two films: they had to react to certain things that happened in it, whereas the other one could be ignored, as it was not needed for the task. It turned out that the participants were incredibly good at doing this. Their performance in reacting to the films dropped only very slightly in comparison to a condition in which they were only watching a single film. Moreover, they barely noticed what was going on in the other film. The experimenters had inserted some unexpected scenes that would have been noticed by anyone who paid attention to the films; however, participants did not recall any of those if they were asked to attend to the other one of the films. This experiment powerfully demonstrates how good we are at consciously directing our attention to whatever is relevant in a given situation. But it also demonstrates how we can totally fail to notice some things if we happen to be distracted.

In common parlance, we recognise this phenomenon as *selective attention* – and we are familiar with it from a range of everyday situations. In a room full of people talking, such as a party, we can focus our attention on the conversation we are currently involved in. It might be challenging and tiring, but it does work. If we catch something from another conversation nearby, our attention might switch – and as a direct effect we will miss something from the conversation that we were supposed to be following. This is essentially the same effect as the visual one demonstrated by Neisser and Becklen (1975), only in the listening domain. If we make an effort to pay attention to certain aspects, we perceive relevant things much more clearly and intensively than if we don't (Kahneman, 1973). There are certainly individual differences; some people get more easily distracted than others, and physical impairments such as hearing difficulties might make it much more difficult to focus. On the whole, though, we know intuitively that we are capable of directing attention to certain things, at the expense of other aspects of a situation. We cannot attend, at the same level, to everything at once – this is clearly impossible.

Likewise, we know that it is very difficult to remember things that we did not pay attention to. It has long been known that memory is directly affected by attention focus (e.g. Moray, 1959) – and this opens up interesting questions about the exact nature of the dependency between the two. For instance, although attention guides what we perceive, there are always aspects that do not quite reach consciousness but that are nevertheless processed to some extent (Corteen & Wood, 1972). If that's the case, to what extent can we learn (and then perhaps subconsciously remember) things that we don't actually pay attention to? Nissen and Bullemer (1987) observed that *awareness* during learning need not be entirely the same as *paying attention* during learning. And indeed, in a series of experiments they found that in order to learn, one need not always be aware of certain aspects. Some information may just be carried by a task, and people don't need to notice it in order to learn it. However, they do need to pay attention to the task as a whole, in general. Thus, it appears that attention is central to cognition in many respects, and while it is intricately related to conscious awareness it is not identical to it.

Another way in which attention plays a role in relation to cognitive task performance concerns the opposite effect of learning: the better we get at a task, the less attention we need to pay to it in order to get it done (Norman & Shallice, 1980). You might remember how much attention you initially had to pay to every single movement or action when you learned how to drive (or to ride a bicycle, or any other acquired skill). The more experience you get, the less you need to think about it. Your responses to different traffic situations become more and more automatic, and you may often not be aware of what you are doing, especially if the situation is not particularly complex. This enables you to engage in deep conversations, or do other things while driving. Naturally, this also involves a danger (Canas et al., 2003): since you're not really paying attention to the current task of driving, some things may escape you. And this might lead to tricky situations, where experienced drivers can make errors that learners, whose attention is fully activated anyway, may not necessarily do. It is therefore important to be flexible enough to switch back to enhanced attentional control, out of the 'autopilot' mode that enables experienced people to do a task without paying much attention to it.

So, from a cognitive science perspective, we can see that attention is one of the most central factors guiding cognitive processes, and it never ceases to be of interest because of its complex relationships to other factors such as awareness and automated processes. Attention also guides performance in cognitively challenging tasks, because solutions sometimes can't be found if the problem solver's attention focuses on something else. And it provides a bottleneck for simultaneously executing certain motor actions – we all know how difficult it is to do one type of motion with one hand and a different one with the other. It can be learned, by paying attention to both motions sequentially and automatising the processes – but the bottleneck is there. There are many further exciting findings in this area. Anderson (2009), for instance, provides a useful review of earlier literature, and more can be discovered by reading up on more recent developments in cognitive science.

4.1.2   *Attention from a Linguistic Perspective*

If attention is central to our thinking, we can expect it to have systematic reflection in language. Language, after all, is the prime way to express our thinking. And indeed: language never represents facts or perceptions neutrally, but rather serves to spotlight and privilege certain aspects while neglecting others. Within cognitive linguistics, all of the main grammatical approaches highlight in some way how attention focus is represented in language. We have already considered some of them in Chapter 3. Now that we're looking directly at the cognitive factor of attention, it is easy to see how linguistic structures systematically account for the fact that some things are more prominent, more in focus, than others. For instance, Langacker (1986) shows in numerous examples how language can be used to *profile* specific aspects of a scene while backgrounding others. Even small and seemingly negligible changes in grammatical structures can be significant in this respect. Consider the difference between the following sentences (Langacker, 1986:15):

Example 4.1   I sent a walrus to Antarctica.
Example 4.2   ? I sent Antarctica a walrus.
Example 4.3   I sent the zoo a walrus.

Something is odd about Example 4.2, as Langacker suggests (indicated by the question mark). In some grammatical approaches that are not cognitively motivated, Examples 4.1 and 4.2 are regarded as entirely equivalent, and therefore they should not differ with respect to acceptability. Also, grammatically, both *Antarctica* and *the zoo* are noun phrases – so there's no grammatical reason for Example 4.3 to be better than Example 4.2.

Langacker's explanation for this puzzle is that there is a slight difference in profiling, which is illustrated in Figure 4.1. Using the preposition *to* profiles a trajectory from an unknown source to the destination indicated in the sentence – *to Antarctica*. This profiles the path, much more than Examples 4.2 and 4.3 do. Without the preposition, the recipient of the transfer is profiled: *Antarctica* in Example 4.2, *the zoo* in Example 4.3. Now, it intuitively makes sense to donate a walrus to a zoo, and this justifies directing attention (linguistically) to the recipient. In contrast, there is something odd about donating anything at all to a continent. The focus on the recipient therefore does not seem to make sense. Shifting focus to the trajectory of the transfer (ever so slightly, by using the preposition *to* as in Example 4.1) makes the sentence acceptable.

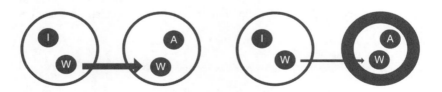

I sent a walrus to Antarctica.   I sent Antarctica a walrus.

Figure 4.1 The different profiles of semantically similar sentences (following Langacker, 1986).

Although the notion of profiling in cognitive grammar clearly accounts for the different ways in which attention can be focused and expressed in language, Langacker (1986) did not himself discuss the relation between profiling and attention as a cognitive phenomenon. Langacker's approach can nevertheless be useful for explaining specific linguistic choices in terms of cognitive focus, in cases where systematic differences in profiling choices are found across sets of language data, related to different kinds of cognitive tasks or task aspects.

As indicated in Chapter 3, Talmy (2000) offered a different approach to explaining linguistic structure from a cognitive perspective, with a stronger focus on semantics. Talmy's distinction between *Figure* and *Ground* in linguistic constructions is entirely compatible with Langacker's notion of profiling and the associated notions of *Trajector* and *Landmark*. This explains differences such as those between *the bike next to the church* and *the church next to the bike*. Some entities are more likely to be profiled as the item to be localised – such as the bike – than others. A church is not movable and normally does not have many competing items looking similar in the nearby environment; therefore, it is fairly difficult to think of a context where it would be natural to identify the church's location as being next to the bike.

It is probably safe to say that every single grammatical distinction somehow reflects a difference in conceptual representation – and thus, a slight difference in just how attention is allocated. Taking these ideas further, Talmy (2007) offered a comprehensive account of more than fifty ways in which linguistic structure highlights attention. Each of these factors introduces a difference in linguistic structure that draws attention to some aspect while decreasing attention to another. For instance, even though *aunt* means *parent's sister*, both *parent* and *sister* are much more in focus when saying *parent's sister* than when simply saying *aunt*. This is because the word *aunt* conflates the notions of *parent* and *sister*, leaving them implicit – and this is different to actually mentioning these terms directly. Similarly, consider the following ways of expressing the fact that some event happens in the past or in the future (Talmy, 2007):

Example 4.4   a. When he arrived, . . . b. When he arrives/will arrive, . . .
Example 4.5   a. On his previous arrival, . . . b. On his upcoming arrival, . . .

On a semantic level, there does not seem to be much difference between these two examples: both of them express an arriving event at a time located before or after the time of speaking. However, while Example 4.4 expresses the notion of past or future simply by using grammatical morphemes (arrive-*d*, arrive-*s, will* arrive), Example 4.5 uses content adjectives (*previous/upcoming*) to do the same. In addition, the action of *arriving* is expressed by a verb in

Example 4.4, but by a noun in Example 4.5. These two factors work together to create the overall impression of a much stronger focus on the event in the future or in the past in Example 4.5.

To illustrate another factor, consider the choice of grammatical roles in the following examples, which are also arguably semantically equivalent:

Example 4.6   The landlord rented the apartment to the tenant.
Example 4.7   The tenant rented the apartment from the landlord.

Although renting could be justifiably regarded as a balanced act, with complementary actions carried out by the people involved, the two examples clearly guide attention to the part played by the landlord in Example 4.6, but to the part played by the tenant in Example 4.7. In each case, the grammatical subject (landlord vs. tenant) is perceived to be more active, more in charge, more accountable for the decisions made.

Further factors include the following, just to cite some inspiring examples from Talmy (2007):

• Lexical choices that highlight different aspects of related terms: compare the different associations of *dirt*, *soil*, *earth*. All of these can occur almost interchangeably in some contexts but not others.
• Order of elements in a sentence, similar to thematic structure in SFG (Halliday & Matthiessen, 2014), as discussed in Chapter 3.
• Linguistic ways of drawing attention to terminology, as in *this gadget is called a 'pie segmenter'*.
• Linguistic ways of drawing attention to the delivery style of an utterance, as in *So then I'm like: Wow, I don't believe this!* – uttered by a young person while telling a story.

And many more. Obviously we cannot and need not reiterate all of the many ways in which linguistic features reflect differences in attention focus identified by Talmy (2007). For current purposes, it suffices to note that language is extremely well equipped and powerful in expressing attention focus and guiding an interaction partner's attention to certain aspects of a situation (including language itself) rather than others.

With respect to CODA, it can be wise (in the absence of more direct predictors from previous literature) to think in the opposite direction: starting from linguistic data collected in an experimental study, rather than from the differences available in the linguistic system. If one data set primarily represents a certain state of affairs in one way, and another data set (perhaps in a different condition, or a different time throughout an experimental procedure) favours a different way, then this may very well have to do with distinctions contributed by the attentional system of language. Talmy's (2007) work, among others, may then serve as a valuable resource to provide a theoretical explanation for the differences found in the data.

Altogether, we can conclude that language offers a wide range of ways in which attention focus can be reflected and communicated. As users of language we normally just accept these features in the language we use and encounter, without giving it much thought. As analysts, it can be highly revealing to examine such features systematically in a linguistic data set.

4.1.3   Attention: Links between Language and Cognition

Attention is central to cognition, as we have seen – and language has multiple ways of reflecting attention shifts. But how much evidence is there to show that language and cognition are actually linked through the attentional system? Various directions of research indicate such a link, and we will look at three examples here: eye movements, child language acquisition, and discourse structure. Although we won't have space for more, this list could be expanded in many ways, showing the intricate relationship between attention and language use.

When we pay attention to something, we are also typically *looking* at it. If you want to direct a partner's attention to something you see, you might say, *Look at this!* – and point in the relevant direction. This concrete experience also extends into non-visible aspects, as when we say things like *Look, what I mean is …* in a more figurative context. And when parents have something very important to say to their children, they will often ask them to *Look at me!* – hoping to make them pay close attention to what they have to say.

So, looking is closely related to paying attention, and this has been utilised for research on attention in cognitive science. Unlike attention itself, eye movements can be observed, recorded using eye-tracking devices, and measured; therefore, they serve as an external representation of the internal phenomenon of attention. In this respect, eye movements are like language: utterances can also be recorded and analysed in detail. Once we have these two measures that both relate to cognition, we can relate them to each other to identify patterns of attention focus.

In an inspiring collection of articles that report research of this kind, Henderson and Ferreira (2004) demonstrate various ways in which eye movements are systematically related to language processing. For instance, attention processes guide reading. We don't read individual letters or even words, but our eyes jump across chunks of text, comprehending meanings rather than visual shapes as we go. Similar findings can be noted for comprehending the real world: as we look at scenes, we process them on the basis of meaningful concepts and relevance, rather than by taking in a lot of details. Indeed, the details may easily get lost as we understand scenes based on what we see.

Sometimes we completely miss unexpected aspects if they are not connected to anything that is relevant to our current situation. This in turn is reflected in the way humans describe scenes through language. What we look at, or have just looked at, gets represented in language. Moreover, the order in which we look at things in a scene is systematically related to the order in which they appear in language. Attention focus, as measured by eye movements, also guides comprehension and processing of language – and sometimes we can even predict what people will say, or how they will interpret an utterance, by observing what they look at.

Looking at something and talking about it starts early in life. Carers frequently name objects when speaking to young children, typically accompanied by a pointing gesture: *Look at this shiny red train, it's nice isn't it?* Expanding on this everyday experience, Tomasello (2003) claimed that child language acquisition, on a very general scale, is guided by joint attention. Children learn language precisely because of their ability to direct their attention to exactly the same thing as their carers do. After all, the world is full of objects and sounds. Without joint attention, how would children be able to understand that the sound of saying *train* has anything to do with a particular shape of object, out of the many objects visible at the time? The early experience of following a carer's attention gradually expands to being able to understand communicative intentions, to follow a train of thought, and to derive meanings from abstract contexts – and along with this, vocabulary and conceptual understanding grows.

As we can see from looking at child language acquisition, joint attention is a central factor for communication: understanding each other's intentions through language works because we can guide each other's attention focus through what we say, and how we say it. Some theories of language and communication use this idea as a fundamental element in spelling out how discourse works. For instance, Grosz and Sidner (1986) introduced a computational theory that models features of discourse structure, capturing elements such as conjunctions, referring expressions, and the like that organise the discourse. According to this theory, discourse is constrained by attention in decisive ways.

For instance, agreeing on a specific referent in dialogue works because the interactants' attention is jointly focused on this particular referent; this enables the speakers to use simple terms like pronouns to refer back to them. This is not entirely foolproof: pronouns like *he*, *she*, *it*, and *they* can be ambiguous in some contexts – particularly if the speakers' attention is not entirely aligned, which means that they may be thinking of a different referent. Thus, pronouns are a frequent source of misunderstandings.

Furthermore, cue phrases such as conjunctions (*but*, *and*, *first*, *moreover*, etc.) serve to guide attention throughout the structure of verbal interaction. For instance, if you hear the phrase *but anyway, ...* you can assume that the attention focus in the discourse has somehow drifted away from the original train of thought, and the cue phrase helps to bring it back. This normally works even though the phrase is very unspecific: it doesn't provide any details as to where exactly attention should be focused instead. The discourse partner will need to listen to the remainder of the utterance and make the connection in their mind, in order to link back to the previous focus of attention.

Altogether, it is safe to say that attention and language are clearly interlinked. This is supported by research on eye movements. In child language acquisition just as well as in everyday language use, joint attention is needed to achieve communication successfully. Specific cues in language can signal clashes of attention in dialogue.

4.1.4 Attention: A CODA Example

Since attention is so central to language use and clearly linked to cognitive phenomena, this aspect of cognition is a natural target in CODA projects. Independent of what kind of task is given to participants, the focus of their attention throughout the task will determine what they say and how they formulate it. If you describe a picture, you will focus on the kinds of things that you pay attention to – it will be almost impossible not to notice where your focus lies when considering how you describe it. Likewise, if you think aloud while solving a problem, your words will reveal your current attention focus in various ways. To illustrate this idea, we will now look at one example from CODA research in more detail.

Imagine you're given a famous picture by a classic artist, and are asked to describe it. What would you pay attention to, what would you focus on? Perhaps your description will reveal something about the extent to which you're interested in paintings of this kind, and perhaps you will linger on aesthetic aspects or those that you find particularly convincing or impressive. Now, what would be different, do you think, if you were a professional painter rather than a layperson admiring a famous picture? As such, describing a picture is not a particularly demanding task – you don't need years of professional training to do that. However, the way in which you do it may very well depend on who you are, and how you think about paintings. Expertise may guide attention, and thereby influence the way in which descriptions are presented in language.

In Cialone, Tenbrink, and Spiers (2018), we took this train of thought a step further and hypothesised that professionals with some kind of spatial expert background would look at pictures showing spatial environments in a different way to how other people do. This idea is related to the Whorfian theory (see Chapter 1), which suggests that societal and cultural background determines structures in language, reflecting structures of thought. Most research in the Whorfian tradition addresses differences in cultural thinking as evidenced in the differences between entire languages. Following a slightly different tack, in Cialone et al. (2018) we set out to test whether thinking, as reflected by language use, may be influenced by particular aspects of a speaker's professional background.

We designed a study with three groups of people who had been working in a spatial profession for at least eight years – sixteen painters, sixteen sculptors, and sixteen architects – plus a control group containing sixteen people with a similar range of experience in non-spatial professions. All participants in the study were interviewed individually, and they were given as much time to respond to the questions as they liked. We gave them three different pictures to look at: a Google Street View screen shot, a famous painting, and a surreal landscape produced by a digital artist. For each picture, participants were asked the same set of three questions:

Question 1 'Could you please describe the environment that you see in this picture?'

Question 2 'How would you explore the space in this image, where would you go?'

Question 3 'If you were given the chance, how would you change the environment in this image?'

These questions were intended to encourage the participants to look at the pictures in some depth, and to think about them in various different ways, none of which required any particular professional expertise. And indeed, the answers did not directly represent professional training – none of the participants tried to educate the experimenter by explaining expert facts about paintings or architecture or anything of that sort. And none of the 'non-spatial' participants had difficulty dealing with the questions. But nevertheless, there were striking differences between the groups: they were indeed looking at the pictures in different ways, depending on their particular expertise. They paid attention to different things, thought about them differently, used different concepts.

Most prominently, it was clear to see that painters, sculptors, and architects produced more elaborate descriptions than the group without any particular spatial expert background. Their descriptions revealed more attention to detail, more willingness to focus on this task for a longer period of time. But then there were also differences between the groups of professionals, revealed by a close CODA analysis that involved the identification of linguistic markers for various conceptual categories throughout the collected language data.

Results of this analysis showed that painters were more likely to describe the depicted space as a two-dimensional (2D) image; they said things like 'It's obvious the image wants you to follow the boat off onto the horizon.' More than others, painters switched between describing the scene as a three-dimensional

(3D) space and as a 2D image. This reveals that they frequently shifted attention between the picture as a picture, and the environment depicted within it. By contrast, architects focused their attention more on barriers and boundaries of space, and this was revealed in utterances such as 'There are voids within walls which become spaces in their own right.' Sculptors' responses were between the two; they were somewhat like architects except for one measure: with respect to describing bounded space, they appeared more like painters.

Altogether, our study showed that even within the same culture, people of different professions differ in how they appreciate the world – in this case, how they focus their attention when looking at pictures that show environmental scenes. The findings also raise the possibility that people who are already inclined to see the world as a 2D image, or who focus on the borders of a space, may be more inclined to pursue painting or architecture. This also makes sense – perhaps we develop our thinking in a particular way, for whatever reasons, and this paves our way towards a particular profession.

4.2   Perspective

As human beings, we live in the 'here and now' – we perceive the world from a certain vantage point in space and time. However, we can adopt a different point of view in our minds. For instance, we can imagine seeing the world from the perspective of our interaction partner, or any other position that we can think of. This is also true in terms of concepts, in various ways (Schober, 1998). Perspective taking means considering different worldviews, beliefs, concepts, physical viewpoints, and more. Our ability to do this means that we can take various perspectives into account when making judgements, or when talking about complex facts or ideas.

Like the speaker's focus of attention, the underlying conceptual perspective is represented systematically in linguistic structure, and it can be highlighted by the analyst in relation to the discourse and task context. In this section, we will start by looking at spatial perspectives and how people choose and switch between them (Section 4.2.1), followed by discussion of a CODA study that addresses this (4.2.2). Section 4.2.3 discusses other types of perspective taking, and this will again be followed by an example study that involves various conceptual perspectives (4.2.4).

4.2.1   Spatial Perspectives

We perceive the world from wherever we are, through our own eyes, or ears, or other sensory organs that might play a role. This simple fact has a direct effect on the ways in which we use language. Clearly, talking about the world is easiest when we can just follow our own perceptions. If I see a dog in front of me, I can simply say, *There is a dog in front of me*. If I happen to be walking along with a friend, this just as simply translates to *There is a dog in front of us*. I can include my friend in this spatial description, relating the dog's position to both of us, as I am aware that we are both roughly sharing the same perception, or perspective, relative to the dog's location.

However, things become a bit more complicated if my friend is not walking beside me, but has a different perspective on the same scene. If my friend is coming towards me, still further away than the dog, I might want to switch from the use of *in front of* to a different spatial term, and might perhaps say, *There is a dog between you and me*. But if they're located at a certain angle, this won't work: the term *between* requires a more or less straight line connecting two locations, with the described object somewhere in the middle. In such a situation, I will have to choose: do I use my own perspective, or my friend's? Would I say that *the dog is in front of me* – or that *the dog is in front of you*?

Incidentally, I do not only choose between perspectives, but also relate the dog to a different person in each case: either to myself, or to my friend. In technical terminology, what I choose is a *relatum*. In our example so far, the relatum (me, or my friend) has their own view of the scene, which provides a certain kind of *direction* (a view direction). Levinson (2003) calls this kind of situation an *intrinsic reference system*. Any entity (object, person, animal, etc.) with some kind of intrinsic direction can be a relatum in an intrinsic reference system, as in Examples 4.8–4.11. This doesn't always have to be based on perception, as we can see in Examples 4.10 and 4.11:

Example 4.8   The dog is in front of me (from my point of view).
Example 4.9   The dog is in front of you (from your point of view).
Example 4.10   The dog is in front of the car (i.e. in front of the headlights and direction of movement).
Example 4.11   The dog is in front of the cupboard (in front of the doors).
Example 4.12   ? The dog is in front of the ball.

Example 4.12 is trickier: the ball doesn't have an intrinsic front, as such. However, it is possible to imagine situations where the sentence makes sense. For instance, if the ball is moving, it establishes a kind of directionality that might provide some kind of perspective (Tenbrink, 2011):

Example 4.13   The dog is in front of the ball that is rolling down the hill.

Also, it might be possible to use the dog's perspective, in this particular example, to make sense of the scene:

Example 4.14   The dog is in front of the ball, examining it.

However, such an interpretation seems to be only possible with *in front*, not with other terms like *behind* or *to the left/right of:*

Example 4.15   ? The dog is behind the ball, touching it with its tail.

Clearly, intrinsic reference frames aren't always available. If the relatum doesn't have an intrinsic perspective, it is difficult to identify a *front, left, right, or back* direction without any further clue. However, there are other options. Levinson (2003) shows that there is another very common type of reference frame, which he calls *relative*. With a relative reference frame, the perspective is not associated with the relatum, but rather with another entity, called the *origin*. This means that there are three entities involved in the spatial configuration: the locatum (object to be located), the relatum, and the origin. With this option, we can say things like:

Example 4.16   The dog is behind the ball from my perspective.
Example 4.17   The box is to the right of the table as you walk into the room.

In Example 4.16, the origin is the speaker, and the perspective is explicitly associated with them. In Example 4.17, the origin is the person walking into the room; they will then use their own perspective to see where the box is, related to the table. There may be further options and interpretations, as evidenced by countless everyday misunderstandings even in cases of fully specified spatial descriptions.

As we can see from these examples, humans have a very flexible range of options for thinking and talking about spatial relationships. We can use our own point of view, but we don't need to do so. It is not too difficult to consider someone else's perspective, or imagine looking at the scene from a different vantage point.

When do we use which perspective, what aspects influence our preferences when we talk about spatial relationships? A lot of research over the past few decades has addressed this question. Getting a clear idea about systematic patterns of usage is, however, hampered by the fact that the literature has used a wide range of different terminologies to describe this same phenomenon (Levinson, 2003). In psychology, for instance, it is far more common to talk about *egocentric* as opposed to *allocentric* reference frames.

As Levinson (2003) demonstrated, this dichotomy can be translated to some extent to his classification of intrinsic and relative reference frames (plus *absolute* ones, as when we use compass directions). However, it is a complicated translation because the reference frame classifications don't allow for a direct match, based on the very different definitions they use. Using an *egocentric* reference frame in the egocentric–allocentric dichotomy means using someone's own point of view, both for intrinsic and for relative reference frames. That is, the person in question would either relate an object to themselves (which would be an intrinsic reference frame in Levinson's classification), or to something else from their own point of view (which would mean a relative reference frame). In contrast, any perspective other than one's own would be *allocentric*.

Egocentric reference frames are easier and more intuitive, as they correspond to our own point of view. Some people seem to be readier than others to rely on allocentric reference frames, that is, to locate things independent of their own point of view. This seems to be related to different abilities in sense of direction, at least in navigational contexts (Wen, Ishikawa, & Sato, 2013). People with a good sense of direction find it easier to understand where things are and how the various spatial locations relate to each other, whereas people with a poor sense of direction can struggle to get a clear idea of the overall environment structure independent of their own location (Sholl, 1988).

In navigational contexts, relying on your own perspective facilitates the acquisition of *route knowledge*: you know how to get to a certain place because you have walked that route several times, and you can remember what the various streets, buildings, and intersections looked like and where you had to turn. In contrast to this, *survey knowledge* is more flexible: you know more generally how places are related to each other, and would be able to find them without necessarily following the same route every time. These two different types of knowledge (Siegel & White, 1975) are related to two different types of perspective as expressed in language, called *route* and *survey perspective* (Examples 4.18 and 4.19 taken from Taylor & Tversky, 1996:379):

Example 4.18   As you come in, turn right. To your right will be the 'personal computers' room. Continue until you're forced to make a left. The 'Stereo components' room will be in front of you as you turn left.

Example 4.19   North of town are the White Mtns. and east of town is the White River, which flows south from the White Mtns. The main road by town runs in the east-west directions and crosses the White River. The stables are on the south side of this road.

These two ways of describing the memory of a spatial scene clearly demonstrate the different types of knowledge related to different perspectives: route knowledge is based on someone's own (egocentric) perspective and serves as the basis for describing a tour through the memorised environment, as in Example 4.18. People who adopted a route perspective in Taylor and Tversky's study often used active verbs such as *enter, walk, head, find, turn, go*, and *continue*, and descriptions that related locations to the viewer, using terms like *left, right, front*, and *back*. In contrast, survey knowledge is not based on a particular perspective, but relies on compass terms and static terms (such as forms of *be*) to describe how locations are related to each other, as in Example 4.19. People have different skills and preferences for acquiring and using each of these, and they also often mix perspectives (Taylor & Tversky, 1996).

What people will do in any specific situation, what perspective they will use, is not entirely determined by skills or random preferences – it also depends on context factors of various kinds. In Taylor and Tversky's (1996) study, speakers preferred particular types of perspectives for different types of environment. Some environments apparently lend themselves well to an imagined tour, whereas others may be more easily described by using a survey perspective, as if seeing the scene from above. This corresponds to findings that speakers may sometimes choose a perspective that allows them to use a relatively simple spatial description over another that would be more complex (Tenbrink, 2007).

As the literature shows, the language that people use to express reference frames depends on the scenario. Whereas Taylor and Tversky (1996) identified linguistic markers for survey and route perspectives, other types of reference system may be reflected in discourse in different ways. Utterances may also be genuinely ambiguous, as in *the ball to the right of the table*: if the perspective is not specified, it is not clear where the ball is. However, an observer hearing the utterance and seeing the scene will normally be able to identify the intended perspective from context. Also, many people will interpret a sentence like *the ball is to your right* as using the addressee's perspective, whereas *the ball is to the right of you* might be relying on the speaker's perspective (Olloqui Redondo, Tenbrink, & Foltz, 2019).

Another important factor for choice of perspective concerns the interaction partner. Tversky and Hard (2009) found that the mere presence of a person induced many people to take that person's perspective, especially when action was involved and the person was ready to act. Speakers are also known to align with interaction partners in dialogue; they agree on a particular way of describing a scene (Clark & Wilkes-Gibbs, 1986). This can either mean sticking to the same perspective throughout, that is, either one of the interaction partners' perspectives, or it could mean that each speaker always uses their own perspective, or that each speaker always uses the partner's perspective. All of these options can be implicitly agreed in dialogue, facilitating interpretation. Schober (1995) found that such decisions are sensitive to task features, in particular the difficulty of adopting a different perspective. Under certain circumstances, speakers choose to avoid using perspective-dependent spatial terms altogether. Thus, again, ease of reference seems to play an important role for the choice of perspective in spatial description.

In sum, perspective plays a major role when we talk about spatial relationships. Most descriptions of space need to be understood from a particular kind of perspective. This is not always clear, as perspective is often not mentioned explicitly, and it may not be shared between interaction partners. Also, the language used to represent underlying perspectives can vary across scenarios.

Identifying patterns of speakers' perspectives in discourse reveals an important aspect of how they conceive of the spatial situation in question.

4.2.2   Spatial Perspectives: A CODA Example

As we have seen, we use our own as well as others' perspectives all the time. Some people are more skilled than others in using perspectives other than their own. For instance, for some of us it is quite easy to think of street networks in terms of a map, knowing how the roads are related to each other as if from above, using an allocentric survey-based reference system. Researchers in cognitive psychology have been interested in preferences for egocentric or allocentric reference systems for a long time; one major goal is to find indicators towards classifying people according to whether they intuitively adopt an allocentric or egocentric perspective when learning environments.

One mechanism in particular had been suggested as a possible instrument for such a classification (Gramann et al., 2005; Schönebeck, Thanhäuser, & Debus, 2001): the so-called *tunnel task*. This task involves a short travel through a simple virtual tunnel. The tunnel has almost no features – there are no landmarks or road signs to orient to, no traffic to distract from the journey. The only change that the observer can perceive is that the tunnel curves, once or twice, until it ends. The task given to experimental participants is then to indicate where the entrance was by choosing an arrow (see Figure 4.2).

According to Gramann et al. (2005), there are always two possible solutions to this task, one of which reflects an egocentric reference system, and the other an allocentric one. However, alternative explanations for the two different kinds of answers have been suggested. For instance, in a similar task, Riecke and Wiener

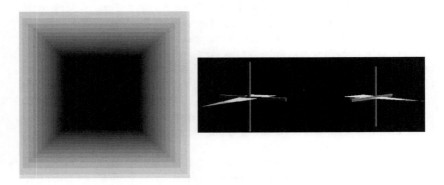

Figure 4.2 Screenshot of a tunnel during the virtual journey in the tunnel task used in Schönebeck et al. (2001), followed by a set of arrows shown when emerging from the tunnel.

(2007) identified further systematic responses that were not consistent with any reference frame, but consistent with a failure to update turn changes.

We (Tenbrink & Salwiczek, 2016) were intrigued by this scenario, and set out to collect verbal data associated with the tunnel task. As outlined above, previous literature had identified several linguistic differences that correspond to certain underlying perspectives and reference frames. Accordingly, we reasoned that if the tunnel task led to two distinct reference frames, then the language that people use to talk about it should reflect this in some way. This might not be the case directly – people wouldn't be saying things like *I am using the allocentric reference frame*, or even *I'm relying on my own point of view*. Actually, reference frame use may not be a matter of conscious decision; speakers may not be aware of the perspective they're using. Nevertheless, people are easily able to use language to express spatial relations in various ways, using different reference frames, and the language they use does typically reveal the underlying frame systematically – as long as it is clear what they are referring to. Therefore, we expected to be able to collect meaningful and informative language data using the tunnel task.

Although the tunnel task scenario had not been previously associated with any specific linguistic terms, we expected that some kind of systematic difference should emerge if people were consistently using distinct (allocentric vs. egocentric) reference systems. We (Tenbrink & Salwiczek, 2016) used the linguistic distinctions suggested by Taylor and Tversky (1996) as a starting point, since their survey perspective corresponded to an allocentric reference frame, and their route perspective to an egocentric one. However, since the scenario was very different in our study, we also did a close qualitative post hoc analysis of the linguistic data we collected in order to allow for the emergence of different patterns from the data.

Apart from recording the responses that our participants gave during the tunnel task, we collected two types of verbal data. First, participants were asked to think aloud while travelling through the tunnel, and also when they gave their response indicating where the tunnel entrance was. Second, after completing twenty short virtual tunnel trips, they were asked the following retrospective question: 'Please describe to me in a few sentences what you think was happening and how you made your decision at the end of each tunnel journey.' This was intended to trigger further thoughts that may have run through the participants' minds, without them necessarily having had time to speak them out loud before. Also, combining think-aloud with retrospective reports allowed us to look at two different kinds of verbalisations, which could be expected to be quite different in nature (see also Chapter 2).

Our results showed that just like in the studies before us that used the tunnel task, most participants consistently chose one of the two possible solutions, associated with the allocentric and the egocentric reference frame by Gramann et al. (2005) and others. However, quite in contrast to this expected behavioural finding, almost all of the linguistic markers of reference systems found in the verbal data fell into the category of route perspective indicators, pointing to an egocentric reference system. This was independent of the behavioural choices. Less than two per cent of the linguistic markers, forty-three in number, fell into the survey category, which contained survey markers found previously in the literature as well as some additional terms identified post hoc in this data set, such as *map* and *compass*. These seemed to be associated with the allocentric response to the tunnel task more often than with the egocentric one.

Nevertheless, the fact that almost all markers indicated a route perspective left us puzzled. Apparently, our participants did not consistently verbalise a survey perspective even when they produced the kind of response that seemed consistent with a survey perspective. What did they actually do? To address this, we conducted a qualitative analysis of several data sets, in terms of individual case studies. This turned out to be particularly illuminating in this study.

The results showed that participants developed highly idiosyncratic strategies to deal with the tunnel task. Only a few participants showed the expected behaviour in a consistent way – conceptualising the tunnel from either a route or a survey perspective, and representing this in the way they talked about it. The others came up with an intriguing set of creative strategies that helped them to cope with the considerable cognitive challenge that the tunnel task apparently poses. This, in itself, was a surprise, as the tunnel task had been proposed as a simple test that could easily be used to identify basic cognitive mechanisms and preferences for choosing between them. Altogether, our data did not confirm that participants were actually using the kinds of (egocentric and allocentric) reference systems that are widely discussed in the literature and known from other contexts. Instead, they seemed to be adopting a range of strategies that were more or less consciously accessible. This suggests that using consistent spatial reference systems in virtual reality settings may be more challenging than previously assumed.

In sum, this example illustrates a study in which perspective was examined systematically on the basis of language data along with a spatial situation in which perspective was decisive. Since perspective was not articulated explicitly, it took various different analysis approaches to draw conclusions about the underlying perspectives. Results were interesting in that they revealed different concepts to those previously expected.

4.2.3   Conceptual Perspectives

Spatial perspectives are intriguing for linguistic research, because it is possible to relate the spatial situation to the linguistic expression chosen by a speaker and thereby to identify the underlying perspective. However, perspective taking can mean much more than this. We take other people's perspectives in many different ways, not just spatially.

In a sense, most misunderstandings mean some kind of clash in perspectives. If your understanding of an utterance or a situation differs from mine, you clearly have a different perspective on it, and we might miscommunicate. Consider the following fictive example:

Example 4.20 Jill: This window really needs cleaning before our guests arrive, and dinner will already be late.
Pete: It's okay for me to eat a bit later!

If, in this example, Jill hoped to get some help from Pete for the household chores, she will be very disappointed with his answer. From Pete's perspective, it's up to Jill to do the window cleaning and also to prepare dinner; it does not occur to him that she might be indirectly asking for some help. From Jill's perspective, there is no such thing as a given task allocation; her aim in mentioning both urgent tasks was to divide the labour, so that both can be accomplished at the same time. Clearly, the perspectives clash and as a result the speakers miscommunicate, leaving Jill disappointed.

What constitutes a speaker's perspective, beyond the spatial perspective already discussed in Sections 4.2.1 and 4.2.2? First, perspective is determined by the *here and now* – by the speaker's time, place, and identity (Schober, 1998). These aspects can be more or less decisive in a speech situation, or may come into play in different ways. As I am writing this book, I write with you in mind as readers – but I have no idea where and when you will read it, or even who you are. Likewise, you will have no idea what time of day or season in the year it was when I wrote it, or what my desk looked like. You might to some extent be interested in the identity of me as the author, or the name might mean nothing to you.

Thus, in this particular instance of communication, the speaker's (or writer's) time, place, and identity seem of little relevance. Books are written to be understood independently, in a relatively context-free way; different readers should ideally be able to understand them at a different time and across different places – though there are limits to this. In contrast, if you talk to your friend about the argument you had yesterday with your partner, it will typically matter quite a lot who you are, when the argument took place, and also perhaps where you talk to your friend.

Language represents such aspects through the class of so-called *deictic* terms: *I*, *you*, *here*, *now*, *then*, *there*, and the like. These terms immediately convey a sense of context dependency; you need to know who *I* is, and where *here* is, when hearing a simple exclamation like *I am here!* Apart from that, it is, of course, also possible to quote someone else saying these words: *Anne shouted, 'I am here!'* Then, the context makes it clear that the word *I* refers to *Anne*, not to the speaker who quotes Anne.

In a literary context, the perspective from which a story is told is one of the most basic features that stand out, affecting the atmosphere created by the narrative. Literary stories can be told from a first-person perspective, and in the most extreme case the reader may never learn the narrator's name at all. As everything is recounted from the narrator's point of view, they might never have any reason to state their own name. This represents the most direct way of expressing someone's perspective from the inside, so to speak. The story will be restricted to the kinds of things that the first-person narrator knows, and we might learn something about their thoughts and feelings that nobody else could know.

Although the first-person pronoun *I* provides a direct mechanism to convey such an inside perspective, very similar effects can be achieved (perhaps less obviously) using third-person pronouns (*he* or *she*). A story told from a third-person perspective, as in *He went to the store, feeling hungry* . . ., also allows the reader to adopt this person's perspective, and to identify, to some extent, with the main character. This will depend on whether the reader learns about the character's thoughts and feelings, and whether the story is told in such a way as to restrict the character's knowledge in a realistic way. In contrast, an 'omniscient' narrator telling the story would not be part of the story as such; they would know things that none of the characters could possibly know, and might be able to report thoughts and feelings of various people.

In literary genres, authors often experiment with these ways of taking perspective. Some stories are narrated, chapter by chapter, by different people. Perspectives can switch in the middle of a story. First-person and third-person pronouns can switch even while using the same person's perspective. And sometimes the reader can be deceived by an untruthful narrator, to be revealed towards the end of a story. There is a lot of room for creativity here, and the distinction in terms of pronoun choice (first- or third-person perspectives, or even second-person where the author pretends to address the reader) only affects the surface, not the scope for perspective taking as such. Readers may identify with a first-person narrator more readily than with a third-person one (Brunyé et al., 2009), but perspective taking takes place all the same.

Just as we are able to take other people's perspectives and imagine their identity when perceiving the world, we can imagine being at other places (*there* rather than *here*) and at other times (*then* rather than *now*). Considering what the world was like during the Middle Ages immediately evokes a range of images of dirt, poverty, horses, perhaps castles – possibly supported by films we may have seen, or books we may have read. We will surely be aware of the technological limitations at that time, allowing us to develop a sense for the perspective of a person in the past who could not travel by car, not communicate by online chat, and not gather information through the Internet. Our minds are incredibly flexible in this regard; as long as we have some information to go by, we can imagine and elaborate on other kinds of perspectives.

Schober (1998) further highlights how our perspectives are revealed by the ways in which we think of objects and people. Any person or object can be referred to in many different ways: we can talk about *Dr Anthony Myers*, or *Uncle Tony*, or *Dad*, or the *Golf Club president*, or *neighbour Anton*, or *my stepson* – this depends on who we are and how we relate to this person. Likewise, we could mention *the school*, or *the workplace*, or *that horrible building over there*, or *the meeting place* – all of these may be relevant in different contexts for a single location, depending on the perspective of the speaker.

In this way, the use of a single noun phrase reveals the underlying conceptual perspective by contrast with the many other ways in which the same person or thing could have been referred to. In this regard, it can be very interesting to focus specifically on phenomena highlighted by cognitive linguists (see Chapter 3): for instance, if a person consistently talks about how *anger boiled up* or *the argument became heated*, this person clearly adopts the metaphorical concept of ANGER IS HEAT – a common concept with many implications (Lakoff & Johnson, 1980). Then, the person's underlying perspective and understanding is revealed in their use of lexical choices, beyond noun phrases used to refer to objects and people.

Schober (1998) furthermore suggests that a speaker's conversational agenda also corresponds to some kind of perspective. To illustrate this idea let's consider the following exchange:

Example 4.21 Mary: I had such fun at the party yesterday.
                        Colin: No need to rub it in!

Here, Mary may have wanted to share the memory of the party experience with Colin, without any further implications. Colin, however, has a different perspective; for some reason, he feels offended by the fact that Mary had fun at the party. Perhaps he feels that he should have been invited; perhaps he is jealous for some other reason. Clearly, Mary's innocent communicative intention is not received very well. She failed to take Colin's perspective, and therefore her conversational goal of sharing a positive experience did not work out.

To really understand what is going on at this level in any given instance, we need to know details about the people involved and their background, their communicative intentions, their relationships to each other, and so on. Failing to understand another person's perspective at the level of an unspoken conversational agenda concerns misunderstandings of a kind that may be fairly hard to clarify. The (semantic) meaning of the utterance itself is clear enough, so there's nothing to clarify there. But explaining communicative intentions (or aspects pertaining to the pragmatic level of language) is not necessarily something that people are used to doing, or willing to do. It takes a lot of perspective taking to really understand a speaker's underlying meaning at this level.

In sum, perspectives are not only decisive in space, but actually underlie all communication in a range of ways. Identifying the conceptual perspectives in a given discourse is not easy, but can be central for making sense of the discourse, for understanding it properly.

4.2.4   Conceptual Perspectives: A CODA Example

We have seen, in the previous section, that a person's perspective has a lot to do with their identity, with their personal background, the time and place they're speaking, their conversational agenda, and so on. In a theoretical essay, Tenbrink et al. (2014) took a closer look at a communication situation where various different perspectives come together, which frequently leads to conceptual clashes and communicative challenges. This is the case in architectural design, especially when designing new complex public buildings such as large railway stations or hospitals.

In our essay, we considered the perspectives of architects, their clients, and building users. *Architects* construe a building from their own professional perspective, which involves aspects such as aesthetics, functionality, innovation, and more, combined in a creative way. Their *clients* are the people tasking them with building construction, and their perspective on this task can be vastly different, and more economically oriented. But the people who will finally end up using the building may not be concerned with any of those things; *users* perceive a building in a different way than architects do; they may or may not identify with its structure, but first, they will need to find their way around. Appreciation of a creative and innovative building has its limits if the building users frequently get lost in it (Carlson et al., 2010). Communication between architects, clients, and users therefore involves a high amount of flexibility in perspective taking – a significant cognitive challenge.

Related to this line of work, we (Tenbrink, Brösamle, & Hölscher, 2012) used a qualitative CODA approach to investigate to what extent trained architects switch perspectives, and in particular how they manage to take a building user's perspective during the architectural design process. We used a set of interviews conducted previously with architects to learn about their conceptualisations during design (Brösamle & Hölscher, 2012).

The interviews included three ways of thinking about buildings. First, the architects were asked to describe and comment on a schematised plan of a basic building structure; this encouraged thoughts and ideas about the *building* as such. Second, they were invited to design the basic building structure further by introducing a circulation system, such as staircases in appropriate places; this induced a *design* perspective. The third question concerned building *users*; architects were asked to imagine a person trying to find their way to an office within the building. Architects' answers were generally very elaborate, and as such provided plenty of evidence for the ability to take different kinds of perspectives related to architectural design.

Our analysis in Tenbrink et al. (2012) focused on the ways in which different perspectives were expressed in language. We speculated that it might be possible to associate pronoun use with different perspectives: *it* for the *building*, *I* for the *design* (as in, *I'd change this aspect*), and *you* for the *user* (as in *to find the office, you'd have to go this way*). However, in actual fact the situation turned out to be rather more complicated. While the different underlying perspectives did find systematic expression in language, all three pronouns could be used with all three perspectives, as shown in the following examples:

Example 4.22 I mean, I don't know what the scale of the drawing is but
              I suppose ...
              Do you have rooms for patients towards the internal corridors?
              Maybe it's some kind of lecture hall or something.

Example 4.23 I'd keep it fairly classical.
              You might put a stair round the back of it.
              It might make sense kind of placing them here.

Example 4.24 I naturally would walk to the third floor.
              If you are meeting someone on the third floor that's not the
              staircase for you.
              The person will try to find a different staircase in order to go up.

In Example 4.22, the *building* is described in various ways: from the observer's point of view (first person), from a metaphorical owner's point of view (second person), and with respect to the buildings features as such (third person). In Example 4.23, the first-person perspective describes the possible *design* changes from the architect's point of view as expected. However, the second- and third-person forms are also available for a similar purpose, where the pronoun *you* represents a less personal way of expressing the possibilities, and the third person is used for impersonal constructions such as passive voice and references to the envisioned state of the building. In Example 4.24, the *user's* perspective could be expressed in either one of the three pronoun types, corresponding to the different ways in which stories can be told as outlined in the previous section.

It can be seen from these brief examples that, although pronoun use as such was not an indicator for perspective, the ways in which pronouns were used in context revealed the different perspectives adopted in each case, with different degrees of personalisation. Interestingly, the second-person form *you* was only rarely used in its core sense, namely to address the interviewer. This shows how immersed the architects were in the task of discussing various perspectives on the architectural design process.

Another interesting finding in Tenbrink et al. (2012) was that while the questions targeted the three different perspectives one by one, architects actually moved freely between them in relation to all three questions. Therefore, we could observe frequent shifts of perspective in a single response, as in this example where the speaker shifts back and forth between the *building* and the *user*:

Example 4.25 ... if you come from there [USER]
              because they don't seem to have entries.
              It seems to be the only one or maybe this is a disabled entry.
              I don't know. [BUILDING]
              Or you could come from here [USER]
              if that's a connection. It only seems to be a connection on the
              first floor.
              So I think this is the entry. [BUILDING]
              So you come in and you see this stair and that goes to nowhere.
              So that's the first problem.
              So you don't – you probably go to – you want to go here. [USER]

This example illustrates a recurring phenomenon that we identified in our data. When the architects shifted perspectives between building, design, and user, they frequently employed causal or conditional conjunctions such as *so*, *so that*, *if*, *in order to*, *because*, and *then*. Also, we noted that shifts between perspectives were frequently necessitated by the nature of the task question given to the architects in the interviews. In Example 4.25, to discuss the challenges a wayfinder faces in the building, the architect's thought process goes back and forth between the wayfinder's actions and the features of the building that the wayfinder encounters along the way. This demonstrates the flexibility with which architects conceptualised and reframed the various scenarios posed to them in the course of the interviews.

This chapter has looked at two main ways in which human thoughts are oriented, as reflected in language use: attention and perspective. Attention means the focus of thoughts on a particular aspect of a situation or idea, whereas perspective is the angle from which such a focus happens. Together, these two cognitive phenomena represent a powerful mechanism for conceptualising the world in an idiosyncratic way, generating the intriguing diversity in both thought and language that cognitive scientists encounter in their quest to understand the human mind.

5   Identifying Cognitive Depth

While the previous chapter looked at the ways in which we cognitively orient towards specific aspects in the world or in our minds, this chapter turns to the *depth* in which we do this. Once more, there are two aspects to this: on the one hand, we can think about things in more or less detail; this is captured by the notion of *granularity* (Section 5.1). On the other hand, our depth of cognition can be limited in terms of understanding and knowledge; here we look at the *certainty* of our thoughts and thought processes (Section 5.2). Together, these two notions complement the insights on cognitive orientation in terms of attention and perspective discussed in Chapter 4. As with the previous chapter, we will find strong links between cognitive science and linguistics, adding to the kinds of insights that we can gain about cognition through a close look at how people speak in a controlled scenario.

5.1   Granularity

Imagine you are in a museum with your friend, looking at a famous picture that was painted centuries ago. You ask your friend whether she likes it, and she replies in either one of the following ways:

Example 5.1   It's a nice painting. I like the colours and the scenery in it.
Example 5.2   It is fantastic, truly intriguing, an inspiring picture. Just look at
              how the depth of blue shifts in the sky in various places, and how
              the leaves on the trees show maybe twenty different versions of
              green, depending on the light intensity, the type of tree, and even
              the freshness of the leaves at springtime!

   Both of these possible answers are perfectly normal, and they could be given by any of us. The answer given in Example 5.2 is perhaps more likely to come from a person who likes art very much, or has some professional background in the area, whereas Example 5.1 sounds some-what less informed. But in general, there is nothing in the answers that actually requires or directly reveals professionality or expertise. Moreover, considering the analysis perspectives discussed in the previous chapter, we don't see many differences in attention or perspective. Both mention positive evaluation, colours, and scenery, and look at the picture as a whole. But they use a different amount of words for the description, and this gives a first indication of the main difference here: namely, that the two examples are very different in how much detail they offer.

Example 5.1 is restricted to fairly general expressions: *nice, colours, scenery*. These terms express three different aspects that your friend has thought about: her general opinion of the painting, and then (somewhat more specifically), the colours and scenery depicted in it. However, she does not go into any more detail, and does not say what she likes in general, or what she thinks about the colours and scenery.

In contrast, Example 5.2 elaborates on each of these three aspects. The general evaluation is more specific in that it adds the adjectives *intriguing* and *inspiring*: she has clearly engaged with the painting intellectually, and that's why she thinks it is *fantastic* (not just *nice*). Then, she provides some details as to how colours are depicted in the scenery. It turns out that both of these aspects actually work together for her. The speaker elaborately points to the ways in which the scenery is represented in colour variations and nuances, going well beyond what might be seen as a *blue sky* and *green leaves*. This reveals a close look at the picture. At first glance, even from a distance, one might discover that the picture is good, and has appealing colours and a fine scenery. However, to be able to describe these aspects in as much detail as your friend does in Example 5.2, one will need to 'zoom in' to the picture – really take a close look at it, discover in detail how the colours shift and vary along with elements of the scenery.

Variability of granularity, as shown in this example, can be understood as *cognitive zoom*. The more you zoom in, the more you will discover, at a more fine-grained level. If you look at a picture from a distance, you might see what it shows in general and perhaps whether you like it. In contrast, a microscope would allow you to see fine-grained details in very small spaces.

However, this comes at a cost: the use of a microscope might prevent you from seeing the picture as a whole, from appreciating its general impression. Therefore, a given level of granularity is not necessarily good or bad. It simply describes the level or scale from which things are considered, and this can be equal to or more or less appropriate than any other level. A coarse description at a general overview level may be useful for some purposes, whereas detailed elaborations of fine-grained insights and ideas serve different ones. When asking your friend about a picture in a museum, you may be entirely happy with an answer like Example 5.1. You may not be interested in dwelling on the topic for longer, or in looking so closely at specific aspects of colour variety.

Too many details can be inappropriate in some situations, or simply boring for the communication partner. And too few details may not suffice.

In the following, we will take a closer look at two notions that are associated with granularity: scale (Section 5.1.1) and elaboration (Section 5.1.2). A CODA example on variable granularity in route descriptions will conclude this section (Section 5.1.3).

5.1.1   Scale

As just outlined, granularity means mentally zooming in, and this very often corresponds to providing more details on a finer scale. What exactly do we associate with the notion of scale? Scales are well known in human society, in many ways, not only as an idea but also as concrete objects. Scales are tools for measuring weight, distance, volume, wind force, and other things, depending on their nature. What they have in common is that they can be used at different levels of granularity. Weight, for instance, can be measured using scales at the levels of tons or micrograms; distances can be miles or millimetres, or measured at an even smaller scale.

Scales can be introduced for all sorts of structures, along various dimensions (Hobbs, 1995). We can effectively carry out comparisons based on the scales we use, and we can use them in a composite way. For instance, if a car is damaged, we can assess the damage on the scale of associated costs, as well as on the scale of loss of functionality. These are two different dimensions, and we may be able to weigh them against each other, or account for their interdependency.

Through multiple experiences in everyday life, we are used to these effects. However, our minds don't offer any precise metrical scales for us to work with. We might have a relatively good idea of what it feels like to hold a 100 gram bar of chocolate in our hands (or perhaps 70 gram, depending on our cultural habits!), but to precisely determine 100 gram of anything, we will need a tool.

Accordingly, the conceptual notion of scale that we are considering for current purposes is not based on exact metric measures. Instead, it is primarily a qualitative notion. Qualitative scales are reflected in language, in the way we speak. Imagine Corinne trying out a new running route without consulting any measuring instruments, and then saying the following to Mike:

Example 5.3   This route was 2.135 miles less of a challenge than my usual route.

Example 5.4   This felt short. My usual route must be longer!

Mike would probably be astonished about Corinne's ability to measure distances without tools if she said something like Example 5.3, whereas

Example 5.4 would seem perfectly normal. We don't feel (or otherwise know) precisely how much shorter a particular route is, but we may feel that it is *short* as compared to something else. Importantly, attributes such as *short* are inherently scalar. They inherently classify something as *less than expected*, compared to something else from our experience, or some cultural or individual norm. How long is a short route? We can't tell unless we have some notion of a distance to compare it against. This will depend on context; what seems long for a walking route may be very short compared to our habitual running distance.

To take a different example, we might have an idea of the approximate size range of a *large mouse* or a *small elephant*; in each case, we intuitively compare the animal in question with an average exemplar of its category. Large mice are larger than the average mouse, and small elephants are smaller than average elephants. However, it would be rather a stretch of imagination to consider even an extremely large mouse to be larger than an extremely small elephant – at least in the real world. Fiction can provide different scales, offering new opportunities for comparison. The fact remains, though, that scalar attributes are relative; without context or associated world knowledge, they do not have any concrete value of their own.

Granularity variations help to identify the underlying cognitive scale that is used implicitly for establishing the contrast that is at stake in a given context (Freksa, 1981). Compare the following with Example 5.4, in the same situation:

Example 5.5   This felt fairly short. My usual route must be longer!
Example 5.6   This felt incredibly short. My usual route must be longer!

If Corinne utters the statement in Example 5.4 (*this felt short*), we might infer that the underlying scale has fairly coarse distinctions between *short, normal, and long*. In Examples 5.5 and 5.6, the words *fairly* and *incredibly* serve as so-called amplifiers (Martin & Rose, 2003); they add further levels of detail to the scale. In Example 5.5, we might assume that the scale not only distinguishes between *short, normal, and long*, but further introduces *fairly short* and possibly *very short* as additional options. Example 5.6 seems to add even further detail, resulting in a possible underlying fine-grained scale such as *incredibly short–very short–short–fairly short–somewhat short–normal* (and so on).

We may not consciously think of all of those possible attributes, but we do understand intuitively that *incredibly short* is further away from *normal* than a simple *short* would be, and also than *very short* would be. As a flexible and simple term, *very* could be expected to serve the purpose of highlighting that something is quite far away from normal; the fact that even this term is not considered sufficient tells us that the distance must be extreme indeed. Alternatively, the speaker might be habitually exaggerating, speaking in extreme terms when a moderate term might have been fine.

If we happen to know the metric information in Example 5.3 to be true, we can infer from Example 5.5 that Corinne typically runs long distances where a difference of 2.135 miles does not matter very much, whereas in Example 5.6, the subtraction of 2.135 miles seems to have reduced the running route to a minimum and consequently, her normal routes may not be longer than three miles. This inference is nowhere to be found in the language itself, and may well be unfounded. Nevertheless, the choice of amplifiers (or their absence) does provide important insight into the conceptualised underlying scale on the part of the speaker. This may allow for hypotheses concerning the reasons for the chosen scale – especially if we have access to metric information, complementing the qualitative measures used by the speaker.

The fact that context-dependent attributes allow for inferences has also been discussed in the context of the Gricean maxim of quantity (Grice, 1975). Grice suggested that speakers generally aim to provide as much information as they perceive to be required in a given context. Therefore, if Corinne utters a statement like Example 5.4, Mike (as the listener) can assume that Corinne does not know exactly, or does not deem it necessary to share, how much shorter the route was – because she would have uttered Example 5.3 if this amount of information was available and relevant. On top of that, if she had felt that the route was not just shorter than normal but extremely so (e.g. because she normally doesn't run more than three miles), she would have uttered Example 5.6. Because of this, Mike can assume that Corinne (uttering Example 5.4) felt the difference but did not perceive it as extreme.

This kind of phenomenon is called *scalar implicature*, and it applies well beyond the use of context-dependent attributes. Carston (1998:179) discusses the following examples:

Example 5.7   a. Bill has got some of Chomsky's papers.
              b. The speaker believes that Bill hasn't got all of Chomsky's papers.

Example 5.8   a. There will be five of us for dinner tonight.
              b. There won't be more than five of us for dinner tonight.

In both cases, the first part (a) includes one word (*some* and *five*, respectively) that licenses the implicature given in (b). If Bill possesses *some papers*, it might be logically possible for him to possess *all papers* – but considering the underlying qualitative scale (e.g. *some–most–all*), it is normally assumed that he does not possess *all* of the papers, or even *most* of them. Likewise, if we use a number like *five*, the normal understanding is that the actual number will not be higher, even though it may be logically true that five people is a subset of six, and therefore a dinner party of six does include five people, strictly speaking. However, like all implicatures, this inference can be cancelled depending on context. For instance, if the speaker in Example 5.8a needs at least five people for some reason, the relevant information would be that the target number has been reached. In such a case, it may be irrelevant to add the exact number, as in Example 5.9:

Example 5.9   There will be five of us for dinner tonight – we've made it! Actually we will have four guests, so we'll be six people, more than enough.

Scales are also relevant in the context of time frames. Consider the following:

Example 5.10   Fanny, what will you do after lunch today?

Example 5.11   Fanny, what will you do after your holidays?

The use of *after* in cases such as these suggests the notion of immediate succession (Tenbrink & Schilder, 2003): the question pertains to the next action that Fanny has in mind, immediately after lunch – and immediately after the holidays. The difference between the two types of action lies in the underlying conceptual scale. The concept *lunch* in Example 5.10 suggests a time frame of hours in a day; Fanny might say that she will go shopping, fitting to the time frame. She might not say that she will do the dishes and put her shoes on, and the like: these actions are more fine-grained, and do not interfere with the idea of 'next action'. In contrast, the use of *holidays* in Example 5.11 invokes a temporal scale of days or weeks; it would be very odd if Fanny answered that she will go shopping. Both questions implicitly ask for the next activity on the same level of granularity, without making the scale explicit. Explicit scales are not necessary, due to our intuitive understanding of the granularity level invoked by concepts such as *lunch* and *holidays*.

For the case of space, Montello (1993) suggested a classification that is now widely accepted and used in the spatial cognition literature. He argued that from a psychological perspective, different scales of space are regularly and systematically important across the contexts in which we live. Also, previous literature on how we understand space had pointed to a number of effects that occur at a particular scale, in contrast to another, as follows.

On the most fine-grained level of granularity, *figural space* concerns everything that is smaller, or is perceived as smaller, than the human body. This includes pictures representing space of any kind; maps (independent of what they show) belong to figural space. This reflects the idea that we think of spatial objects and pictures differently if they appear smaller than ourselves. We can handle them differently, manipulate them with our hands, and so on. Not every figural-space object can or needs to be touched directly in order to be fully understood, but the small scale of space still matters conceptually.

On the next level, *vista space* concerns everything that we can perceive from a current vantage point. This will naturally depend on the environment that we happen to be in; indoor vista space is naturally restricted by walls, but if you're standing on the seashore or looking at the mountains, your vista space may include fairly large distances and objects.

Next, *environmental space* includes space surrounding us that is too large (and partially occluded) to be perceived at once, but it can be apprehended and learned over an extended length of time. Knowledge about environmental space includes knowledge of areas like cities and the interior of complex buildings; it must be gradually accumulated, but is still based on personal experience.

Finally, *geographical space* is a scale of space that is too large to be apprehended by a human being's experience. Our knowledge of geographical relationships between entire countries, or relations between oceans and land masses, is never based entirely on our own experience. Instead, such knowledge is acquired through maps or models that help us understand what we cannot perceive directly. As Montello (1993) pointed out, such maps or models only *represent* geographical space, but they are themselves objects in figural space. Thus, when we consider knowledge at this scale, it is useful to keep in mind that this kind of knowledge has been acquired through figural space rather than through the actual large-scale space of geographical relationships.

Altogether, the notion of scale is a powerful mechanism that provides multiple ways of conceptualising the world at different levels of granularity. The use of a particular linguistic term to describe a concept or attribute frequently reveals the underlying conceptual level of granularity, based on the scale that is associated with it. In the case of space, references to diverse kinds of spatial objects or relationships reveal the underlying scale just as reliably. A person referring to a map relies on the figural space that a map provides, whereas a person who recounts the relative location of not currently perceivable places from memory would rely on experientially acquired knowledge of environmental space. In practice, these different types of knowledge at different scales often interact and are combined in useful ways.

5.1.2   Elaboration

We can think about and describe the world at different scale levels, as just described – but this is not the only way in which cognitive detail can be revealed.

Even at the same scale level, our thoughts can expand to varying degrees, leading to more or less detail in thoughts and descriptions. Further to the examples given above, consider the following two ways of expressing very similar ideas:

Example 5.12   This felt short. My usual route must be longer!

Example 5.13   I really had the impression that this route was short, it felt shorter than usual. The route that I normally run must be longer, it makes me more tired, today I did not really feel exhausted after this route.

Intuitively, there is not much difference in content of these two utterances – they both make the point that the route was shorter than usual. Example 5.13 is simply more elaborate than Example 5.12; it provides more details, spells out in more words what exactly was felt.

Providing further elaboration is a common discourse feature that combines textual elements (utterances, clauses, sentences) in sequence. In Example 5.12, the main point is already conveyed in the first three-word sentence – 'this felt short': if the route felt short, the implication is that there must be a longer route that feels normal. The scalar nature of the adjective suggests this; *short* is understood in relation to an implicit norm on this scale, as described above. The second sentence in the same utterance does not introduce any substantial changes or new elements; rather, it serves to provide further details on the same idea. In short, it *elaborates* the first sentence. In Example 5.13, all follow-up clauses elaborate the first one, and this results in the overall impression of a fairly elaborate representation of the experience.

Elaboration plays a central role in expressing granularity. It is a discourse feature that allows the speaker to go into more depth without necessarily changing scale (in the sense of the previous section). This simply means that the speaker provides further details, further evidence of the same point, perhaps different perspectives and aspects that play into it (as in Example 5.13). Halliday and Matthiessen (2014:461) offer the following very useful definition (annotation and symbols removed from the examples they give; my numbering):

In **elaboration**, one clause elaborates on the meaning of another by further specifying or describing it; for example:

Example 5.14   Is there any way of disputing when a priest, any priest, says, 'This is my conviction, this is what the god I serve thinks about this.'

Example 5.15   Moo, however, and the novel I'm writing now, which is a racehorse novel, are comic. They are set in a more stable time, where things aren't crushed and lost, they simply go on.

The secondary clause does not introduce a new element into the picture but rather provides a further characterization of one that is already there, restating it, clarifying it, refining it, or adding a descriptive attribute or comment. Thus in the first example above, *This is my conviction* is elaborated through restatement by *this is what the god I serve thinks about this*. The thing that is elaborated may be the primary clause as a whole, or it may be just some part of it – one or more of its constituents. Thus *which is a racehorse novel* elaborates part of the clause *Moo, however, and the novel I'm writing now are comic*; it elaborates *the novel I'm writing now* and, being a hypotactic elaboration, it follows its domain of elaboration directly and is as a result included within the dominant clause (the traditional category of 'non-defining relative clause').

Elaboration is very common in everyday discourse; we frequently elaborate what we've just said. We do not want to say the same thing twice, but there may be more details to be added, more to be said on the subject. And we usually want to make sure that we have been understood; elaboration often helps to clarify what has been said. Teachers frequently ask students to elaborate on a statement they have made, testing the depth of their knowledge – or the extent to which they are simply repeating something they have heard. If students cannot elaborate, the chances are that they haven't properly understood a concept or phenomenon. Elaboration doesn't necessarily add anything new, and may therefore sometimes be considered redundant, but in fact it is quite essential in order to communicate successfully. We need a certain amount of cognitive depth in order to exchange our thoughts effectively, and elaboration is an important discourse tool to achieve this.

In the verbalisation of thought, elaboration would not necessarily be understood primarily as a tool for better communication. After all, CODA means looking at cognition, not communication. A CODA study design that involves representing experience through language is not primarily aimed towards successful communication, but towards the expression of cognition. In this light, a speaker who further elaborates something that has been said before may simply be expressing increasing depth of understanding. They may start out thinking about something in a tentative way, and then go on to discover and understand more and more aspects of it that allow them to elaborate their thoughts. This would then be reflected in their language in terms of increasing elaboration, revealing increasing cognitive depth.

5.1.3   A CODA Example: Variable Granularity in Route Descriptions

How much cognitive depth do we need, or employ, when describing routes? Previous literature on wayfinding suggested that route descriptions are characterised by a set of essential elements, such as landmarks, direction changes, segments, and the like (Denis et al., 1999). These are particularly pronounced at critical decision points. In effect, this means that there may be differences in terms of granularity. In Tenbrink and Winter (2009) we specifically pursued this point in a number of ways. We explored the notion of granularity in this context, and proposed a model that enabled us to explore the phenomenon systematically. The model distinguishes between granularity at one-dimensional (1D) and two-dimensional (2D) levels as well as elaboration. The following examples are cases in point.

Example 5.16   At the first intersection, turn right. Then at the next intersection, walk straight on. Turn right at the next intersection after that.
Example 5.17   Turn right at the first intersection and then again at the second intersection after that.
Example 5.18   I live in the city centre, close to the cathedral, in a small building next to a little shop.
Example 5.19   You will need to turn right at a nearly 120-degree angle.

Examples 5.16 and 5.17 describe the same situation, but they do so in different ways. Example 5.16 describes each individual segment of the route separately, from decision point to decision point, even if it means just walking straight on. Example 5.17 groups two intersections together by referring to the *second intersection*. This effect is known as *chunking*, and it leads to coarser 1D granularity, that is, less detail with respect to the linear progression of the route.

Example 5.18 shows a shift in 2D granularity within the same utterance. The speaker describes the location of a building, their home, by narrowing down to it in a gradual fashion. They start out with a reference to a relatively large area, the *city centre*, then zoom in to a smaller area relative to a large landmark, the *cathedral*. The last step is to refer directly to the target building itself, locating it next to a different, smaller landmark, the *little shop*.

Example 5.19 illustrates elaboration of a specific route element, a direction change. It is fairly typical for route directions to leave the angles of turns unmentioned; commonly, one would hear *turn right* without any further specification. In this example, the speaker chooses to elaborate the turn information by noting the angle, possibly because this particular turn is unusually sharp. Because a prototypical right turn would have something like a 90-degree angle, 120 degrees is sufficiently different to be mentioned. This would support the listener in identifying the correct road into which they need to turn.

In Tenbrink and Winter (2009), we further specified and operationalised this classification of three types of granularity changes – 1D, 2D, and Elaboration – to enable rigorous annotation of natural language data. We were interested in patterns of granularity changes in route descriptions of two very different kinds: one automatically generated by a web-based system (provided by German railway at www.bahn.de), and another produced by young adults who were asked to write them down on a piece of paper. For this purpose, we chose a route that contained various modes of travel (walking, train, and tram) as well as more and less familiar sections for the traveller. The web-based system produced a description that used the same route as the young adults in our study, enabling direct comparison.

Our results showed some interesting patterns. First, we noted that the essential information required to find the way was provided across the board, both by the system and by the young adults. This means that each leg of the route was reliably identified in some way.

Next, both types of route directions exhibited a hierarchical structure. In the web-based system, this was realised by the option of learning further details by clicking into particular elements of the route. In the human route directions, the hierarchy was realised by route elements at different levels of importance. Our analysis started from the identification of *spatial units*, which we defined as abstract, spatially based categories that reflected the basic level of 1D granularity without elaboration. Some of these spatial units were *crucial*; they were mentioned by everyone rather than being subsumed in some kind of chunking or left out altogether. Others were integrated by shifts to coarser levels of 1D granularity, marking them as less crucial. Yet other segments were described in more detail than the basic information needed for a spatial unit, showing finer granularity in the 1D, 2D, or Elaboration categories.

Both the web-based system and the young adults thus provided further details, offering aspects of the route that were not strictly crucial for successful travel. However, they did so in very different ways. The web-based system primarily offered alternatives in terms of time and travel mode, whereas the handwritten route descriptions almost completely ignored such details, and only referred to the fact that the train left at a particular time every hour.

Most importantly, however, the young adults clearly accounted for the information needs of the traveller in a much more flexible way than the system did. While the system generated the same information independent of travel direction, the young adults recognised details that depended on the direction of travel: for instance, finding the exit of a large railway station when arriving by train is easier than finding the correct track on departure. The young adults' descriptions offered detailed information precisely for the more difficult parts of the route, showing that they recognised a higher need for elaboration. This was the case, for instance, when changing mode of travel, or when identifying the correct turn after a lengthy footpath. The automatic system, in contrast, was much more rigid and incapable of accounting for different degrees of information needs; elaboration (wherever it was offered) did little to clarify a complex or challenging situation. Instead, the automatically generated information was sometimes redundant in the way it was presented, creating information clutter rather than providing useful support at the level of granularity required for travel.

In conclusion, CODA as applied in Tenbrink and Winter (2009) supported the identification of specific features of human route descriptions by contrasting them with the features of a system that was developed to support human wayfinding. The results highlighted various ways in which the system did not match how humans think and talk about routes. For humans, different aspects of a route come with different challenge levels, and this is reflected by variable granularity in route descriptions, going into further cognitive depth wherever and whenever required. Clearly, a substantial amount of everyday background knowledge is needed to develop adequate intuitions about flexible information needs. Our young adults had no trouble doing this, in clearly identifiable systematic and meaningful ways. In spite of accessing a rich database of spatial information, the web-based system turned out to be far less adaptable.

More generally, with this analysis perspective we can see how much detail is provided by a speaker in a given situation. More detail does not necessarily mean more knowledge, but it does mean that the speaker dwells on the thought in more depth. The represented details may not be altogether correct or lead to more insight (this is the topic of the next section), but they do reflect the fact that speaker is cognitively 'zooming in'. Note that some speakers may still 'zoom in' but not represent this fact in language – this is always a possibility. However, we can only analyse the data that are available to us, and identify significant patterns across speakers in relation to specific situations.

5.2   Certainty

How do we know how much another person knows? One way is to ask them; most people will be able to assess their own wisdom to some extent. However, knowledge is hard to quantify. If asked how much you know about tap dancing, you might say, 'nothing' or 'a little', or you might start explaining the things you know. If you don't know much, your words will soon start to reveal uncertainty about the subject – unless you're really good at making things up as you go.

Even though it is difficult to quantify knowledge and certainty, we still tend to have a good sense of our own, or other people's, level of expertise on a particular topic. If someone starts talking about a subject of general interest or skill, it may not take us long to assess whether the person is knowledgeable or a newcomer to the subject. This is especially true if we are experts ourselves; newcomers reveal themselves through simplifications and slight misrepresentations of facts. If we're not experts, we can often recognise their lack of knowledge by the way they're formulating things. Alternatively, we might be impressed by the level of certainty and confidence in the speaker, but there's always the chance that this is 'put on' – a fraud; the speaker may be pretending to know more than they actually do, hiding their uncertainty.

But how do we do this in the first place? How do we assess another person's level of knowledge, or degree of certainty, concerning the concepts they are talking about? What factors help us when we make these judgements? More specifically, what is there in the language that people use that might serve as clues to identify certainty and depth of insight? In CODA, our everyday intuitions are taken a step further, as with all other levels of analysis. Rather than aiming for a general estimate about the speaker's expertise, CODA seeks to systematically identify linguistic markers that reflect cognitive aspects pertaining to the speaker's knowledge and certainty. To get a better idea of how this can be achieved reliably, in Section 5.2.1 we will look at relevant insights from cognitive psychology, turn to linguistic markers of certainty in Section 5.2.2, and finally discuss a CODA study in Section 5.2.3.

5.2.1 Expertise and Certainty in Cognitive Psychology

Generally, we would expect that experts can speak with confidence about a topic, or use a skill more accurately and efficiently than others, based on their extensive knowledge of it. Experts have spent years in the realm of their expertise, have talked many times about it, have used their skills in multiple ways, know all the details, and may have trained others to learn it. However, not all of the seemingly trivial conclusions that one might draw from this general understanding of expertise are actually valid. In some domains, expertise does not necessarily lead to better performance of a skill.

In a study by McManus et al. (2011), for instance, people varied in how good they were at cropping photographs, according to independent judgements of the croppings. Surprisingly, the skilled people weren't necessarily experts, and experts' croppings weren't judged to be any better than non-experts' croppings. Experts mostly differed from non-experts in that their croppings were systematically different in some ways, and they took longer to do it, taking more factors into account. Clearly, their performance was affected by expertise, and they exhibited greater cognitive depth in approaching the task. Nevertheless, this did not lead to a preference for their croppings by either expert or non-expert viewers of the cropped photographs.

Another expectation that could be associated with expertise, but does not necessarily hold, concerns the kinds of strategies used for doing a challenging task. One might expect that non-experts are more naïve, less knowledgeable, and therefore might not be aware of some expert strategies for solving the task. However, Chi, Glaser, and Rees (1982) reviewed previous work in which this is demonstrably not the case. For instance, the strategies that expert chess players employ are not substantially different from those of novices, and they do not look any further ahead either. Their expertise is reflected in other ways, such as a better ability than novices to handle and memorise specific chess positions. The reason for this is that they have seen certain kinds of configurations so often that they can think of them as wholes, or *chunks* of information, rather than having to conceptualise and memorise the details. This makes it much easier to recall the structure later, and to work with it during the game play.

Cognitive chunking processes are also known from other domains. As it happens, the use of language is a case in point. Compare the following two utterances, heard in an everyday context:

Example 5.20   Better to have loved and lost than never to have loved at all!

Example 5.21   Paul asked Nina first, but Adrian threw in many stupid remarks.

Can you remember both of these sentences with your eyes shut? Chances are that you have no problem recalling the first one, even verbatim, but not the second – or at least not the details. This is because the first is a well-known quote that you are likely to have encountered many times before. If you're familiar with it, you'll have glanced at it, recognised it, and stored it in short-term memory in an instant, without any processing effort. The second one, Example 5.21, is a novel combination of words; to memorise it you'd need to process every detail and possibly make a conscious effort of remembering the exact words.

Experts, therefore, require less processing effort for familiar situations or configurations within their area of expertise. They can assess the significance of a particular detail or constellation because they are trained, explicitly or by experience, to recognise it. Moreover, they are able to structure aspects of a situation in a hierarchical way, based on the chunks they are familiar with (Chi et al., 1982). This is remarkably similar to the observations on hierarchical thought processes observed in Section 5.1. Experts find it easier to structure a domain into different layers, and handle each challenge by conceptualising appropriate levels of detail. Clearly, cognitive depth, whether situational or expertise based, enables us to establish several layers of thought, to be drawn upon and referred to when we need it. In contrast, lack of depth or expertise leaves all aspects of a situation at the same level of importance, due to an inability to impose a useful structure or identify priorities.

We can expect knowledge of entire chunks, or thinking at this level, to be reflected in verbal protocols in systematic ways. In problem-solving studies in the domain of physics (Chi et al., 1982), experts used the same formula as novices to derive the solution. While experts simply stated the result in a quick one-step solution, novices evoked the formula, spelled it out, and gradually came to a solution on this basis. This reflects how problem-solving speed is enhanced by expertise, and it also shows that consciously thinking about fine details is no longer required in the case of experts – they simply *know*. Our everyday experience is likely to be similar. If Emily knows what is required to bake an apple cake, she may simply be asked to *buy the ingredients* – no further details are needed. But someone who has never baked a cake, or even not gone shopping before, will need a lot of details before they can carry out this particular task.

Again, therefore, we see how granularity is related to cognition. Whereas a more detailed verbal description reflects enhanced cognitive depth as discussed in Section 5.1, a short and crisp, seemingly superficial description that goes into no details may simply be a matter of expertise. Someone who is very familiar with all the details may not see the need to spell them out, or may not even be aware of the details any more because they are simply too normal, too common to be noticed. Nevertheless, the expert will be able to speak with confidence, and to elaborate if needed in a particular situation.

Indeed, people may be more or less verbose, but this does not necessarily reflect how much knowledge they have on a subject. Experts are able to restrict their attention to the highest level of relevant chunks in the hierarchy, in contrast to novices who would not be able to recognise them. Thus, a shorter verbal protocol by a novice may remain on the surface of aspects in a situation just like the expert's, but these may not be the same kind of aspects that an expert would identify in the same amount of words. Chi et al. (1982) confirmed that quantitative measures (such as word count) do not reflect expertise – it is *what* people say, not *how much* they say, that reveals their knowledge level. Novices may leave out decisive aspects, overlook crucial relationships, or misrepresent facts, whereas experts would be able to crisply mention everything essential, including details where required.

Experts can confidently verbalise their thoughts within the domain of their expertise, but they are also more aware of the limits of their knowledge, or of the subtle aspects that might sometimes complicate things – more than novices may be aware of. For this reason, a novice may sometimes sound overly confident or certain of what they are doing, simply because of a lack of recognition of subtler aspects. For instance, Mercier and Sperber (2011) noted that people who are not aware of counterarguments to a particular position tend to be overconfident; their lack of knowledge is exhibited precisely by the confidence with which they present a problematic position, one that can be challenged given a bit more knowledge. Experts may be more cautious and conservative in such cases. This is especially true when expressing estimates about future developments. For instance, in the domain of weather forecasts, uncertainty is pervasive and inevitable (Hoffman, Trafton, & Roebber, 2005). Long-term forecasts are therefore purposely vague and coarse, rather than attempting to provide precise details for specific time spans or small spatial areas.

However, even experts can be overconfident within their own area (Chi, 2006). This seems to become most apparent when they are asked to rate their own performance or assess their degree of comprehension. In such a situation, novices may be more aware of their own limitations, enabling them to judge their own level of knowledge more accurately.

In conclusion, we can observe that expertise can be manifest in a range of ways, and is sometimes – but not always – reflected in degree of confidence. Lack of certainty expressed in language can therefore have various different reasons. Expertise is often a strong reason for confidence, but clearly not the only one – and even experts may become overly confident. Novices may pretend they know more than they do, or they may simply lack awareness of the associated complications. And some expert domains are characterised by a high degree of uncertainty, which may be represented in the language used by experts when they speak about a situation in which not all factors are available, such as future developments. In such a case, uncertainty is more a feature of the situation than a feature of expertise.

5.2.2   Linguistic Markers of Certainty

As outlined in Section 5.2.1, we cannot equate expertise or knowledge with the certainty expressed in language. However, if the level of knowledge is assessed independently (e.g. based on previous experience or training), linguistic indications of certainty can be highly revealing with respect to the cognitive processes in a novice or expert. For instance, some aspects of a situation may be described with more confidence than others. Such patterns may differ between experts and novices. Experts would be more confident about central aspects that are clear enough in the situation at hand, and their uncertainty markers would be mainly related to aspects that are truly underspecified by the situational parameters. Novices, in contrast, may be uncertain about any aspect of the situation, or they may confidently misrepresent certain aspects due to lack of knowledge about the potential complications and subtleties. This section reviews the kinds of linguistic features that may be relevant in this regard – those aspects of language that reflect confidence and certainty in a speaker.

In Chapter 3, we looked at Systemic Functional Grammar (SFG) as a framework that distinguishes between different levels of analysis: the ideational level (for content), the interpersonal level (for aspects pertaining to the speaker and hearer), and the textual level (for discourse structure) (Halliday & Matthiessen, 2014). For the purposes of current concerns, it is the interpersonal level that is most relevant, as this is where we see the speaker's 'intrusion' (in Hallidayan terms) into the situation. This level of analysis therefore highlights various ways in which a speaker can assess their own certainty about the represented facts.

Neutral and undisputed poles of certainty are represented as clear positive and negative statements, such as those in Examples 5.22 and 5.23. The speaker is confident about the future, and can make a clear prediction about the rain the following Tuesday. In SFG terminology, *will* and *won't* are temporal operators indicating the future, with either positive (Example 5.22) or negative (Example 5.23) polarity. The following examples then add a degree of indeterminacy, ranging from low confidence (Example 5.24 positive, and 5.25 negative) via median (Examples 5.26 and 5.27) to high (Examples 5.28 and 5.29):

Example 5.22   It will rain on Tuesday.

Example 5.23   It won't rain on Tuesday.

Example 5.24   It can rain on Tuesday.

Example 5.25   It needn't rain on Tuesday.

Example 5.26   It should rain on Tuesday.

Example 5.27   It shouldn't rain on Tuesday.

Example 5.28   It ought to rain on Tuesday.

Example 5.29   It can't rain on Tuesday.

All of these variations tell us something about the speaker's certainty that this event will happen in the future. Events in the past and the present can be expressed likewise, with different reasons for the represented level of confidence. Whereas nobody can be entirely certain about the future (because it simply hasn't happened yet), lack of confidence about something in the present or past would be related to lack of specific knowledge. Examples 5.30–5.33 show some of the options for the present tense. Note that the modal *will* can either express clear certainty (positive polarity) for the future (Example 5.22), or high probability for the present (Example 5.31). Context is needed to determine which of these options is intended by the speaker.

Example 5.30   This is/is not the right solution.

Example 5.31   This must be/will be/may be/should be/can't be the right
               solution.

Example 5.32   This is possibly/probably/certainly/probably not the right
               solution.

Example 5.33   This will probably be the right solution.

If we don't know for certain whether something is, was, or will be true, we can express the level of certainty by using suitable modal operators. We might use variations of the modal Finite as in Examples 5.22–5.29 and Example 5.31, or modal adjuncts as in Example 5.32. Example 5.33 demonstrates that these two distinct grammatical options can be combined, making the element of indeterminacy more transparent.

There are further ways of expressing the speaker's stance, beyond these options, that are directly related to the interpersonal level of analysis in SFG. Certainty can also be expressed as an attribute of the speaker as in Example 5.34, as an expression of mental processes as in Examples 5.35 and 5.36, or through nominalisations of such processes as in Example 5.37. With options such as these, the English lexicon contains a wide range of opportunities to express degree of determinacy.

Example 5.34   I am sure/certain/convinced that this is the right solution.

Example 5.35   I expect/believe/assume that this is the right solution.

Example 5.36   I wonder/doubt that this is the right solution.

Example 5.37   My expectation/conviction/hunch is that this is the right solution.

Analysis of certainty in CODA should therefore address a range of ways of expressing indeterminacy: modal Finites and modal adjuncts as the main grammatical indicators, plus further lexical items and constructions that express related notions.

It is worth noting that the same grammatical options can also express other concepts, such as obligation or inclination, in addition to probability. Consider the following:

Example 5.38   Should I write a book?

Example 5.39   We ought to be on our way.

Example 5.40   Mary will help.

As Halliday and Matthiessen (2014) point out, Example 5.40 is on the surface a statement of positive polarity about an event in the future – but if Mary is listening, it will now be very difficult for her to refuse to help. In this sense, the statement can express a degree of obligation rather than mere certainty. In spite of their clear modal function, modal verbs (like any other linguistic feature) therefore need to be interpreted in light of their pragmatic meaning in context.

Uncertainty can furthermore be conveyed through hesitation markers, hedges, and other tell-tale aspects that may make speakers seem not entirely sure of themselves or of what they are saying. Hesitation markers include non-lexical fillers such as *uh*, *uhm*, *um, er*, and *ah*, as well as lexical devices such as *like*, *okay*, *right*, and *you know*, which are commonly perceived as semantically empty when they're used as fillers. Hedges are similar in that they can also fill gaps of speech, but they can also indicate vagueness, for instance *sort of*, *kind of*, *technically*, *somewhat*, *I think*, *though*, *well*, and various others (e.g. Culpeper & Kytö, 2010).

Together with pauses in the speech flow and delays in starting an utterance, all of these features indicate fluency interruptions of some sort, and are therefore perceived as indicating some kind of hesitation. There may be various reasons for this. Lack of confidence about the topic at hand or about the appropriateness of the choice of words are major possibilities, which is why it makes sense to consider these features as potential indicators of uncertainty. However, there are plenty of other possible reasons for their occurrence. For instance, people may simply be considerate of their communication partner's concerns; if they are talking about a sensitive issue, they may want to package their message carefully, not wanting to sound overwhelming or over-assertive. Consider the following examples, which can be interpreted as indicating hesitation for different reasons:

Example 5.41   Um, I don't really know what to do next, uh, (3) sort of stuck now.

Example 5.42   Um, did you, uh, realise that you (3) sort of messed this up?

Example 5.41 could be part of a think-aloud protocol in which the speaker verbalises a problem-solving process. Since there is no communicative task here, there is no reason for social hedging. The hesitation markers in this example (*um*, *really*, *uh*, *sort of*, 3-second pause) match well with the lexical indications of uncertainty (*don't know what to do*, *stuck*). Together, the indications for uncertainty in this particular phase of the problem-solving process are therefore very strong and fairly unambiguous.

Example 5.42, in contrast, would more likely be heard in a communicative context; the speaker is addressing someone else who has in their opinion done something wrong. Alerting the person to the problem is socially problematic, and could lead to a loss of face. As a result, the speaker hedges and tries to skirt around the problem as much as possible; the pragmatic markers (*um*, *uh*, *sort of*, 3-second pause) accompany the explicit goal of making the person realise (*did you realise*) that something went wrong. The use of colloquial language (*messed this up*) further supports the speaker's solidarity with the listener, in the hope of avoiding this coming across as a formal reproach.

Further frequent reasons for displaying hesitation is *cognitive load* as well as dispersion. Someone who is confronted with a complex task or with several tasks at once will speak less fluently than otherwise. Lindsey et al. (1995) designed a study to identify reasons for temporal non-fluency (pauses and delayed speech onset). In particular, they looked at social reasons for non-fluency as opposed to cognitive load. Their results showed that while people do sometimes employ non-fluency markers for social purposes, cognitive load plays a major role in challenging situations, for instance if the speaker needs to convey several communicative goals at once. Non-fluency markers were considerably reduced when people got a chance to prepare their messages in advance, indicating that they weren't simply strategic. With respect to Example 5.42, it is therefore possible that the various hesitation markers reflect the cognitive challenge of getting a communicatively problematic thought across, along with the possibility of strategic hedging in order to avoid overwhelming the listener.

Generally, we may note that hesitation markers, hedges, pauses, and the like are typically indicators of some kind of problem. Something is there that slows the speaker down, or makes them formulate their messages with caution, in a less than assertive style. Further aspects of the linguistic data, or of the context, typically provide indications as to the nature of the problem. This can be uncertainty about the task at hand, or about the associated thoughts, or about suitable words, as well as cognitive load and communicative concerns about the relationship to the interaction partner.

Finally, the tone of voice can reveal the speaker's degree of certainty in various ways, ranging from individual variability in assertiveness to systematic differences in tone patterns. Because speakers differ a lot in the habitual degree of forcefulness in their voice, it will often be difficult to determine a specific degree of certainty in a particular situation. Differences can often be subtle, and will be a matter of degree, relative to other situations. However, Halliday and Matthiessen (2014) suggest that patterns of falling and rising tone can reveal degrees of certainty across individuals, with a falling tone indicating more certainty than a rising tone. For instance, questions are typically associated with a rising tone, and this would reflect the highest degree of uncertainty: an explicit request to learn about some facts which the speaker is not certain about (except in rhetorical or educational questions). Combinations of rising and falling tones, according to Halliday and Matthiessen (2014), indicate various intermediate degrees of certainty, such as 'seems to be certain but isn't' with a falling–rising pattern, and 'seems not to be certain but is' with a rising–falling pattern.

However, even though these patterns are presented in SFG as part of the grammar, there are huge individual and sociolectal variations in this regard. In certain dialects or sociolects, it is common to end statements with a rising tone, simply as a matter of convention, rather than an expression of uncertainty (Ladd, 1996). This is known as *uptalk*, and is seen as associated particularly with female speakers in North America, Australia, and New Zealand (although the actual picture can be a bit more complex than this; see, e.g., Warren, 2005). It stands to reason that a rising tone in conversation invites the listener to agree with a statement and thus enhances interaction; this would then be a dialogue function rather than a marker of uncertainty.

To conclude, language is rich with resources for expressing levels of certainty in many ways. Expressions of uncertainty are often very prominent in language, and may intuitively seem worth focusing on in analysis. However, it is critical to distinguish between different levels and sources for uncertainty, not all of which may be directly relevant to the goals of a research study. We will now turn to a CODA study in which certainty was targeted directly.

5.2.3   Certainty and Expertise: A CODA Study

Since expertise is an important topic in cognitive science and language offers many different ways of conveying certainty, the interplay of these two factors is a fruitful target of analysis in CODA studies. To exemplify this, we will now look at a study on the strategies people use to find their way in a complex building, relative to how well they know the building (Tenbrink, Bergmann, & Konieczny, 2011a).

Imagine it's your first day at the university, and you've just managed to find the room where you're expected, somewhere on the first floor in the confusing building complex. Now someone asks you to take them to the cafeteria. Or something happens and you need to find a way out – quickly. Since you don't know your way around in the building, you may not be sure about either one of these goals. However, chances are that you wouldn't just give up. Somehow you would manage to find the cafeteria, or an exit within reasonable distance – even though you might not get there on the shortest possible route. But how do you do this? What are the strategies that you might use to find your way around in an unfamiliar building?

In our study, we confronted two different groups of participants with just this kind of task, namely novices and experts. Novices were students during their first week at university, and experts were employees with offices in the building. We expected that these two groups would solve the task in very different ways, and that the differences in expertise should be reflected in their language use. All participants were asked the following two questions, in balanced order (translated from the German original):

- Imagine you have to leave this building as quickly as possible. Please explain to me as well as you can how you would do that.
- Imagine you want to go to the cafeteria in this building. How do you get there using the shortest route?

Following this verbal task, participants were asked if they were willing to do more, and those who consented received the following instruction:

- Please walk to [the goal they described last: cafeteria/nearest exit] using the shortest route. It is not important to us whether you walk the same route that you just described or take a route that is even shorter. However, it is important to us that you *think aloud* while you are walking. Please say everything that crosses your mind.

This short think-aloud description, without a chance to practise, was used to keep things simple. Participants had not been given any prior warning about the study and took part spontaneously on an entirely voluntary basis; therefore, we did not wish to use more of their time than absolutely necessary. With a more complex study design where participants are prepared to spend some time in the lab, it is useful to elaborate on the think-aloud procedure and let participants practise before doing the actual task (see Chapter 8). For the purposes of this wayfinding study, we hoped that the task would be simple enough for the participants to verbalise without further elaboration. And indeed, the verbalisations were adequate for the purposes of our study.

In this way, we collected two types of verbal data (two planning descriptions per participant, plus an optional think-aloud protocol) along with associated behavioural data for each data set, that is, the route that participants chose in each case. The route choices revealed participants' performance in the sense of route efficiency, whereas the verbal data reflected their certainty in relation to the task.

Results showed, unsurprisingly, that experts found shorter routes than novices did (see Figure 5.1), and they also assessed their own knowledge to be higher than novices did. Also, novices sometimes did not verbalise any specific route at all, but referred to generic wayfinding strategies instead. These results confirmed that linguistic features in the language data sets could indeed be traced back to differences in certainty about the routes involved, because novices were unable to identify the shortest route.

The linguistic analysis was qualitative as well as quantitative, and distinguished between the two types of data sets (planning and think-aloud) as well as between experts and novices. For the quantitative analysis, we counted a range of operationalised features in the language data, which were motivated in part by the previous literature and in part by inspection of the data (as it is not always possible to predict the kinds of features speakers will employ in free language production). Our operationalised features included uncertainty markers of a generic kind, as well as more scenario-specific indicators of different degrees

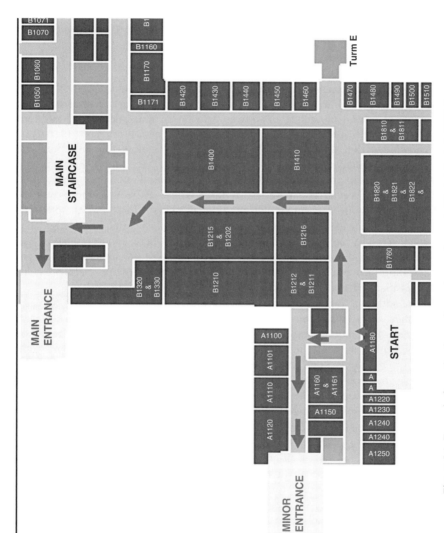

Figure 5.1 Example for paths chosen by novices and experts (Tenbrink et al., 2011a).
Experts described a quick route to the nearest exit, while the novice's path leads to the main entrance via the main staircase.

of spatial knowledge, namely concrete spatial elements (such as specific references to landmarks, start and endpoint, distances, changes of direction, etc.) as well as markers of orientation (such as public orientation aids including signage, verbs of orientation including *look out for* and *search*, etc.). Generic uncertainty markers, in this study, fell into the following categories:

- vagueness: words that include the morpheme *some*: *somehow, something, somewhere, sometime,* etc.
- restarts: incomplete words or sentences followed by a fresh start
- referential problems (indicated by specific markers in German)
- modal verbs: *could, may, might, should, would,* etc.
- hedges: *in a sense, probably, possibly, maybe,* etc.
- mental processes/stance: *believe, think, know,* etc.

The quantitative results revealed very clear patterns, indicating how expertise is reflected in language in this scenario. Experts produced more concrete spatial elements, but fewer orientation and uncertainty markers, than novices. This confirms that the experts had more specific spatial knowledge that they could rely on during wayfinding, that they had less need for orientation, and less reason to express uncertainty. Furthermore, planning protocols included more concrete spatial elements than think-aloud data, associated with more uncertainty. However, there was no difference with respect to orientation markers. Thus, when planning ahead, there was more need to verbalise specific spatial knowledge than when actually navigating in the environment, where concrete spatial elements were directly visible. The higher amount of uncertainty in the planning process reflects the fact that the environment itself provided clues that reduced uncertainty and supported wayfinding.

In addition, our qualitative analysis of the protocols' content revealed a range of different strategies that included the above markers to different degrees. People with very little knowledge of the building typically relied on basic generic strategies that could be used anywhere, such as *looking for signs* or *asking people*. Such descriptions do not contain any concrete spatial elements, but could include orientation and uncertainty markers. People with limited knowledge of the building referred to environment-specific elements, such as the *signs above doors* or the *nearest staircase*. People with somewhat more knowledge would refer to central elements of the building such as the *main staircase*, adding a limited number of concrete spatial elements to the description. This central point–oriented strategy is known from previous literature to be common in wayfinding tasks in unfamiliar environments: if you don't know much, orient towards landmarks of high saliency that you can always come back to. With even more specific knowledge of the building, our participants were finally able to employ turn-by-turn directions of the kind one would expect in familiar environments: *turn right at the next corner, take the staircase down, it will be on your left.* Such descriptions were based on fairly elaborate knowledge of the building, and accordingly contained plenty of concrete spatial elements, and few uncertainty or orientation markers. Naturally, they were more frequently produced by experts than by novices.

In sum, our study in Tenbrink et al. (2011a) identified various cognitive strategies that participants employed in a situation of potential uncertainty, along with a range of verbal devices that revealed the degree of confidence. The speakers' language use reflected aspects of their minds (their expertise) in systematic but subtle ways, not by explicit statements declaring lack of knowledge, but by signalling uncertainty and vagueness through the choice of words and use of suitable spatial strategies.

This chapter has highlighted two major ways in which cognitive depth is manifest in the way we speak. On the one hand, differences in granularity levels reveal the extent to which a speaker conceptualises elaborate details and fine-grained aspects of a situation, as opposed to employing a more abstract and general perspective. On the other hand, cognitive depth can mean depth of knowledge based on expertise. Lack of confidence, related to extensive knowledge or other factors including indeterminacy of the scenario itself, is regularly expressed in verbalisations by various markers of uncertainty.

These two aspects of cognitive depth, granularity and certainty, are not directly interdependent, but interrelate systematically. Experts who are certain of a particular fact are normally able to describe this fact either in much detail, or in abstract terms (e.g. as a 'chunk', a familiar pattern expressed as a whole), depending on context. Similarly, uncertainty can be expressed either in relation to general ideas, or in relation to fine details as the speaker zooms in to the issue at stake. In this sense, looking at the two aspects of cognitive depth jointly may be highly revealing to the analyst.

6   Identifying Cognitive Constructiveness

This chapter will address *inference* and *transformation* – two processes of human cognition that are often involved in problem-solving tasks, and which may also be part of mental representations to some extent. Both of them are ways in which the human mind creatively *constructs* reality, rather than simply observing and representing objective facts in the brain. Inference involves taking observable facts and combining them with further knowledge or assumptions, in order to come to new insights or conclusions that aren't directly observable. Transformation, on the other hand, involves taking observable facts or objects and turning them into something different, something that isn't yet there but that can be accomplished using available tools and operators. The following sections will look at each of these processes of cognitive constructiveness in turn.

6.1   Inference

Imagine you read the following beginning of a story:

Example 6.1   Helena lived in a farmhouse with her parents. She didn't have many friends, and was often bored.

A simple and easy-to-read text such as this one immediately invites you to make a range of assumptions. Readers may differ in the extent to which they jump to conclusions, but at least the following three inferences are fairly likely:
• This story will be about Helena as the main character.
• Helena is a child.
• The farmhouse is located in a rural area, definitely not in a city.
How do we know all this? None of it is directly mentioned in the two sentences of Example 6.1. In fact, all of these assumptions could be wrong. The story could be about somebody else, with Helena introduced as a minor character for reasons that will become apparent later. Helena could be grown up and still living with her parents in the farmhouse. And there's nothing to prevent farmhouses being located in cities, even though it does not seem likely – the city might have grown around the house over centuries. So, all of the inferences that the reader makes may be unfounded and proven wrong as the story unfolds.

But how do we get to these inferences in the first place? Why do we make assumptions such as these, and what are the principles behind this? For this particular example, we can note that the reader builds on a number of conventions as well as background knowledge. Since the style of the two sentences is relatively simple, readers will naturally assume that the story follows a conventional pattern in which the main character is introduced up front. The easy-to-read style also supports the assumption that Helena is a child, as this could be the start of a story for children. This is reinforced by the mention of *parents*, *friends*, and *bored* – familiar elements in a child's world, even though they are by no means restricted to children. Since children's stories are conventionally told around such elements, the semantic field of a child's life is evoked, and supports the idea of a child's story in the reader. Finally, farmhouses are typically (though not inevitably) located in rural areas, and the mention of boredom fits very well with the lack of busy urban life.

Thus, there is an abundance of associations that jointly support the three assumptions above. Not every reader may have exactly the same associations, but as long as the cultural background is shared, it is likely that inferences are made, to some extent, in fairly similar ways.

Inferences such as these happen all the time, and for the most part we're not aware of this. We may read a story and build up a mental image of the represented world without ever realising that half of our insights are mere assumptions. With stories, this is usually not a problem since we're only a passive recipient, we aren't supposed to act on what we read, and any erroneous inferences will be corrected as the story unfolds. However, in other scenarios, inferences can be quite serious and affect future actions in non-trivial ways.

Consider the two main areas that we're concerned with in this book – problem-solving tasks and mental representations. When we solve problems, inferences are often crucial because not all facts may be explicitly represented. Indeed, if all the facts were clearly described, there may not be much of a problem left to solve! So problem solving is very much about having suitable thoughts about the information at hand, so that solutions can be generated. And concerning mental representations, even when we merely describe what we observe, some aspects may well be based on inferences rather than objectively observable facts. For instance, if part of an object is hidden, we may just guess what the hidden part looks like – and we will often be right, since we're relying on common sense and relevant world knowledge.

Clearly, then, inferences are frequent in our lives in the way we think. Focusing on inferences when using CODA can provide a host of insights relevant for the research question at hand. In the following, we will first explore cognitive processes of inference (Section 6.1.1), and then look at inference processes specifically in the area of problem solving (Section 6.1.2). Section

6.1.3 addresses the role of inferences in language use, and Section 6.1.4 gives an example of a CODA study that addresses inferences through linguistic analysis.

6.1.1   Cognitive Processes of Inference

In our introductory Example 6.1, one of the assumptions involved expansion from previous experience or background knowledge, namely that farmhouses are normally found in rural areas. Generalisations such as these are very common, and they regularly lead to inferences that may or may not be true. Here, the generalisation that farmhouses are *normally* found in rural areas suggests to the reader that the location of *this particular* farmhouse is in a rural area, too. Readers may quickly forget that this is only an inference from a generalisation, rather than explicit information from the text itself. Typically, after little more than a minute, readers are unable to distinguish between the exact words they read and a paraphrase (Sachs, 1974). Based on rapid comprehension processes, inferences are quickly absorbed and taken for granted.

Overgeneralisations happen in other contexts as well; they are frequent processes in everyday thinking (Sternberg & Ben-Zeev, 2001). When confronted with a new challenge, people often recall previous experiences of a similar nature, and then attempt to deal with the new challenge in a similar way. In this process, one might go too far and fail to realise that the new situation might need a different approach. Or one might become confused, if the new challenge comes with unfamiliar aspects. Consider the following sample of a think-aloud protocol recorded in an origami paper-folding study (Tenbrink & Taylor, 2015):

Example 6.2   I usually look at pictures only but sometimes because this is a more tradition- a more modern way of teaching origami as opposed to a normal diagram, I took a look, at first I was disoriented once again so what I ended up doing was I looked back at the original thing to see that we had to fold it back to the original position.

Here, the (male) participant refers to his previous experience with origami. According to this protocol he is used to doing origami folding tasks on the basis of pictures alone, without the help of accompanying verbal descriptions. What he saw in this task, however, was a different kind of picture, which did not contain all the information he needed to solve the task; therefore, reading the instructions was essential – contrary to his previous experience. This explains the disorientation in this instance. Relying on previous experience was not sufficient; this task had to be solved differently.

Why do we rely on previous experience so much – why do we base our actions and decisions on inferences gained from other contexts? Gentner (2010) suggests that this ability is one of the basic prerequisites for thinking and learning throughout our lives. We experience something specific and are then immediately able to transfer the experience to other situations by analogy. All we need is some kind of parallel with the new situation, some common structure that we can recognise, so that we can do the transfer. After identifying similarities and differences between situations, we try to map their structures by aligning them as far as possible. As part of this process, we may fill some gaps by transferring some aspects of one situation to the other, without requiring all the details to be specified explicitly. And this can mean that we make inferences that we're not aware of, since much of this process is habitual and automatic.

For instance, Gentner et al. (2009) showed children two models of a skyscraper. One of them was stabilised by a diagonal brace, whereas the other only had a horizontal brace that provided no stability. Once the children had understood the difference between the models, they were able to transfer the insight to a different model building. This transfer was facilitated if the two models shown to the children were otherwise similar. If they were different in further respects (other than the brace), the children were less able to identify the decisive difference between the two models that led to the increase in stability. The transfer to a new building requires abstraction and generalisation abilities, as well as inferences as to how the brace might work with the new building. Remarkably, even young children were able to achieve this transfer following very brief training, involving just one pair of models for demonstration. And they could transfer the insight to a different-looking building, assuming implicitly that the principle would still work – as it did.

Transferring insights from previous experience is thus crucial for learning, and for understanding the world. The ability leads to generalisations of individual situations, and likewise to specific solutions for new kinds of challenges – as long as they are similar enough, in some structural way, to a familiar kind of challenge. We do this all the time, it is central to how we think. The world would be far too complex for us to cope with if we were unable to categorise, generalise, transfer, and abstract from insignificant differences.

In fact, the same principle is at work for acquiring concepts. Children start by learning the names of categories such as *chair* or *dog*, often based on a single instance. They might use the new word right away when they see another one that seems similar. And the more exemplars of a category they see, the more accurate they will be in transferring the concept to a new exemplar. In the meantime, children often overgeneralise – they may call a *dog* a *cat*, and a *sofa* a *bed*. This reflects the thinking behind concept acquisition: cats look similar enough to dogs that they may be classified in the same category at a particular stage of development (Tomasello, 2003). And sofas can be used for sitting and lying on, just as beds. However, as the child sees and hears more about the world, concept classifications will become more stable.

As adults, the same principle is still at work. We learn new words and concepts all the time, for instance from context when we read or listen to the radio, or as new technology introduces novelties. For instance, we learned the meanings of *iPad* and *virtual reality* along with their functions as technology developed. In some instances, just seeing and understanding one exemplar will be sufficient to acquire the new concept, whereas other concepts may be too abstract and complicated to grasp, and we may be unsure of them for a long time. In any case, the underlying process involves understanding which aspects of a particular instance are relevant and can be transferred to another instance by analogy, allowing for the inference that the next item that looks like an *iPad* is, in fact, also an *iPad*, with similar features.

Although central to human cognition in many respects, the ability to make inferences from past experience comes with a few problems. Generalising too much, filling in too many gaps by analogy, means jumping to conclusions. We could easily expect the features of an *iPad* in another item that is in fact an *iPod*, resulting in some unwelcome surprises. Or, to take another example: if three of our four best friends have long black hair, and two people who we don't like have short hair, we may start to assume that people with long black hair are generally nicer. Logically, this can only make sense if there is some character trait or cultural preference directly associated with this hairstyle. Even if there was, taking the inference further to the point of assuming that short-haired people are all awful would definitely be disastrous. There are so many other factors to take into account, and a stereotype of this sort could have all sorts of negative consequences.

Also, over-reliance on analogy may under certain circumstances reduce creative thinking and cloud judgement. For instance, Sternberg and Ben-Zeev (2001) reported that teachers often encourage children to establish a pattern for solving a mathematical task in a particular way. With word problems such as 'Tom has 5 apples, Jerry takes away 3. How many apples are left?' (Sternberg & Ben-Zeev, 2001:163), they may be taught to use the word *left* as a cue to perform a subtraction, as necessary for this task. However, if a child takes this analogy-based strategy too far, they might assume that subtractions are also required for other tasks involving the word *left* – including 'Tom sits to the left of Jerry.' Then, the established task-solving procedure actually keeps the child from processing a new task properly, and hampers identifying suitable solution paths for it.

We can conclude that inferences happen frequently in our everyday thinking, allowing us to think and act quickly based on our life experience. The ability to transfer from something known to something (slightly) new is useful, and it works well as long as there are sufficient parallels to allow for a suitable analogy. The more inconsistencies there are between situations, or the less complete information is available, the more we will have to rely on inferences to fill in the gaps. And then, inevitably, overgeneralisations and erroneous assumptions become more frequent.

6.1.2   Inferences in Problem-Solving Tasks

In problem-solving situations, or when we are confronted with a complex decision to be made, one of the challenges that people are typically confronted with concerns the lack of a clear strategy or basis for acting. The available information is often either incomplete in some way or too complex, and previous experience may not allow for a direct and complete transfer without considerable gaps. This is an essential aspect of why there's a problem or why making a decision can be really hard. How do we cope with this kind of situation? Would we try to analyse all aspects and details of the situation before proceeding, or what else can we do?

Famously, Simon (1956) suggested that we use cognitive 'shortcuts' to accomplish our goals in an efficient way when confronted with complex challenges. Our rational minds are limited, and we cannot account for all relevant aspects of complicated situations. Simon (1956) refers to this fact as *bounded rationality*; our minds have very clear boundaries, and they do not work quite as fast as modern computers. What makes us superior to computers, however, is our efficient way of dealing with information gaps or overload, which enables us to function well in an infinitely complex world. That is, we use a range of useful heuristics and strategies that we establish throughout our lives and then have at our disposal for new situations.

For instance, when we find our way to a new location in a familiar complex urban environment, we do not need to plan the entire route to perfection in our head before setting off. The spatial information that we have in our heads about streets and landmarks in the city is inevitably incomplete (as we never have access to all the facts), and it may at the same time be too complex to account for every aspect if we know the urban environment well. Instead of attempting to optimise the route in advance, therefore, we just estimate the rough direction of the goal location and start moving towards it, using suitable roads and turns as we go (Hölscher et al., 2011). This heuristic works really well for most wayfinding situations in familiar environments, even though there may be occasional challenges such as blocked roads.

Such heuristics and strategies are employed in more or less conscious ways. In challenging situations, we typically need to consider a high number of factors, but we may not be aware of the kinds of cognitive shortcuts that we employ when we get to a solution. Due to our bounded rationality, we cannot take everything into account. But we do consider a relevant subset of the aspects involved, such as our knowledge of the general goal direction, and use this as the basis for a fast and efficient strategy.

These procedures often imply a range of generalised underlying assumptions. To return to the example cited in the previous section, the children trained in Gentner's (2009) study generalised from the single example they saw that diagonal braces stabilise buildings. From this experience, they could apply a diagonal brace to a different building, based on the (correct) assumption that the spatial arrangement of the brace mattered. There clearly wasn't enough evidence available to show that this was indeed the case across many kinds of buildings; the children did not have access to any static facts or calculations that would enable them to work out the optimal positioning and size required of the brace in a new building. However, the cognitive shortcut of focusing on the diagonal arrangement worked well enough for the purposes at hand.

In this way, cognitive shortcuts mean that we attach our assumptions from previous experience to the currently available information, in order to reach a conclusion that will typically correspond to the actual state of affairs closely enough to lead to the desired effect. Following Toulmin's (1958) terminology of human reasoning processes, we use the available information as *data*, and connect it with some kinds of *warrants* (principles or rules – including cognitive heuristics) in order to come up with *claims* (inferences or conclusions). In Toulmin's theory this then leads to the formulation of *arguments* in order to persuade other people of the claims made.

Even without considering arguments, the notions of *data*, *warrants*, and *claims* are very useful as cognitive components that can be identified in language data in the realm of CODA studies. They reflect the cognitive process of reasoning on the basis of background knowledge and cognitive heuristics, and they can be applied across many different kinds of scenarios. Verbalisations are often very useful resources to identify corresponding evidence as part of inference processes.

For instance, in one study, expert geologists and undergraduate students were asked to identify plausible geological structures from artificial rock outcrops (Kastens, Agrawal, & Liben, 2009). The students combined the available evidence with their background knowledge to form hypotheses that could be valid or not. This study showed that well-founded reasoning processes, as represented in language, were associated with valid claims, and also that experts produced far more evidence-supported claims than non-experts. In contrast, students produced more unsupported claims, that is, hypotheses that were not based on data and warrants. Further, some of the valid inferences (claims) required geological knowledge as warrants during the interpretation process of the evidence (data); as predicted, students were rarely able to refer to this kind of warrant. Altogether, the study provided extensive evidence concerning the relevance of inferences for reasoning processes in a complex task situation involving incomplete information.

Across many kinds of scenarios, it can be very enlightening to focus directly on the *claims* and inferences humans make based on the data available. However, perhaps the most interesting part of a reasoning process is the intermediate step: augmenting the given *data* using some kind of *warrant*. Such warrants may often be related to mental imagery (Johnson-Laird, 1983). For instance, if we think of our spatial surroundings, our mind quickly fills in any gaps concerning aspects or areas that we haven't actually observed, or don't remember in detail. We only have the most essential information available, but we may well be able to visualise some aspects that we don't have direct evidence for.

This kind of filled-in information comes from our previous experience, which we transfer to our mental image of the spatial environment. Identifying such processes through linguistic data analysis can be highly enlightening, as it can reveal where and how inferences are warranted or based on overgeneralisation of previous experience. Then, these inferences can be evaluated against actual facts, as they may be correct or incorrect. Also, they may be more or less detailed, revealing different degrees of imagination involved in the thought process.

In sum, problem-solving processes are based on inferences of various kinds. Making the right inferences from the available information in combination with prior knowledge may often be the main challenge when solving a problem. Therefore, a focus on inferences in analysis can be highly revealing.

6.1.3   The Role of Inferences in Language Use

So far in this chapter, we have looked at various ways in which we draw on incomplete information in order to learn language, to act, to make decisions, to solve problems, or generally to understand the world. The world is far too complex for us to understand in full detail – but we can manage quite well based on generalised and vague knowledge as well as some practical heuristics.

The same is true for language use. Communication is never perfect and spelled out to the last detail. In dialogue, speakers don't ever reach complete understanding, but they are satisfied if they can understand each other 'well enough for current purposes' (Clark, 1996:226). For instance, if Anne encourages Greg to *sit down* she might be alluding to a specific chair to sit on, but she won't need to say this explicitly unless it's really important that he doesn't sit down somewhere else. Indeed, the more important it is to choose the intended place to sit, the more explicitly her intention will be communicated. If it doesn't matter at all, Anne will just say *sit down*. If she intends Greg to sit in a specific area, a vague gesture might accompany the verbal encouragement. If she wants him to sit on a specific chair, she might touch the chair and point him directly to it. And if she wants to make her point in a decisive way, she will accompany this non-verbal gesture by a clearly pronounced ... *here*.

In general, instead of telling each other everything explicitly, we draw on a number of communicative principles such as those formulated famously by Grice (1975). Grice suggested that we *normally* aim to be truthful, orderly, informative enough for the topic at hand, and relevant to the context of the situation. However, we might sometimes break those 'maxims' for a specific purpose, or it might seem that we do. If this is the case, this communicates to the listener that there is some additional meaning that needs to be inferred.

Example 6.3   George: What time is the meeting?
              Jenny: You'll have to hurry up after class.

In Example 6.3, George asks for a specific clock time, but Jenny responds in a way that might seem to be irrelevant to the question at first sight. She does not provide a specific time as asked, but instead informs him about a certain consequence for George's future action. In a way, Jenny goes beyond the question. Rather than merely sticking to the conventional question–answer pattern, she makes some inferences about George's plans: he'll want to attend the meeting; but he is in class directly before; in order to get there in time he will have to hurry. Then she informs him about the outcome of this train of thought.

George, on the other hand, will have to retrace Jenny's thoughts in order to derive the answer to his question. He needs to infer that Jenny is aware of his class, and that he actually intends to go to the meeting; based on this inference, George can finally infer the answer to his question: that the meeting takes place at a time shortly after his class ends. All this happens quickly and normally without the speakers' awareness. Successful communication can be hard cognitive work, but we're rarely bothered by it because we are very much used to the principles of conversation that are normal for our culture.

One reason why we communicate in this way is because we aim to be economic, or to follow a 'principle of least communicative effort' (Clark, 1996). If speakers share a lot of background knowledge, they do not need to invest much effort into spelling everything out. Allusions and minimal pointers can be enough to understand each other easily. What guides understanding in the absence of explicit communication is our expectation of *relevance*. We can understand minimal contributions mostly because they happen in a certain context and are relevant to it.

George can make the correct inferences on hearing Jenny's utterance in Example 6.3 because he has just asked about the meeting. In a different context, the utterance *you'll have to hurry up after class* would not tell anybody the time of the meeting. Thus, somebody who does not share the knowledge about George's class time would learn nothing from this statement.

Understanding utterances out of a specific context is much harder and leads to misinterpretations and miscommunication far more easily. Compare Examples 6.4 and 6.5. In each case, the initial statement provides a context that we can use to understand the following (identical) evaluation of a film's story.

Example 6.4   Kate: This film had a deep message. This guy had cheated everyone, and he was surrounded by friends who accepted all of that. How nice to be forgiven!

Example 6.5   Kate: I really didn't like this film. This guy had cheated everyone, and he was surrounded by friends who accepted all of that. How nice to be forgiven!

Example 6.6   Tom: I agree with Kate – forgiveness is really important.

In Example 6.4, Kate liked the film and then elaborates the kind of deep message she saw in it – namely how it is *nice to be forgiven*. In Example 6.5, the same elaboration is used to explain why Kate did *not* like the film. The concluding statement, *How nice to be forgiven*, can now be understood as sarcastic: the speaker does not believe that forgiveness can or should happen this way, after cheating everyone. In Example 6.6, Tom might have overheard the last sentence, without its context, so he infers that Kate made a statement about the importance of forgiveness. While this may be true in the context of Example 6.4, it certainly is a wrong inference in Example 6.5.

Considering Tom's and Kate's utterances together, then, allows the analyst to identify the source for misinterpretation, based on Tom's inference. Tom lacks the context of how Kate actually judges the film, and therefore cannot know whether Kate's concluding statement is sincere or sarcastic. He does not know, in effect, what the statement is about. He infers that it must be about forgiveness, but in Example 6.5 at least it is actually a statement about the film – namely, how it (in Kate's opinion) oversimplifies forgiveness.

As noted in Chapter 3, Sperber and Wilson (1986) suggested that communication is altogether dependent on relevance, and they built an entire theory around this notion (relevance theory). They claimed that speakers always aim towards maximal relevance, and that without this principle we would be unable to interpret each other's utterances at all. In effect, no utterance is entirely context-free: everything we see or read is embedded in some context, which enables us to make sense of it. And this sense-making process involves inferences: both on the side of the speaker, whose contributions reveal what they have inferred from the context, and on the side of the addressee, who interprets the contribution based on their own inferences according to context.

These insights are quite decisive when interpreting language in a discourse analysis context, such as CODA. Analysts need to be aware of their own inference processes and treat interpretations with caution. However, they can also gain valuable insights about speakers' inference processes by adopting this kind of analysis perspective. As in the study by Kastens et al. (2009), cited in the previous section, verbal protocols often reflect participants' thought processes in problem-solving studies in such a way that inference processes become apparent. Sometimes speakers will make their inferences explicit in some way. In Example 6.7 the speaker explicitly derives a specific inference (*this* bottle is heavy) based on general knowledge (*green bottles* are heavy).

Example 6.7   Here is a green bottle. I know green bottles are heavier than white bottles; therefore I expect this bottle to be quite heavy.
Example 6.8   Ah, here is a heavy bottle.

At other times, the inferences may be entirely implicit, as in Example 6.8: the speaker does not spell out how they know that this bottle is heavy – it is simply referred to as such. If the analyst knows that the speaker has not touched the bottle, it is clear that this judgement must be based on an inference, such as the one made explicit in Example 6.7.

Since speakers aim towards minimal effort and maximal relevance, it is actually rather likely that they will only utter something minimal like Example 6.8 in an experimental setting, at least after some experience. When asked to think aloud while solving a problem, speakers are not required or expected to explain their inference processes to an addressee, and therefore will only say what is relevant to themselves as they solve the problem. In Example 6.8 there is no need for the speaker to say why they think the bottle is heavy. But the idea that it is heavy is relevant enough for the speaker to say out loud, as a proper part of their conscious thought process.

Along these lines, speakers will linguistically represent those aspects of a perceived scene or problem-solving process that they judge to be important. They may neglect things that they are unsure about unless these become relevant for a given goal. As a result, linguistic descriptions reflect what is prominent and relevant for the speaker while (or after) processing available and inferred information. It is then up to the analyst to identify which parts of the utterances are based on directly observable information, and which are inferred (as in Example 6.8 if the speaker hasn't actually touched the bottle). If inferred, they may be either accurate or inaccurate, which can lead to interesting analysis results. We will now look at a CODA study in which inferences played a major role.

6.1.4   Inferences and Linguistic Analysis: A CODA Study

Imagine the following scenario. You're a rescue worker, trained to find and help people in need. A large building collapses, and you're called on the scene to search for survivors trapped underneath the debris. You can't enter the scene yourself, as the debris may collapse further, causing further harm. Instead, you use a certain type of camera that has been developed for this kind of situation. The camera works like an endoscope: you can guide it into the debris and it sends pictures to your screen.

What you see on the screen is unfortunately very hard to understand and interpret. The camera twists and turns, the scene is cluttered, things are upside down or partially obscured. Detecting people in this challenging scenario can be extremely difficult, and success will depend crucially on your ability to make the right kinds of inferences. Your eyes will not tell you all the details – your brain will have to fill in some gaps, make sense of what you see.

In a recent study (Tenbrink et al., 2016), we addressed this urban search-and-rescue scenario to find out how much untrained people understand what they're seeing in such a scenario, and what this might depend on: is it just a matter of having enough time for the search, or is it rather a matter of skill? We designed a scenario that matched the described emergency in crucial respects but did not require any technological knowledge or prior expertise. Rather than hiding people under real debris, we hid small objects in a cluttered Styrofoam construction that was made to look very similar to a (small-scale) collapsed room (see Figure 6.1). This mock-up construction was filmed with a camera of the kind used in rescue scenarios, moving slowly through the scene. Participants were shown the film and asked to find all eight objects hidden in the debris, and to memorise where they found them so that they could describe their position later. Afterwards, they were asked what they remembered, and prompted to describe where and how the objects were positioned. Also, they were asked to describe the shape of the room if they could, and to draw a sketch of it together with the objects that they remembered.

To measure the effects of time constraints, we used one condition in which participants were under time pressure, and another where they had as much time as they needed. To measure the effects of skill, our participants did a spatial ability test that was matched to the kind of challenge given in the study. To measure participants' success in identifying objects,

Figure 6.1 Screenshot from the film in Tenbrink et al. (2016), showing a tilted view with artificial horizon. Note the lamp on the right.

we counted the objects that participants detected during the film and described later.

Further, we aimed to assess participants' success in making sense of the cluttered scene they saw. To operationalise this idea, we did three things. First, we addressed the extent to which descriptions of the scene were coherent, in that they represented the cluttered room as one consistent whole with a structure of some kind, rather than individual disconnected bits and pieces. Here, we found a wide range of variety. Some descriptions consistently started from one particular object, and then related the following objects to its position. Others related their object locations to the room area as a whole. In contrast, some descriptions did not follow any consistent description strategy at all, but rather reflected the confusion that participants clearly felt concerning this complicated task.

Second, we looked at how specific descriptions were. A description like *at the wall* could apply anywhere and did not count as specific, in contrast to more precise spatial relations such as *to the left of the tennis ball*, or *on the right side of the room*. And some objects were simply mentioned, without any further specification. Third, we rated the coherence of room drawings, which sometimes looked rather chaotic; this reflected the high degree of challenge in making sense of the scene.

Comparing these various measures and relating them to each other led to a number of insights. Most interestingly, people with higher spatial skills were more able to describe the specific location of objects in the scene, and to draw coherent sketches of the cluttered room and its contents. Unexpectedly, the time constraint factor did not matter at all; the quality of descriptions and drawings was not affected by introducing time pressure to the task.

It appears that spatial ability is a good skill to have when confronted with a complex scene requiring a lot of inferences about how things add up to a coherent whole. If you're not good at this kind of spatial understanding, you might stare at the pictures for a long time and still not be able to make sense of it. You might detect more objects with time – which can be very useful – but you might not be able to explain where they are, since you don't understand the overall configuration. This doesn't mean that these skills can't be acquired. All our participants were inexperienced and untrained; they only differed with respect to general spatial skills, not specific experience. In fact, it is well known that specific cognitive abilities can be trained very effectively, and there is no reason to assume that this wouldn't also be the case for the skills needed for search and rescue scenarios.

It can be concluded from this example study (Tenbrink et al., 2016) that the analysis of inference in empirical research can be challenging, because people won't directly mark a thought as being inferred. However, there are ways of operationalising analysis in such a way as to identify underlying inferences, based on a targeted comparison between available information and conclusions drawn by the participants.

6.2   Transformation

Many real-world tasks involve transformation of some kind: a child learns to tie her shoes by transforming two ends of a string into a knot; a piece of paper can be transformed into a flower or bird using origami folding procedures; pieces of wood can be transformed into furniture items. Transformation can be action, as part of a task or problem-solving process. But transformation can also happen in the mind, as part of a mental process. For instance, if you look at a picture and try to imagine what it would be like to be there and what you would like to do once you're there, you're already going beyond the picture itself – your mind takes you further towards a transformed alternative version of what you actually see.

Transformation is thus another way in which our minds construct reality beyond input. Inference, as explored in Section 6.1, means to 'read between the lines', fill in the gaps of available or perceivable information through background knowledge and logic. Transformation, on the other hand, means to 'go beyond the lines' – to take the available or perceivable information creatively towards something that *could* be there, but isn't yet, or isn't there as such. Our minds are incredibly flexible in this regard, and the world wouldn't be the way it is today if they weren't. Ultimately, the ability to creatively transform existing things and ideas into new ones lies at the heart of invention and improvement, or any kind of advancement from the status quo.

Transformation can be entirely creative; this is the case whenever something truly novel is created without a prior example. However, most transformation processes are guided in some way, either by prior experience or training, or by direct instruction. Transformation, in the sense considered here, is therefore not identical to creativity, although an element of creativity certainly supports transformative processes effectively.

What is happening in our minds during transformation, and how can we find out? Depending on what is being transformed, the process will often include a range of complex cognitive procedures. If we are confronted with a set of pieces that we wish to transform into one larger item, we will need to find out how specific parts can be assigned specific functions. In this way, a wooden board might become an outer wall in a doll's house (Gralla & Tenbrink, 2013). We will also need to think about the goal state, to decide (or clarify) what the result of the transformation should be. And we may need to anticipate manual actions that affect objects in the desired way.

Language often plays a crucial role for transformation. Frequently, we will be able to follow explicit instructions that tell us, more or less exactly, how the transformation can be carried out and what steps will need to be taken. Also, we may be able to describe the actions before we do them, or after having done them. Language is a useful medium to represent our thoughts about the transformation process, and it may sometimes be the main way to specify them. People may think aloud while doing transformations, or report how they did them, or simply represent the mental transformation itself in words – for example, describing what they would do if they were inside the scene shown in a picture (Cialone et al., 2018). Verbalised thought can represent a range of crucial cognitive aspects that are involved in transformation. For this reason, a focus on transformation in linguistic analysis can lead to exciting insights, highlighting how the flexibility of human thought affects the real world and interacts with it.

In the following, we will take a closer look at transformation processes from a cognitive science point of view (Section 6.2.1), and then turn to two CODA studies that explored different aspects of transformation: assigning functions to objects when assembling a doll's house without instructions (Gralla & Tenbrink, 2013; Section 6.2.2), and the challenges for transformation when following instructions in an origami paper-folding task (Tenbrink & Taylor, 2015; Section 6.2.3).

6.2.1 Insights on Transformation from Cognitive Science

Evidence for human ability to transform given input is abundant – it happens at all levels of cognition, at all stages of development, with all types of input. Transformation skills can be measured to some extent, using tasks that specify precisely what type of transformation is expected. For instance, to test the ability to mentally transform some visual input, people may be shown a picture of an object to compare with another picture – for instance a rotated version of the first (Smith & Dror, 2001). To successfully compare the two, they need to mentally rotate the first object to see if it matches the second one.

Mental rotation is one way to transform given input; the visual information is changed towards a different orientation in order to accomplish another cognitive task (the comparison with another object). Mental rotation tasks have been used extensively to test various aspects associated with this type of transformation. For instance, Shepard and Metzler (1971) found that the more the angle of the rotated object departs from the original, the more time it takes to mentally perform the transformation. And Mast and Kosslyn (2002) discovered that mental rotation can help identify different interpretations of the same picture. Because of insights such as these, the task designed by Shepard and Metzler (1971) is frequently used to measure participants' ability to do mental rotations in their head, in order to compare this skill with performance in some other task.

The study by Smith and Dror (2001) specifically looked at what happens when we mentally rotate an object, and what this might depend on. Previous literature had shown that mental rotation can be either holistic or piecemeal: either we conceptualise the entire shape as a whole, or we look at specific parts of it to perform the mental rotation. The authors speculated that this might depend on whether the objects to be rotated were meaningful or not, so they showed participants sketches of either meaningful objects (e.g. a ship or a helicopter) or meaningless objects (similar size and style of line drawing, but depicting no specific object). Their results showed that meaningless objects seemed to be mentally rotated as a whole, in holistic fashion, whereas meaningful objects were considered in terms of their specific parts. This reflects the flexibility of mental transformation processes, which can be adapted to the purposes at hand.

Mental rotation can be the basis of more complex imaginative processes, as shown by an intriguing experiment by Finke, Pinker, and Farah (1989). Rather than simply asking people to mentally rotate objects, they added further instructions that could lead to new meanings, as in Example 6.9 (Finke et al., 1989:62). The result of this particular mental transformation is the letter 'T'. All of these transformations happened in the mind only, but participants had little trouble identifying the new meanings created in this way, reflecting the versatility of human imagination.

Example 6.9   Imagine the number '7'. Make the diagonal line vertical. Move the horizontal line down to the middle of the vertical line. Now rotate the figure 90 degrees to the left.

While mental rotation is a typical example of transformation that has been explored in much depth, our minds are capable of doing more complex transformations – and we frequently need to do so. Taking the idea of mental rotation to another level, Atit, Shipley, and Tikoff (2013) observed that traditional mental rotation tasks only involve rigid transformations, unlike many tasks in the real world that involve non-rigid objects that can bend or break. In their study, they showed participants three-dimensional pictures of bent sheets, and asked them what the sheets would look like if they were unbent. Results showed that performance varied according to how exactly the sheet was bent, with some ways of bending harder than others. Also, interestingly, performance in this particular task did not correlate with performance in a rigid mental rotation task. This shows that mentally transforming non-rigid objects requires different skills to mentally rotating rigid objects – and it indicates that focusing research on rotation alone, as a prime example of mental transformation of visual images, is not sufficient to account for human transformation abilities.

Outside the visual domain, transformation can take a wide range of different forms. Any mathematical equation is a transformation that changes a sequence of numbers to a different one that is mathematically related to the first. Many transformation outcomes in the realm of numbers can be visualised as graphs or diagrams. Interpreting such visualisations is then a matter of making sense of the transformation.

In fact, while diagrams are useful ways to represent aspects of the world by transforming them into a visual scheme, observers may often fail to identify crucial information that the diagram is meant to display. Also, they may misinterpret accidental features of a diagram as representing specific facts about the displayed numbers. For instance, if some parts of a diagram use salient bright colours while others are displayed in grey, observers may think that the coloured ones are more important or decisive for their purposes. But both of these are merely transformations of a particular aspect of reality into the abstract schematic space of a diagram. Relevant aspects of the represented facts will be carried over, such as quantity of a particular measure: if a number is higher than others, the diagram will display it in some way, for instance by a larger bar. However, other aspects will be neglected or may change – such as colours.

As can be seen from this example, transformation is a matter of preserving some aspects while changing others. The challenge, then, is to find out what changes and what doesn't. In a series of experiments that have become famous, Piaget (1952) observed how children gradually learn about object permanence – the fact that objects remain in the world even if you can't see them. At first, children immediately lose interest as soon as an object is hidden. Later, they start looking for it, and thereby demonstrate that they know it still exists. But they may still not be able to keep track of it if it changes location or undergoes other transformations. Even later, the ability to keep track of quantity emerges. For instance, if the same number of objects are placed with equal distance between them in each of two rows, children may recognise that the number of objects is the same in each row. But if the experimenter transforms the situation slightly, and pushes the objects in one row closer together, the child (at a certain stage of development) would think that the number has been reduced. The transformation of the situation has led to confusion: the *space* covered by the objects has been reduced by the transformation, but not the *number* of objects. Similar to misinterpreting colours in a diagram, it is clearly not always easy to see which aspects of reality change with transformation, and which remain constant.

Most actions we undertake in the world are associated with some kind of change or transformation. Whenever we do something with objects, even just turn the page of a book, we have changed the shape of the book ever so slightly – not necessarily permanently, but definitely relative to how it looked before. When we turn around to look in the opposite direction, we have transformed nothing else but our own view direction – but as a result, the visual input we receive has changed completely. Changes can be permanent or temporary, and transformational opportunities are abundant. In this section, we have only touched the surface of the wide range of aspects involved in these phenomena. Rather than aiming to cover the field more exhaustively, we will now turn to two specific case studies that exemplify how CODA can be used to address research questions related to transformation.

6.2.2 Transforming Separate Objects into a Coherent Whole: Assembling a Doll's House without Instructions

Imagine you've just bought a dissembled set of wooden pieces on the flea market, which you were told fit together to make a cupboard. Unfortunately, there is no manual – you'll have to figure it out yourself. How do you go about this task? This kind of situation challenges you to a kind of transformation that is considerably more complex than the ones discussed in Section 6.2.1. Rather than changing just one object in a limited way, you're tasked with creating new meaning by assembling an entire set of objects together in a particular way, so as to serve a coherent function. You'll probably keep the overall function of the goal object in mind as you go along, making sure that what emerges from your transformation will actually be useful as a cupboard. One of the main challenges, however, is to assign specific functions to individual parts. Which of the pieces could serve as a shelf, which one goes on top, which one could be a door? How do you know, and how certain can you be in your decisions about which part will serve which function?

As described in Gralla and Tenbrink (2013), we created a similar scenario by giving participants a set of objects that together constituted a doll's house and asking them to assemble them. We were particularly interested in the effects of how much information people had in advance. Assigning functions to object parts should work best if you have a fairly good idea what your goal object should look like. You might even be able to name individual functions specifically if you know where the object parts will end up in the overall structure. In contrast, if you have no information other than the dissembled object parts as you see them, you will have to think creatively about the possible ways of fitting them together, with a possible overall function.

We tested this assumption by using three different conditions (Gralla & Tenbrink, 2013), with sixteen or seventeen participants each. In one condition called 'verbal & visual goal', participants were shown a photograph of the assembled doll's house and asked to *assemble the pictured doll's house*. In another condition, called 'verbal goal', they were not shown a picture but asked to *assemble a two-storey doll's house*. In the 'underspecified goal' condition, they were merely asked to *assemble a meaningful object*. On this basis, even though the transformation goal as such remained the same, the challenges for achieving it were very different in each of the conditions. Participants were asked to think aloud as they worked, so as to represent their thoughts during the process.

In addition, we were interested in effects of communication – how do people instruct others to accomplish the same task? For this purpose, we asked another sixteen participants to assemble the doll's house as in the 'verbal & visual goal' condition, but without thinking aloud. After successful assembly, their main task was to instruct another person to assemble the same doll's house. This person was able to watch and listen through a one-way video connection that did not allow for any responses.

We were interested to see if linguistic data would reflect differences in how people assigned functions to object parts under these various circumstances. Accordingly, our analysis focused on the matching process of object parts to functions. Since this particular aspect had not been addressed as such before, our analysis started on a qualitative basis, identifying what kinds of linguistic expressions were used to describe the function assignments, and annotating them throughout the data. This systematic procedure enabled us, in a next step, to identify quantitative frequencies in the three conditions.

Results showed that mapping phrases often consisted of a set of three elements: two noun phrases or pronouns that were related in some way to each other by a mapping term. Consider the following examples:

Example 6.10   This is a wall.

Example 6.11   This could also be storeys.

Example 6.12   The red building part looks like the roof of a house.

Example 6.13   (...) each with a small piece uhm a wall element.

While Examples 6.10 and 6.11 start with a demonstrative pronoun (*this*), Examples 6.12 and 6.13 use a more elaborate description of a specific object (*the red building part*; *a small piece*). The object function is expressed in terms of a noun (*wall*; *storeys*) in Examples 6.10 and 6.11, and a more complex noun phrase (*the roof of a house*; *a wall element*) in Examples 6.12 and 6.13. Whereas terms like *roof* and *wall* or *wall element* point to specific functional parts of the house, references to the entire structure or larger parts of it, such as *storey*, refer to structural aspects of the house that consist of multiple objects.

To relate the first reference term to the second, Example 6.10 uses a simple relational verb (*is*), whereas Example 6.11 and 6.12 reveal a more tentative assignment (*could be*, *looks like*). However, Example 6.10 and 6.11 both use forms of *be*, as opposed to *look like* in Example 6.12, which expresses a representational mapping rather than a direct relation. In contrast, Example 6.13 does not explicitly express any mapping at all – there is no mapping term. Yet, just as in the other examples the same object is referred to twice: first as an undefined *small piece*, then in terms of its function (*a wall element*). This is a case of implicitly *reframing* an object within the same utterance.

Our quantitative analysis accounted for each of these differences systematically. For objects, we looked at occurrences of demonstratives (e.g. *this*, *that*) as opposed to nominal references, and also looked at how specific the nominal references were. Mapping verbs were annotated with respect to whether they directly mapped objects to functions (which mostly happened using the verb *be*) or treated the objects as *representing* a function (as in *look like* or *use as*). Further, we looked for occurrences of modal verbs (such as *could*, *must*, and *should*), which express certainty to different degrees, and for cases of reframing without explicit mapping verbs.

Taken together, our analysis revealed three different mapping strategies as represented in language, which were used under different circumstances. First, the strategy shown in Examples 6.10 and 6.11 reveals *direct mapping* of an object to its function. The certainty with which this strategy is applied is indicated by the choice or lack of a modal verb such as *could*. Second, Example 6.12 illustrates *representational mapping*, which was less frequent than direct mapping; here, uncertainty is expressed by the choice of verb, rather than by modals.

Across these two strategies, higher certainty was expressed most frequently through the modal verb *must* where participants had most information – in the verbal and visual goal condition. In the underspecified goal condition, where participants had least information, they referred to structures (*house, storey*) more often than to specific object parts (*wall, roof, floor*).

Third, the *reframing* strategy shown in Example 6.13 only occurred with instructions, rather than during assembly. In instructions, all occurrences of direct mapping expressed high certainty without any modals. Furthermore, the representational mapping strategy was used more frequently than in the assembly conditions, and instructors used more nominal references (as opposed to demonstratives) than assemblers. Thus, the verbalisation of object-to-function mappings differed markedly between think-aloud and communicative tasks.

What can we learn from this study about transforming separate objects into a coherent whole without instructions? A number of insights highlight the cognitive processes that characterise this task. First, mapping objects to functions is one of the clearly represented conceptual processes in this kind of task; its regular presence in the verbal protocols as well as instructions reflects its importance during the unaided (instruction-less) assembly process. Second, mapping is preferably conceptualised directly as a relation (*this is*, or *could be*) that is asserted with either more or less certainty depending on circumstances, but it can also take the form of a representation (*this is used as*, or *looks like*). Third, when giving instructions, the conceptual challenge of assigning functions as such has disappeared; instructors primarily *communicate* the result of the mapping process to their interaction partner.

One of the strategies to communicate mapping is by reframing. Rather than expecting that the addressee knows which *object* functions as a *wall*, speakers frequently used both expressions, as in Example 6.13. Even though explicit mapping was not deemed necessary, the addressee still needed to be informed. It appears that hesitation markers such as *uhm* in Example 6.13 serve to replace the mapping term: since simply placing both terms together yields an ungrammatical sentence, the hesitation marker indicates a restart, following conventions of spoken language. It would be interesting to see if this particular strategy would simply disappear in written language or take a different form.

In sum, our study showed how participants verbalised the transformation from a set of objects to an assembled doll's house, based on the assignment of a specific function to each individual object. Obviously not every single object was explicitly marked in this way, but the verbalised data revealed a range of systematic ways in which function assignment was accomplished.

6.2.3   Transforming a Piece of Paper into a Complex Object: Following Origami Instructions

Transformation can take many forms, and the cognitive processes involved in this process will depend on what exactly is accomplished. While our previous example demonstrated the importance of assigning functions to object parts when transforming separate objects into a coherent whole, this section illustrates a different kind of challenge. This time, we are looking at a situation where only one object (a piece of paper, without specific meaning or function) is transformed into a different, now meaningful, object.

If you have ever tried origami paper folding, you will be familiar with the difficulties that may arise while following the instructions. You know that you are supposed to transform your piece of paper into something nice, such as a flower, and you are given a range of steps that tell you exactly how to do that, through pictures and words. Nevertheless, you may very quickly get to a point where your own product does not look quite the same as the one in the pictures. You might then try out various ways of improving your object: you could reread instructions, reinterpret them, refold the paper, try again. In the extreme case, which is not uncommon, you may be forced to give up, frustrated: this problem has become too hard for you to solve, you just cannot figure it out.

Most research on problem solving targets situations in which only the goal state is known (such as an origami flower), and the problem solver faces a range of constraints as to what can or cannot be done (e.g. in origami, the paper is not to be cut or torn into pieces). Research then typically addresses the kinds of intermediate steps that the problem solver undertakes to reach that goal, given the constraints (Ericsson & Simon, 1993). These intermediate steps could then be turned into step-by-step instructions that anyone could follow easily, without being confronted with the problem of figuring them out themselves.

However, origami paper folding is hard; it would be unrealistic to assume that anyone could figure out how to transform a piece of paper into a flower without step-by-step instructions. In fact, we (Tenbrink & Taylor, 2015) argued that even just following the instructions is hard enough to constitute a considerable conceptual challenge. In contrast to most previous research in the area, we therefore treated the process of following step-by-step instructions as a problem, while otherwise following traditions of problem-solving research by analysing think-aloud protocols (Ericsson & Simon, 1993). We were interested in the kinds of thought processes that were associated with the various steps in the problem-solving process.

Our twenty-four participants were trained to think aloud and then asked to do so while folding a relatively simple origami object, a tulip, following verbal and visual instructions shown on a computer screen. They did not receive any help from the experimenter except brief hints when they admitted to being stuck, which happened to less than half of the participants at some point during the task. In this study (Tenbrink & Taylor, 2015), we looked only at the paper stem of the tulip, as this was sufficiently complicated to reveal a range of interesting cognitive phenomena.

On average, participants folded the stem within five minutes, but the range of variety was impressive: some needed twice as much, and some managed the task in only three minutes. Similarly, they differed very much in the extent to which they verbalised their thoughts, producing between 113 and 1,738 words each. Altogether this resulted in a rich corpus of unconstrained language production data, allowing us to examine participants' verbalised thoughts both on the level of content and with respect to linguistic features and patterns.

First of all, we were interested in how much the speakers were actually verbalising their own thoughts, as opposed to merely reading the task instructions aloud – which they did quite frequently, as a natural part of the problem-solving process. To determine this, we identified content categories and annotated each language data unit according to whether:

- participants read the task instructions aloud
- participants reformulated the task instructions without adding their own thoughts in any way
- participants verbalised additional ideas about a paper-folding step
- participants evaluated their own work with respect to success of paper folding
- participants referred to background knowledge, such as experience with origami paper folding
- participants expressed problems with the current problem-solving step
- participants commented on what they were currently doing, describing their own actions.

We also included an 'Other' category, to capture further types of content that did not fit into these categories but did not reoccur frequently enough to warrant a further content category. While all of the identified types of content occurred frequently in the data, 'reading' was the most frequent category, followed by 'comments on current actions'. However, 'additional ideas about the paper-folding step' also occurred quite frequently, and this was a category we found highly intriguing. We wished to know more about what these additional ideas were, and what could be learned from them about the participants' problem-solving processes. It is in this category that the conceptual challenge of transforming a piece of paper into a meaningful object is represented most directly, as it highlights the creative process of following the instructions.

Based on what we found in the language data, we subcategorised the instances of 'additional ideas' further according to their content. We discovered many comments on quality (e.g. trying to get a nice result, making sharp and nicely aligning folds, or matching one's own results to the instruction), and various observations associating some meaning with the object, as in *This looks like a crane*. Aside from these, we took a closer look at those comments that observed some sort of structure: either the structure of the folded paper, or the structure of the folding process. These included the following categories:

- spatial description: patterns in the current status of the object (e.g. *it's in a diamond shape*; or *each corner goes to the opposite corner*)
- orientation of the folding paper (e.g. *that means it's still on this side that we have to fold*)
- within-step repetition: doing the same action twice (e.g. for left and right sides) within a folding step (e.g. *I gotta do it with the other side*)
- across-step repetition: recognising that an action repeats a previous step (e.g. *I have to do that same thing again*).

The presence of these various recurring types of comment is an interesting qualitative result as it highlights the kinds of conceptual patterns that participants attended to during the paper-folding process. Structural thinking clearly mattered; for many participants, the recognition of some sort of pattern was an integral part of the transformational process of paper folding.

To gain further insight into the role of *spatial* thinking within this kind of problem-solving process, we next took a closer look at the specific spatial language employed by the participants. Although this analysis was inspired by the category of 'spatial description', we decided to analyse the spatial language across all content categories, as spatial thinking might influence other aspects of verbalised content as well.

Again, the analysis required a clear differentiation between what people simply read from the instructions, as opposed to what they came up with themselves as part of the creative thought process. We identified all spatial terms in the data and determined whether they were part of the instruction for the current paper-folding step. If they weren't, we counted them as 'new spatial terms' that highlighted the spatial thinking in this transformational task. It turned out that some terms (particularly prepositions such as *in, on, down*, but also *side*) were used extremely frequently in this way, while others (such as *bisect, overlap, parallelogram*) occurred only once or twice. Moreover, participants differed very much as to how many new spatial terms they used. Some were very creative, with one participant using as many as fifty-two different spatial terms – whereas another participant did not produce a single new spatial term that wasn't part of the instruction in the current step. This reflects an astonishing range of variety in how the participants approached the task in a spatial sense.

Next, we were interested in the order in which the various kinds of content were produced while thinking about a paper folding step. To assess this, we identified the sequence of content categories for each participant within each folding step. Overall, a pattern emerged that suggested the following structure of verbalised thoughts, namely:

reading–reformulating–reconceptualising–evaluating

In other words, people started out, in each step, by reading the instruction. Next, they might reformulate the wording by adapting it to their current situation without adding content (as in *turn the paper towards 'me'*, instead of '*you*' in the instruction). This was followed by adding their own ideas to the instruction, that is, reconceptualising them, for instance by identifying spatial structures or relationships to previous steps. Finally, they might evaluate the results, judging whether or not their folding step was successful in this instance. Participants did not verbalise each category for every step. It was also possible for them to encounter problems that meant they had to go back to *reading*. Therefore, the pattern is by no means strict or entirely predictable. Nevertheless, statistical tests verified that this pattern did indeed reflect the order of content categories as a general structure, which was adhered to significantly more often than not.

Altogether, our origami paper-folding research (Tenbrink & Taylor, 2015) highlighted the fact that following instructions can indeed pose a problem, involving substantial high-level thought processes that can be verbalised. This is contrary to the traditional idea that think-aloud protocols are best suited to identify separate steps in a problem-solving process. Furthermore, it showed the wide range of individual variability in this regard, along with a consistent basic pattern of conceptualisation: namely, starting with a close look at the given information and gradually moving away from it and towards cognitive flexibility, leading up to a result worth evaluating.

Incidentally, moving away from the original instruction towards one's own formulation is closely related to the cognitive effect discussed in the first half of this chapter – inference processes. If simply following the instructions had been sufficient, no further conceptual flexibility would have been required. Instead, they frequently verbalised their own thoughts based on what they read, revealing a range of inferences made while applying the written instruction to the transformation task at hand. In this sense, cognitive constructiveness works both ways: we use it to interpret the information we are given, and we use it also to transform the current status to something else. Our origami study revealed how these two processes worked together by making inferences from instructions while transforming a piece of paper into a meaningful object.

In summary, this chapter has dealt with two ways in which people frequently add to and change reality, so to speak: on the one hand, we add to reality by making inferences from what we actually perceive or know; we fill in the gaps in the available information based on what we have experienced previously. More often than not, such inferences are useful and valid, allowing us to think and act naturally and efficiently even in the absence of complete information. On the other hand, we change reality by transforming an existing situation into something different – we assemble objects to build a larger one, or manipulate one object to turn it into something else. Transformation depends on the cognitive ability to identify meaningful changes, to see the potential of certain manipulations.

A sculptor, as the myth goes, doesn't create a statue out of a brick – they simply 'see' it underneath, and liberate it from the excess material around it. This process, to some extent, is the basis of all transformation, and our language reflects to a high degree just how we accomplish this. Human ability to change reality in these two respects is remarkable, and it is certainly worth focusing on as a target in CODA analysis.

7   Using Language to Convey Thoughts

This chapter returns to a more general level as compared to previous chapters. Here, we will consider the purposes and contexts in which humans use language to convey thought. Whenever we put our thoughts into words, we do this for a specific purpose. More often than not, the expression of thoughts is part of everyday communication: we talk about our thoughts with our partners and friends. But other contexts are possible, as we will see in this chapter.

Section 7.1 discusses *communication* and considers how we interact with others to exchange our thoughts through dialogue. When we do that, we normally take into account who we talk to, what is relevant in the context, and much else. All of this goes beyond the mere expression of thought, because it pertains to the communicative function of language. When we communicate, we express our thoughts for the purpose of making them accessible to others – getting our thoughts across to our interaction partner.

Section 7.2 turns to situations in which thoughts are expressed aloud without aiming for communication, namely when thinking aloud. Even though this is not an established social convention, it does happen sometimes – especially in children, who don't always need a conversation partner to chat aloud. In cognitive science, thinking aloud has been established as a technique; in empirical studies, participants are encouraged to simply say out loud what they are thinking as they solve a problem. Therefore, they don't need to worry about formulating their thoughts for an interaction partner. The resulting language then reveals the problem-solving steps that emerge in the mind of the participant, in a particular sequence.

Similar to the previous chapters, both areas covered here – communication and cognitive strategies – relate to distinct analysis perspectives, and they are associated with extensive research communities and traditions. This chapter lays out some of the main associated insights, and thereby highlights two distinct ways in which language is used to convey thought.

7.1   Communication

Language is central to our existence. In most people's lives, not a single day passes without using language for some purpose or other: we read, we listen, we chat, we write, we talk – to one person or more at a time. Language serves multiple purposes in our everyday lives, and it is hard to imagine what human life would be like without it. Without doubt, the most prominent goal of using language is to *communicate*. Communication is the primary function of language. It helps us connect with other people, to exchange information, thoughts, and ideas, and to share our insights about the world.

Communication can take many forms, and language is only one of them: we can also communicate by gestures, mimics, sketches, pictures, signs, diagrams, music, and more. There is no limit to the forms that communication can take, and each mode of communication has its own merit. But notably, language typically comes along with these other communication modes, or is an essential aspect of them. Moreover, language is the most developed and complex mode of communication. It is therefore often more suited to convey insights than other modes – especially if these insights are abstract, complicated, or theoretical. Sign language is a full-fledged language in this regard, while spontaneous gestures are more limited in what they can express.

If communication is the primary purpose for language use, it is clear that using language will mean more than simply producing verbal representations of thought. In everyday use of language, we do not only want to externalise our inner thoughts, but we want to do this for a particular addressee – for an interaction partner or a larger audience, related to a particular context. This will have effects on how we use language, as we will see in several examples below. Many theories of language and communication focus on these effects. Since the area cannot be covered exhaustively here, we will focus on some major insights that are particularly relevant for CODA studies.

To provide just one example of a theoretical framework, Halliday's Systemic Functional Grammar (SFG) (Halliday & Matthiessen, 2014; see Chapter 3 and elsewhere in this book) was developed precisely for the purpose of capturing how the different elements of language serve different functions in communication, across diverse social contexts. Halliday suggested that every piece of discourse is characterised by three situational parameters – field, tenor, and mode – and each of these have a direct reflection in language. *Field* is what the discourse is about (the general topic, what portion of the world is being represented in the discourse). *Tenor* concerns the relationship between speaker and hearer, or writer and reader. *Mode* means the basic distinction between spoken and written, plus finer distinctions of intermediate modes and subtypes (such as the special features of Internet chat, or of lectures as opposed to face-to

-face dialogue). The mode systematically affects how the discourse is structured and organised.

The fact that Halliday's SFG is geared towards the communicative purposes of language makes it useful for understanding what language does when it represents thought. This is one of the main reasons why SFG theory serves as one of the main resources for CODA, in spite of the fact that it makes no claims, as a theory, about the relationship between language and thought. Instead, it helps us recognise that certain linguistic features pertain to certain communicative functions, whereas others are predominantly means of representing the world, or thoughts about the world.

In this section, we will now turn to other insights and theories beyond SFG, in order to explore a range of effects that have been identified as crucial for language use during interactions with others, where the purpose of communication is prominent. Section 7.1.1 will start by looking at how it matters who we talk to, that is, effects of the intended addressee on the verbalisation of thought. Then we will turn to aspects pertaining to face-to-face dialogue more specifically. In Section 7.1.2, we will consider how speakers adapt their language to each other's way of speaking (and, arguably, thinking), and in Section 7.1.3 we discuss the structure of dialogues, that is, regular patterns of exchanging thoughts with an interaction partner. Section 7.1.4 reports an empirical study designed to collect dialogue data in a situation involving spatial thinking.

7.1.1   How Interaction Partners Matter

It matters who we talk to – we know this from everyday experience. Compare the following two ways of getting someone to shut the door:

Example 7.1   Shut the door, love, will you.
Example 7.2   Please, might it be possible for you to close the door?

As we're all familiar with social conventions of politeness, we intuitively know that the relationship between speaker and addressee must be very different in these two examples. In Example 7.1, a family relationship is likely; the term of endearment 'love' suggests this just as much as the absence of any politeness markers. The close relationship between the interaction partners allows for the use of a direct command in imperative form ('shut'). In Example 7.2, in contrast, the speaker carefully seeks to avoid imposing an obligation on the addressee. This is indicated by the modal 'might', by the indirect mood (a question about possibility rather than a command), and by the politeness marker 'please'. It seems likely that the addressee is socially superior, perhaps the speaker's boss. The intended effect of the utterance is the same, but the utterance is very different depending on who the speaker talks to. Outside of suitable contexts, the same formulations may be perceived as rude (in the case of Example 7.1) or as sarcastic (if Example 7.2 is used in a familiar context).

If there hadn't been any addressee at all, the speaker might have formulated their thoughts aloud, for example by saying either of these:

Example 7.3   I wish someone would shut the door.
Example 7.4   If only the door was shut.

In this instance, the mere fact that there is no addressee turns the direct command of Example 7.1, or the indirect question of Example 7.2, into an expression of a desire. This desire can, again, be expressed in different ways, as shown in the differences between Examples 7.3 and 7.4. Crucially, the linguistic features distinguishing Examples 7.3 and 7.4 will not depend on the nature of the addressee, but rather on the nature of the desire – that is, the cognitive side of the utterance, rather than the communicative side. For instance, Example 7.3 expresses a wish that involves the idea of a person ('someone') acting, whereas Example 7.4 represents a desired state of affairs. (Note that this is the basic idea in think-aloud protocols: to avoid, as much as possible, situations in which the differences between Examples 7.1 and 7.2 matter, so as to be able to focus on differences such as those between Examples 7.3 and 7.4. We will get back to this idea in Section 7.2.)

A focus on communication as an analysis perspective can be extremely valuable when using CODA. There are many ways in which the intended addressee can affect linguistic choices, and this fact has motivated many empirical studies over the past decades. For instance, we (Tenbrink et al., 2010) looked at how speakers verbalise spatial concepts when they talk to a computer, as opposed to a human interaction partner. We used a dialogue system that was designed to follow spatial instructions in a setup resembling a typed chat situation. When chatting with another human being, our speakers used a fairly wide range of communicative strategies, switching perspectives and levels of granularity freely. This resulted in very efficient dialogues. In contrast, when chatting with an automatic dialogue system, the speakers' linguistic choices became much more limited. Speakers now formulated very brief and simple instructions, and employed only a small subset of the linguistic variety that they used when talking to a human. This was simply triggered by their beliefs about the computers' abilities, not by their direct experience of what the system might have been capable of – they didn't try!

Addressees affect linguistic choices by virtue of who they are, as we have seen, but also by what they do. Imagine you are telling your friend a story on the phone. After a while you notice that there has not been any response for a while.

Inevitably you will ask, *Are you still there?* It would be very surprising if you heard back, *Sure, I am – but you're the one telling the story so I have nothing to say!* While this statement is correct in terms of describing the situation objectively, it may bother you. Addressees normally show their interest by reacting in various ways to the speaker's utterances. They would say *Really?* or *Okay*, or use simple back channels such as *m-hm* or *uh-huh*, or just grunt or nod (which you wouldn't hear on the phone) – anything to show they are with you as you tell your story. Typically, these back-channelling reactions come in a very subtle and time-specific way (Bavelas, Gerwing, & Healing, 2017). So if you don't hear anything at all in response to your story on the phone, this is a clear sign that something is wrong. Maybe your addressee is distracted and not paying much attention, or your story has become too long-winded, and lack of responsiveness is used to subtly suggest this.

Speakers don't just expect addressees to react in those conventional ways to what they're saying, but they also notice how exactly they do so. It may be hard to pinpoint, but you may have experienced this yourself: although your partner used back-channelling signals in a seemingly normal way, you were sure that they weren't really listening. As a child, I could tell from the way my father used *m-hm* whether he was paying attention or not; there was a slight but noticeable change in the tone or intonation pattern. In contrast, addressees who listen closely might enact in their reactions the mood of the topic appropriately (*RE-ally?!?!*), showing cooperation on the level of intonation. Also, they frequently contribute more than just generic back channels, by asking questions and rephrasing or even extending the speaker's utterances.

Clark and Krych (2004) showed that monitoring addressees is a crucial part of dialogue, in particular in an instruction situation. The more access people had to their interaction partner's reactions in their study, the more precisely they could react to them and adapt their speech accordingly. The best case was if the partners could see each other and their workspace; then, the dialogues were characterised by precisely timed pointing gestures, eye gazes, head nods, head shakes, and the like. Sometimes speakers even altered their utterances mid-course in reaction to their partner's signals of understanding. Other scenarios, such as giving instructions by audiotape without the partner present, or being unable to see the partner's workspace, led to less communicative success.

Speakers' awareness of their interaction partner's understanding affects their communication in many ways. When referring to objects, people can use many different kinds of expressions, ranging from pronouns like *it* or demonstratives like *this one* to complex explicit descriptions such as *the hat with curly feathers on the window sill*. What speakers say to refer to an object very much depends on who they talk to, and what the situation is (Arnold, 2008). Typically, when we refer to an object, we want to enable our interaction partner to identify what we are talking about. This will guide the expression we choose. Therefore, the speakers' attention to their addressee's needs explains many of the linguistic choices they make in object reference.

However, there are also some limits to this effect. Under certain circumstances, speakers fail to adjust their choices as precisely to their addressee's needs as they could. For example, they may choose a complex description in a situation where a simple one would have been sufficient. Arnold (2008) concluded from her literature review that speakers often make decisions for the benefit of their addressee, but not all of the time – not all of their choices are precisely tailored to their interaction partner. This makes sense if we consider that communication is only one aspect of using language, alongside cognitive aspects. When we speak, we first of all represent our thoughts. To some extent we do this for our interaction partner, but we also express what we need to say, not just what our addressees need to hear. Within limits, we can assume that the addressee knows that our perspective may be different from their own.

In sum, there are many ways in which communicative aspects affect the way we speak. Our beliefs about the interaction partner and their needs are central at many levels of interaction: the words we choose, the details we provide, the level of politeness we adopt, and so on. Interaction partners readily signal back what they have understood, and we, as speakers, readily react to these signals. In this sense, communication is a complex collaborative process (Clark & Wilkes-Gibbs, 1986).

7.1.2   Mutual Adaptation in Dialogue

As we have just explored, speakers are aware of who they talk to, and they adjust their linguistic choices according to their addressee's needs and reactions. But there are further ways in which speakers influence each other in dialogue. Talking to somebody else is an opportunity to express one's own thoughts for the benefit of another, but not only that. It is also an opportunity to exchange ideas, to gain insights into the interaction partner's views, and to negotiate thoughts where they differ.

Dialogue therefore means mutual influence and adaptation, and this happens on several levels (Pickering & Garrod, 2004). Speakers adapt to each other's contributions on the level of sound, by making their words sound similar to the way the dialogue partner produced them, or by placing the stress in similar ways. Also, they typically use the same words to refer to things – sometimes so much so that the particular reference term chosen is specific to a particular dialogue (Clark & Wilkes-Gibbs, 1986). Thus, speakers would agree to use a specific term during the course of an exchange, but with a different dialogue partner they would use other words. Furthermore, the syntax of sentences often matches previous ones in cases where similar content is expressed. For instance, Cleland and Pickering (2003) found that when participants heard a description like *The door that's red*, they were more likely to refer to a picture of a red sheep as *The sheep that's red* than to say *The red sheep*.

Further, there is also evidence that speakers align their understanding of specific meanings, or of the entire topic being talked about, based on their exchange of concepts (Pickering & Garrod, 2004). If you have particular associations about a concept, say for instance *cat*, after a while of talking to you I might begin to share some of these associations – or at least understand that you have them, and account for that in the way I talk about it. If cats, for you, are dangerous creatures, my utterances to you might incorporate that idea, and perhaps refer to claws and teeth. Or if you describe your home to me, my mind may start creating a mental image that to some extent resembles the mental image that you have in your mind.

The fact that mutual influence is so pervasive in dialogue has led to various theories and debates about the nature of this influence, and about its precise effects on speaking. Pickering and Garrod (2004) advocate a mechanistic view on dialogue according to which alignment in dialogue happens automatically, without the speakers' conscious control. In their view, we align to each other because it is a simple and helpful mechanism: alignment makes it easy to communicate, as it reduces cognitive load when processing language (Garrod & Pickering, 2004) – less work to do for our minds.

In social science, very similar effects have traditionally been examined under the heading of *accommodation* (e.g. Giles & Coupland, 1991): speakers align to each other in social contexts – not only on the level of language – because they wish to show solidarity with each other. Crucially, according to this theory, they can also fail to do so, and this can be taken to signal quite the opposite, namely dissociation from the interaction partner. Imagine that you sit opposite someone you like, and you see that they cross their legs and sit back. You might then do the same, and show by your posture that you agree with their relaxed attitude. In contrast, if you don't like someone, you'll be less likely to mimic any of their gestures or linguistic choices. If they use a strong American accent you might prefer to speak in your best standard British English, and so on. Not all of these effects may at all times be entirely conscious, but they are under the speakers' control and can be adjusted at will, with the primary purpose of showing distance or association with others.

In Clark's (1996) view, the notion of *negotiating common ground* is central. When speakers start talking, they normally already share a certain amount of common ground. They often belong to the same or a similar culture, and perhaps share further aspects of everyday life that they might have in common. The better we know each other, the more we share common ground. We are to some extent aware of this, and we formulate our utterances accordingly.

Therefore, I would not refer to our mutual friend *Lydia* as *the curly-haired woman over there* – this would be decidedly odd if my dialogue partner knows her as well as I do.

As dialogue develops, speakers constantly extend the common ground that they already share further. Every utterance that is heard and understood adds to the common ground. Sometimes this process isn't straightforward and requires some negotiation, such as repairing and reformulating some expressions, clarification questions, and the like. Speakers like to achieve some kind of closure at the end of these processes – some kind of evidence that their message has come across, and information has been added to the common ground. That's why the following dialogue sequence may seem somewhat incomplete:

Example 7.5   Heidi: Let's meet at 12 o'clock.
               Jerry: Okay, in the town centre.
               Heidi: Bye!

It could be expected that Heidi should confirm the location of the meeting before closing the conversation, similar to the way Jerry confirms the time of the meeting by saying *okay*. Likewise, one might expect Jerry to respond to Heidi's suggestion of closing the conversation (*Bye*) by responding likewise (*Bye*). Every aspect of dialogue thus implies some amount of negotiation. Without the expected response to an initiation (e.g. a suggestion to close the conversation, like Heidi's *Bye*), there is no sense of closure. In the case of Example 7.5, this may either mean that communication has failed, or that Heidi is in a hurry to go and simply assumes that common ground has been reached sufficiently, without signalling this explicitly. This view of dialogue suggests that speakers are to a high extent in charge of the relevant negotiation processes (Clark, 1996). Rather than following entirely mechanistic and automatic processes, speakers actively monitor and adapt their reactions to each other in discourse. As a result, the words and concepts they choose when expressing meaning very often align with those of their interaction partner.

Altogether, we can conclude that interaction partners mutually adapt to each other in dialogue in many ways. While theories in the literature do not always agree on how exactly this happens, there is little doubt that mutual influence is a very strong factor that drives and affects interpersonal communication, more than we are usually aware of.

7.1.3   Dialogue Structure

Example 7.5, in the previous section, indicates another important fact about dialogue: that it is not random, but follows certain structural principles. Halliday and Matthiessen (2014) offered a 'metaphor of symbolic exchange' to describe this idea. In their view, each grammatical mood type suggests a specific type of exchange between speakers: the interrogative mood is used for (direct) questions, the declarative mood for statements and offers, and the imperative mood for commands. Questions and statements indicate an exchange of information: questions are used to demand information, and statements are used to give information. Similarly, offers and commands are used to give or demand goods and services.

Each of these four types of exchange (giving or demanding information, and giving or demanding goods and services) can also be expressed indirectly (or *incongruently*, as Halliday and Matthiessen, 2014, put it). For instance, it is possible to demand information in the declarative mood, or to command someone using interrogatives. Particularly in the case of commands, indirect forms are considered to be far more polite. This is illustrated by two examples that we saw earlier in this chapter – let's take another look:

Example 7.6   Shut the door, love, will you.
Example 7.7   Please, might it be possible for you to close the door?

Example 7.6 uses the direct imperative form for commands, whereas Example 7.7 uses the polite (indirect) interrogative form. However, the function of the utterance remains the same: in both cases, the speaker wants (or 'commands') the addressee to shut the door.

Developing these examples further, each utterance comes with an expected response. In Example 7.6, the most likely response will be the wordless action of shutting the door. No politeness is required in this familiar context, and a verbal response is not necessary as long as the service is given as demanded. In Example 7.7, politeness will probably lead the addressee to do both: shut the door and say something like *Of course, no problem.* If these are preferred responses, the alternative is clear: in both cases, the addressee would refuse to do the requested action. They could do this by saying *No* or using a more polite formula, perhaps with a reason for the refusal – or they could simply fail to do as requested.

Failure to respond at all is perhaps the most surprising or disconcerting reaction. And this is not only true for commands. Recall the situation described earlier in this chapter: if you tell a story, you will expect your interaction partner to at least provide some minimal responses, even if there are no questions and no way in which your partner could actively contribute to the story. This expectation reveals just how much we expect dialogue to be structured. Each utterance comes with a certain expected reaction; these may be as varied as minimal responses (back-channelling, nods, mimics), actions following a command, or answers to explicit questions. Moreover, conventions and expectations vary substantially across different contexts and modes of communication. In remote-chat conversations (text or instant messaging, Skype, etc.), it is not uncommon for reactions to come with significant delay, or not at

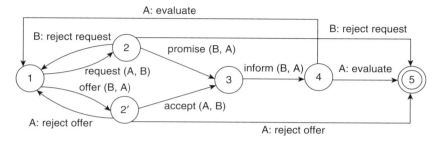

Figure 7.1 An example for a dialogue situation modelled by COR (Shi et al., 2010).

all, without causing much concern. As communication technologies change and develop, people demonstrate considerable flexibility and creativity for making use of them in everyday life.

In the literature, these effects have been studied in a range of ways, for various purposes. One such purpose is to implement dialogue models in artificial communication systems, such as automatic telephone services or assistance robots. In the context of information-seeking dialogues, Sitter and Stein (1996) developed a model that is exemplary for various subsequent approaches. Their 'COnversational Roles' (COR) model structures dialogues in the form of recursive networks. Let's look at a couple of examples that the COR model can represent (see Figure 7.1).

Example 7.8   Customer: Can you tell me how to get to the airport, please?
             Assistant: I certainly can. Tram number 5 will take you there.
             Customer: That's excellent, thank you very much.

Example 7.9   Assistant: How can I help you?
             Customer: I'd like to know how to get to the airport.
             Assistant: Tram number 5 will take you there.
             Customer: Okay. But how do I find tram number 5?
             Assistant: Sorry, I can't help you there.

In Example 7.8, the customer initiates the dialogue by an information request. The request is followed up by the assistant's promise to provide the information, followed by the information itself. The customer evaluates the information, and as they are satisfied, the dialogue ends there. In contrast, the dialogue in Example 7.9 starts with information being offered by the assistant. This offer is accepted by the customer, who specifies what kind of information is required. The assistant provides the information, and the customer evaluates it. However, the dialogue does not end there due to a need for further information, which the customer requests from the

178 Using Language to Convey Thoughts

assistant. Instead of providing the information, this request is rejected, and the dialogue terminates.

The COR model (as sketched in Figure 7.1) represents these sequences and allows for several variations of them, as well as for iteration based on the information seeker's evaluation of the information provided. The dialogue will last until they are satisfied, or until the information giver rejects a request for information. It is also possible that further information is offered but rejected, which also causes the dialogue to end.

It is clear to see that a basic model like this one may capture dialogue structures in clearly defined situational contexts quite well. The precise formulation of a dialogue contribution does not matter; rather, the model captures the function of each contribution within the information-seeking context. Automatic dialogue systems use this kind of basic model to fill in various pre-formulated utterances (e.g. 'How can I help you?') at an appropriate time in the dialogue.

As information exchange is one of the most basic functions of language (Halliday & Matthiessen, 2014), such implementations can be quite useful across a number of contexts. By now, most people living in digitally advanced cultures will have had an opportunity to talk to some variant of a dialogue system. After decades of telephone services at various levels of quality, automatic dialogue systems have now become sophisticated enough to be allowed in our households, in the form of smartphone apps or specifically developed devices.

However, natural dialogues between humans have a much wider range of functions, and the structure of everyday conversations may not be as predictable as the structure of information-seeking dialogues. For instance, the COR model (Sitter & Stein, 1996) suggests that a dialogue starts either by the information seeker requesting information, or by the information giver providing information. But what happens if both start speaking at the same time?

Obviously, there must be mechanisms that allow for negotiation of such possible conflicts. Fan and Heeman (2010) took a closer look at such situations and found that they are actually quite rare; they concluded that whenever they do happen, this must be unintentional and exceptional. Overlap in initiating utterances only occurs if speakers actually start speaking at pretty much exactly the same time. That makes sense: if we notice that our interaction partner has already started speaking, we will wait to hear what they have to say before starting our own utterance. Notice, however, that such principles are culture dependent; overlap is much more normal in some cultures than it is in others. Even British and American English differ in this regard, with overlap being more acceptable in American than in British English.

Once overlap in initiating utterances happens, Fan and Heeman (2010) found that it is normally resolved fairly quickly – overlap typically isn't allowed to last much longer than two syllables. The person who 'wins' is normally the person speaking more loudly: volume is used as a device to organise the sequence of turn taking in situations of conflict. Also, the overlapped part is often repeated, to make sure the interaction partner hears what was said while they were also speaking.

One of the most challenging problems for automatic systems is that most discourse is context dependent. Face-to-face conversations between humans take place in a spatial environment, and this is not easy to transfer to speech technology. A lot of work has gone into ways of capturing dialogic interaction that is situated in spatial contexts. How can a computer, which hasn't lived and grown up in a spatial environment as all humans have, even begin to understand and talk about the world in a similar way to humans? Only if we understand human spatial (or contextual) thinking thoroughly can we implement suitable representations in computers. With this complex challenge in mind, CODA is a useful tool to gain insights about how humans do actually understand the world, and how they represent it in language. In Shi et al. (2010) we did just that: we used results from a CODA study to inform a dialogue model following Sitter and Stein's (1996) method. This CODA study will be outlined in the next section.

In sum, far from being random, dialogue is structured to a high degree. We expect certain kinds of reactions at certain times, and feel that communication fails when this does not happen. However, these structures depend on culture and experience in complex ways. This makes the implementation in automatic systems extremely difficult.

7.1.4   *The Exchange of Spatial Thinking in Dialogue: An Empirical Study*

To conclude this section, let's take a brief look at natural dialogue between humans, in a situation involving exchange of spatial thinking. Our research team collected a large corpus of language data in a situation where two people talked about furnishing a doll's house (Tenbrink et al., 2008, 2017). One of the two was assigned the role of 'director', and the other one the role of 'matcher'. Each director instructed their interaction partner, the matcher, to furnish a doll's house in a specific way. Like previous examples discussed in this book, this scenario requires the use of spatial expressions, which are often highly ambiguous. While the director saw a fully furnished doll's house, the matcher looked at the partially furnished one that they were trying to complete. Therefore, their relevant common ground was incomplete and needed to be negotiated.

In our early paper (Tenbrink et al., 2008) we aimed to find out how the negotiation of spatial relationships works in this kind of situation, and in particular in what ways the matcher contributed to this process. One might expect that they would only listen to the director's instructions and carry them out, perhaps giving minimal responses or asking the occasional clarification question. However, we found they were actually quite active. Matchers contributed to the spatial communication in a range of interesting ways. For instance, they offered specific suggestions as to where objects should be placed, based on but extending the instructors' descriptions. For this, they used their own conceptual perspective, and they often described different object relations. Thus, if the director described an object in relation to the *wall*, the matcher might find that this wasn't precise enough or was perhaps ambiguous, and they might ask how it related to another object like the sink – as in the following example.

Example 7.10   Matcher: (...) and this one is put directly beside it.
                Director: Yes, at the wall.
                Matcher: That is, at the back left of the sink?
                Director: Yes, but at the wall (...)

Thus, the matchers used their own understanding of the visual scene in front of them to come up with meaningful suggestions. They made inferences on the basis of what they saw, and in particular on the basis of how objects normally relate to each other (Tenbrink et al., 2017). This enabled them to participate actively in negotiation processes that ultimately resulted in fairly accurate object placements, in spite of the fact that the spatial descriptions given by the director were frequently underspecified.

In Tenbrink et al. (2017) we further explored the effects of how objects relate to each other to serve a particular function. In the recorded dialogue scenarios, we had used two different versions. In one version, the rooms in the doll's house were conventionally furnished: as a bathroom, a kitchen, a living room, and a bedroom. In the other version, the furniture was placed randomly in the rooms – bed next to shower, and so on. Our expectation was that this would make a difference for the way people solved the task of furnishing the doll's house. If objects are meaningfully related to each other, we can use our everyday knowledge to fill in some information gaps. If they aren't, this might mean that directors need to provide more explicit information as to where and how objects should be placed, or it may lead to communication failure and lower levels of task success. And in fact, our analysis showed that success rates were higher in the functional version of the task. Also, the random arrangements led to more elaborate descriptions, giving more information that helped cope with the unexpected configurations (Tenbrink et al., 2017).

Altogether, the situated dialogue data represent an excellent resource for the effects of communication on how spatial relationships are perceived and described. Both the speakers' spatial concepts and the dialogic negotiation structures can be traced directly across a large set of linguistic data. CODA helps to do this systematically, in order to identify dialogic and cognitive principles that are reflected in the discourse.

7.2   Cognitive Strategies

CODA is certainly useful for analysing thoughts communicated through language across many scenarios, including dialogue, as we have seen in the first part of this chapter. However, the development of the methodology was inspired from a primarily non-communicative approach to verbal data in cognitive psychology. Ericsson and Simon (1993) outlined a paradigm for using verbal protocols as data in the context of studies on problem solving and decision making (see Chapter 8 for details on this method). These cognitive challenges have been of interest to researchers for a very long time; after all, the ability to solve problems and make decisions is central to being human. With Ericsson and Simon's method, people are asked to say out loud what they are or were thinking, without engaging in dialogue with anyone else.

The paradigm has proved very useful, and it has been employed frequently in cognitive science to address people's strategies across various kinds of complex cognitive tasks. Such tasks have in common that they involve time and require several steps in the development of thought. If problems are solved on the spot, or decisions are made in a flash, there is not much to verbalise beyond the instant result itself. Verbal protocols are useful for analysing more complex, sequential thought processes that undergo several stages until completion.

Traditionally, verbal protocol analysis is done by cognitive psychologists who do not normally draw on specific linguistic expertise. Analysis of verbal protocols typically concerns the content of what people are saying, rather than any patterns of linguistic features. In fact, Ericsson and Simon (1993) recommended summarising people's utterances into a limited number of content categories and then discarding the original utterances in order to simplify the analysis process. The basic tenet in CODA, in contrast, is that it matters how people formulate things; we have seen this in many examples throughout this book. Just as with any other type of language data, verbal protocol analysis can therefore clearly benefit from a closer look at the linguistic features of people's utterances.

In the remainder of this chapter, we will look at a range of ways in which CODA can be used to examine the verbalisation of cognitive strategies. Section 7.2.1 starts by examining the types of content that are frequently expressed in verbal protocols, and the role of language in them. Section 7.2.2 addresses how linguistic indicators can be used for the operationalisation of coding categories. Section 7.2.3 turns to conceptual aspects that are typically expressed through discourse markers, such as temporal expressions representing sequence, or causal markers expressing a sense of interdependency. Section 7.2.4 looks at mental switches between task domains and other variations in attention focus. Concluding this chapter, in Section 7.2.5 we will examine the interplay of cognitive strategies and communication in a wayfinding study (Hölscher et al., 2011).

7.2.1   Content and Language Use in Verbal Protocols

Perhaps the most challenging aspect of verbal protocols is their complexity. Confronted with a complex task, people verbalise all sorts of things as they think aloud – and not all of it can be easily interpreted by a researcher. Many thoughts are incomplete and context dependent, and they may not make sense for any other person than the speakers themselves. It is easy for a researcher to get lost in this kind of data, or to spend a lot of time trying to make sense of confusing language. I have met countless researchers who invested major effort, time, and money into collecting and transcribing verbal data in relation to cognitively challenging tasks – and then they gave up trying to gather any meaningful insights from them, as they realised just how complex the verbalisations were. This is clearly a trap that is all too easy to fall into. For some researchers, the only alternative appears to be to refrain from using verbal data altogether – despite the limitations of other methods, and despite the availability of Ericsson and Simon's (1993) useful paradigm.

However, if verbal data were generally too complex and challenging to be useful at all, I wouldn't be writing this book. From a CODA perspective, the key to meaningful and feasible analysis is to establish a focus that sheds light on the targeted research question. Since language is always complex and can be analysed in multiple ways, it is one of the most central goals for a discourse analyst to identify a suitable analysis perspective, and to identify those parts of the data that are meaningfully addressed using this perspective.

For Ericsson and Simon (1993), the main focus of analysis was typically the identification of cognitive steps. Verbalisations of problem-solving procedures reveal what cognitive operations people perform, and in what order. This perspective guides the entire analysis in their paradigm. With such an analysis focus, any verbalisations that do not relate to specific cognitive operations can be ignored. Also, the specific form of a verbalisation is not crucial with this approach, as only the operation itself and its place in the overall process would be of interest to the researcher. CODA, in contrast, focuses on linguistic features. Nevertheless, it is important to keep in mind that complex cognitive processes develop over time, which means that the content of what people express can vary across different stages during their thought process. Thus, it is not always useful to treat the entire data set as a homogeneous resource for linguistic features (see Chapter 8).

Beyond cognitive operations (i.e. what is done in what order during problem solving), people often verbalise relevant aspects of their thought processes such as conscious strategies and decisions, or plans for possible future actions. For instance, when confronted with a search task as part of a problem-solving process, people may decide to search in a particular area first, possibly for a specific reason that they may also verbalise. How such decisions and strategies are expressed in language can vary considerably, depending on the nature of the task. For the analysis, it can be useful to highlight the fact that such strategies are expressed, along with a brief characterisation of the main linguistic features involved. Searching in a particular area could involve a combination of perception verbs (expressing the search) with locational terms (expressing the area). A high frequency of such a combination would therefore indicate a cognitive focus on this particular aspect of the process.

In Tenbrink and Wiener (2009), for instance, we were interested in the cognitive strategies involved in a particular type of spatial task called the travelling salesperson problem. A travelling salesperson must visit many different places to achieve their daily goals. In order to avoid wasting travel time, they will try to find the shortest path that connects all of the places before returning home. From a cognitive perspective, this poses a major challenge. As there are many ways in which places can be connected, it is by no means easy to find the shortest path. In our study, we used a version of this task in small-scale space. In our think-aloud data, we could identify various cognitive operations and processes that were verbalised and represented by recurring verbs such as *searching (for a suitable path trajectory)*, *planning, imagining, path building, ticking off (places), making choices*, and so on. Beyond this, most participants reported visualising the entire trajectory of their chosen path in the field. This observation was crucial, as it indicated a specific problem-solving approach in this kind of task that had been previously debated in the literature.

Naturally, what types of content can be meaningfully verbalised, and which ones are of interest to research, will depend directly on the task at hand. In some cases, participants may spend time considering and describing certain states of affairs. This would then resemble simpler scenarios in which people verbalise mental representations, for instance their perception of a picture (rather than solving a problem). However, in contrast to a simpler task, such a description would merely represent one certain stage in the process. States of affairs might change throughout a problem-solving process. As a result, various verbalisations of mental representations at different stages can be found in verbal protocols.

In other cases, people may consider how different situations relate to each other, for instance if one was caused by the other (see Section 7.2.3). People also sometimes reconsider the same situation in a different way, possibly as a result of a change in the scenario or due to a sudden insight. Such effects are frequently characterised by systematic linguistic features that can be traced in the verbal protocols (see Section 7.2.4).

In sum, the content of language data is often highly revealing when analysing verbal protocols of complex cognitive processes. Many insights in cognitive science have been gained on this basis. A systematic analysis of relevant content, and its expression in language, can allow the researcher to trace the participants' cognitive steps as they solve their task.

7.2.2   Linguistic Indicators and Coding Categories

Coding (or annotation) is a central part of any systematic discourse or content analysis, and verbal protocols are no exception (Ericsson & Simon, 1993). Coding means assigning codes to relevant parts of the data (see Chapter 8 for practical details), in other words, annotating the data according to predefined features. For instance, when annotating content categories, the analyst might identify all utterances that pertain to a certain step in the procedure, such as 'searching', and assign a label, such as 'search', to each of these utterances. The choice of annotation features or categories can be based on content or on linguistic aspects; they can be systematically determined on the basis of previous literature, or identified post hoc, following inspection of the data. These decisions are important, and they need to be made in light of the research question at hand as well as the language data available. More often than not, the final set of annotation criteria will be a combination of predetermined features with new ones that arose from data inspection.

One of the most crucial aspects of this process is the *definition* of categories. If categories are poorly defined, the annotation will be weak and unreliable; different coders will come to different conclusions, and it will be difficult to convincingly report and publish the results. Because of this, the intuitive element of most coding procedures is frequently attacked by opponents of verbal protocol analysis. Their argument is that scientific rigour suffers if the analyst's intuitions are required to interpret the data. And they have a point. The less intuition and subjective interpretation is required, the more reliable the analysis will be. Ideally, definitions should be found that enable the analyst to identify each instance clearly and unambiguously, leading to consistently annotated data.

Linguistic analysis can support this process. In some cases, it is possible to identify and define categories entirely on the basis of objectively identifiable linguistic features, rather than the analyst's intuitions. For instance, when identifying utterances that pertain to a specific cognitive process, it may become apparent that this particular cognitive process is typically expressed in the same way in language. Then, the range of linguistic terms can be specified that indicate this particular category – such as linguistic indicators for a search process (e.g. *look for*).

Other possible analysis categories move away from the idea of content types altogether, and focus entirely on the occurrence and distribution of linguistic features. For instance, you might find that perception verbs (such as *see*, *look*, *hear*, *listen*, *smell*) occur in different contexts throughout your data. If you wish to follow this up by systematic analysis, you will need a clear definition of perception verbs, informed by the relevant literature and further supported by the types of verbs you find in your data. Crucially, you will need to make clear decisions as to which verbs to include, and you will need to justify these decisions in a publication. Once these decisions have been made, the analysis itself is fairly straightforward, and can often be done automatically (or semi-automatically) using suitable tools. This removes intuitive interpretations and subjectivity almost entirely from the coding process.

Intuitive content categories (which are highly subjective) and automatic search for linguistic features (which is objective) represent two ends of a scale. Mostly, you will need to define your categories on a precise but relatively intuitive basis. Linguistic features support this process but do not necessarily remove subjectivity altogether. For instance, when we analysed cognitive processes in the travelling salesperson problem (Tenbrink & Wiener, 2009), we identified a range of linguistic terms that could be associated with certain cognitive strategies rather than others. Thus, nouns like *path*, *route*, *connection*, *detour*, *circle*, and *pattern* referred to the path as trajectory, and they were associated with verbs like *searching*, *finding*, *determining*, *planning,* and so on. However, these word lists were not exhaustive. In verbal protocols, it is often the case that participants creatively use different terminology to describe similar things. Linguistic analysis must allow for this possibility, and remain flexible to account for variations in verbalisations appropriately.

In sum, suitable annotation categories are essential for making sense of complex linguistic data collected in relation to complex cognitive processes. The linguistic annotation of verbal protocols depends crucially on suitable category definitions, identified and specified on the basis of the state of the art along with preliminary data inspection. Final annotation definitions, as reported in a publication, are often the result of an iterative process, aimed to capture relevant phenomena as systematically and objectively as possible.

7.2.3   *Discourse Markers as Indicators of Complex Cognitive Processes*

While any linguistic markers can be revealing in the analysis of verbal proto-cols (as in any CODA study, depending on the research question), complex cognitive processes crucially unfold over time, and this leads to meaningful sequences of thoughts. Therefore, it is often useful to look out specifically for linguistic indicators marking the connections between thoughts and actions. This helps with understanding the structure of the verbalisations in relation to behavioural data.

Caron-Pargue and Caron (1995) were among the first authors to examine this idea systematically in relation to a problem-solving study. Their participants solved the Tower of Hanoi task, which involves placing disks on pegs following certain constraints. The think-aloud protocols clearly reflected the fact that the speakers structured their actions sequentially. Distinct linguistic markers signalled various kinds of connections between the actions, and thus reflected a range of cognitively significant states and transitions.

To highlight a specific example, in the same line of research, Bégoin-Augerau and Caron-Pargue (2003) examined the role of various kinds of connective markers (such as *and, then, next, because, since, but*). A speaker connecting two units with *so that* clearly has a subsequent effect in mind by pursuing a certain action. Example 7.11 is taken from Bégoin-Augerau and Caron-Pargue (2003:83), who stress the fact that the actions are clearly integrated by using the complex connective *so that after* (*pour qu'apres* in French, the language of their study).

Example 7.11   the yellow disk I put it on the B *so that after* the black one I leave it where it is (le disque jaune je le mets sur le B *pour qu'après* le noir je le laisse ou il est)

Apart from connectives, similar effects of demarcating units can be achieved by another class of linguistic markers, namely interjections such as *oh, well, okay, m-hm, yeah*, and so on. These small and seemingly negligible items appear to have little linguistic meaning, but their occurrence in context can be surprisingly meaningful. This is true both for communicative contexts, where interjections bring across substantial interpersonal meaning (e.g. as minimal responses within a dialogue, as we have seen above), and for verbal protocols. Caron-Pargue and Caron (1995) looked specifically at various meanings of the French interjection *bon* in think-aloud data, and established how its use during the problem-solving process related to different stages of insight and evaluation of the situation. Often, the occurrence of an interjection marked the participant's surprise, or an opening or closing of a situation (Bégoin-Augerau & Caron-Pargue, 2003).

In Tenbrink (2008), I compared different types of linguistic data to see how the representations of thought varied (see also Chapter 2). The task given to participants was a version of the travelling salesperson problem (see Section

7.2.1), and they were asked to think aloud while solving the problem, to write a retrospective report after having solved it, and finally to write an instruction for a friend to explain how best to solve it. It turned out that while the three discourse types were compatible and together represented thought processes accurately (as far as this could be determined in relation to behavioural data), there were a number of systematic differences in the representations.

One major way in which the three text types differed most markedly was the use of connectives and interjections. While all text types contained multiple temporal markers, their meaning differed on the level of granularity. When thinking aloud, temporal connectives (such as the German *als erstes*, *zuerst*, *danach*, *dann*, *jetzt*, which are diverse equivalents of the English *first*, *then*, *now*) marked immediate individual actions. However, when describing the procedure as a whole in the two other tasks, temporal markers referred to generalised subtasks and procedures, never to individual actions. The instruction to a friend, in particular, contained a clear temporal sequence, a general action plan to carry out when solving the task.

Connectives of a more complex kind, that is, those marking semantic rather than purely temporal relationships, were less evenly distributed across the three text types. In the instruction task, markers of conceptual complexity (such as the German *jedoch*, *allerdings*, *obwohl* – equivalents of the English *however*, *while*, *nevertheless*) were most frequent, but there were no markers for causality – no reasons for actions were provided to the friend. In contrast, thinking aloud was characterised most markedly by interjections structuring the problem-solving process, such as *okay* and *so*, plus the German discourse marker *ja* (which indicates that something is already known). None of these appeared in the other two tasks.

In sum, discourse markers can be valuable indicators of certain aspects of cognitive processes, making it worthwhile to focus on them in the course of a CODA analysis. Seemingly insignificant words like *so*, with its various discourse meanings, can be highly revealing with respect to the participants' conceptual state or progress.

7.2.4   Conceptual Switches

Another aspect that is specific to verbal protocol analysis is the fact that speakers sometimes shift between different levels of meaning, in ways unlikely to be found with less complex representations of thought. As the task proceeds, people will often adopt different kinds of perspectives on the situation, and regard it in more than one way over time. This leads to variations in attention focus, as well as shifts between various semantic domains. Verbal protocols of complex cognitive processes are far more varied in this respect than representations of concepts and perceived scenes, allowing for rich and multi-layered analysis.

To gain insights about how their participants' focus of attention unfolds, analysts may aim to identify linguistic representations of key concepts within the data, and trace their distribution over time. Different stages of a problem-solving process may require paying attention to different aspects and features of the situation. Also, shifts of attention may lead to insights and decisions that would not otherwise have been possible. For instance, people may start out by focusing on one specific visual aspect – say, the colour of objects, which tends to be cognitively prominent independent of its significance for the task. Then at some point, they may realise that some other feature, such as shape or weight or texture, has a significance for the task that they had not been aware of. This might then lead to further insights or decisions. Such shifts in perceptual attention would be reflected in language, by references to colour being replaced by references to other object features.

Attention shifts can go beyond the level of objects, and concern entire domains. To examine this, let's return to a study introduced in Chapter 1. In Tenbrink and Seifert (2011), we were interested in how people plan a holiday route based on a map, when the actual environmental situation is remote and unknown to the traveller during the planning phase. As part of the analysis, we looked at how people switch between the spatial domain of the map in front of them, and the large-scale domain of the real-world environment envisioned for the holiday trip. Such a domain discrepancy is an integral part of any kind of in-advance travel planning (see Pick et al., 1995, for a verbal protocol study of this challenge).

Planning is what happens 'here' and 'now' – it's what the planner is doing at present: sitting at a table, with a map in front of them, considering options on the basis of whatever insights the map offers. The information on the map is typically limited to a few abstract symbols that the planner can neither feel nor hear nor smell – they can only imagine what the represented things will be like in reality. Travelling happens in the future; it is something that the planner may or may not end up doing. All going well, objects and places shown in the map will then become real-world objects and locations that one can sense in multiple ways. A representation of a beach on a map is not relaxing, but the beach itself may well be.

In this sense, a travel planning scenario combines two very different 'worlds'. Successful planning might relate to the planner's ability to imagine the travelling world suitably, avoiding any travel situations that might spoil the actual trip in the future. While it was unlikely that participants would directly comment on this challenge, we expected that the required conceptual shifts should be represented in the language used to describe the problem-solving procedure in some way.

To operationalise this idea, we first segmented the language data into informational units. Each unit contained a proposition like Examples 7.12 and 7.13 (here translated from the German original).

Example 7.12   The map was helpful because important things were plotted there.
Example 7.13   In order to keep the trip from getting boring, some breaks of up to 2 days are taken.

Then, we identified linguistic markers. Example 7.12 shows an informational unit that belongs entirely in the planning domain, as indicated by the terms *map*, *helpful*, *important*, and *plotted*. In contrast, Example 7.13 indicates the travelling domain by the use of *trip*, *boring*, *breaks*, and *2 days*. It is important to note that the verbal data also contained many instances that were not clearly attributable to either one of the domains. Consider Example 7.14:

Example 7.14   One resort at the south coast and one at the north coast. Both have larger towns nearby. [Einen Badeort an der Südküste und einen an der Nordküste. Beide haben in der Nähe größere Ortschaften.]

While the words *coast* and *towns* arguably represent locations in the real world, they are also clearly identifiable from the map. In fact, there is no simple alternative way of referring to these places in reference to the map. For this reason, references to places were not counted as indicating either of the domains. Example 7.14 can be understood as relevant for travelling just as well as for planning, as the description of spatial relationships is true for both.

While the examples so far could be attributed to either the travelling or planning domain, or neither, some of the informational units contained markers of both domains. These turned out to be particularly interesting, as they marked conceptual shifts between the domains. Here are a few examples:

Example 7.15   I wanted to let the couple travel once round the western part of the island [ich wollte das Paar einmal um den westlichen Inselteil reisen lassen]
Example 7.16   After that I looked for a route that could be travelled [Danach habe ich geschaut, wo man langfahren könnte]
Example 7.17   in order to design the travel so that it is as diversified as possible [um die Fahrt möglichst abwechslungsreich zu gestalten]

Example 7.15 contains references to two different agents: *I* and *the couple*. They are linked through the verb *let*, which semantically indicates the effects of planning on future actions in the real world. Other typical indicators of conceptual shifts are modal verbs such as *could* in Example 7.16, and final connectors such as *in order to* in Example 7.17. These linguistic devices mark the fact that planning is not a conceptual activity in and of itself, but rather involves a constant awareness of the real-world situation that is invoked by the planning. Even though our study was hypothetical in the sense that no actual travelling ever happened, the verbal reports clearly reflected the planner's recognition of this second conceptual layer.

To summarise, conceptual switches appear to be a frequent phenomenon in complex cognitive tasks. They are systematically reflected in language, and indicate how the participants change back and forth between distinct levels or aspects of the task. A close analysis of linguistic indicators of conceptual switches can therefore provide valuable insights into multilayered cognitive processes.

7.2.5   Cognitive Strategies and Communication in Wayfinding

So far in this chapter, we have treated the verbalisation of cognitive strategies as distinct from communication as the normal function of language. According to the paradigm established by Ericsson and Simon (1993), communicative purposes are reduced to a minimum when thinking aloud or formulating a retrospective report. However, some of the verbal data we have reported in this chapter do involve some communicative aspects, such as writing instructions for a friend. More generally, it is important to keep in mind that communicative purposes can never be entirely ruled out, even though they may not be in the foreground of attention. Even well-trained participants in an empirical study will ultimately think aloud for the purposes of the experiment, and accordingly communicate, to a degree, with the experimenter. There is probably no way around that. It is not necessarily a bad thing, but it is a fact that shouldn't be ignored or denied.

With this in mind, it is useful to consider the relationship between cognitive strategies and communication more directly. How does the verbalisation of thought interact with communicative purposes? There are two ways of thinking about this. On the one hand, communication can affect problem solving. We have all experienced situations where we couldn't see the solution to a problem on our own, but once we started talking about it to a friend, the situation gradually became clearer until it was resolved. On the other hand, the verbalisation of the problem-solving process or the problem's solution can change depending on who we talk to, in light of the goals of communication. Both effects can be significant and are worth taking into account, as we will see in the following.

The first effect (how communication affects problem-solving) was addressed by Trognon, Batt, and Laux (2011), who asked why problems can sometimes be solved more effectively in dialogue than individually. They gave participants a logical puzzle to solve, which required some thought before the solution came to mind. Just like in earlier related research, participants who worked with a partner did better than those who solved the puzzle on their own. By looking more closely at the strategies represented in language, Trognon et al. (2011) found that they truly emerged through the dialogic interaction itself. Thus, rather than getting help and knowledgeable advice from the interaction partner, the cognitive strategies emerged jointly based on the exchange of thought, focused on the logical problem that they were both trying to solve. Based on this study, we may speculate that the active and partner-oriented formulation of thought, bouncing ideas off somebody else, triggers a range of thought processes that may otherwise not emerge – or at least not as efficiently.

In Hölscher et al. (2011) we addressed the second effect (how verbalisations of thought are affected by the communicative situation), and asked how cognitive strategies interacted with purposes of communication. Imagine for a moment that you are in a town you are familiar with, and you need to get to the train station. There are multiple paths, as it is a town with many small and labyrinthine streets, but there are also some major roads that you could follow. Knowing your way around town, which path would you choose?

Now imagine a stranger asks you for the way to the train station from that same supermarket. Again, which path would you choose to help the person? And how would you explain it to them? In our study, we reasoned that wayfinding and communicative strategies may both be at stake in such a situation. We would want the stranger to find their way, just as we'd like to find our way. But in addition to this, we'd also need to *communicate* the navigation information to the stranger, which isn't necessary for ourselves. In fact, we may not even want or need to make complete plans before we set out towards the train station at all. This might lead to different planning and verbalisation outcomes.

In order to disentangle these various factors, we conducted two studies. In the first one, we tested the effects of planning in advance as opposed to navigating directly to the goal. Taking the example just used further, imagine you would first describe the path to the train station from where you are, and then you would walk there, trying to find the shortest path. Do you think you would use the same route as the one you just described? Perhaps you'd find a better one as you're walking, seeing as the town has so many different options. And indeed, none of our participants actually used the route they described in advance. All of them found shorter routes when they walked to the goal. This result clearly demonstrates that wayfinding happens to a high degree on the spot – we change and adjust our plans as we go along.

In the second study, we added the communicative factor as follows. Each of our participants was confronted with three different navigation tasks to different goals. In one of these tasks, they walked directly to the goal. In another, they were asked to write down how they would walk to the goal. And in the third, they were asked to write down a route description for a stranger, as if they had been asked on the street how to get there. Conditions were randomised in a way that allowed us to directly compare the routes and descriptions, depending on the task given in each case.

Results showed an interesting pattern. The paths people chose were most efficient when they walked directly to the goal. As with the first experiment, this showed that people were best able to find the shortest route when they had a chance to actually see where they were going. But there was also something else. In both of the written tasks, but particularly when writing the route for a stranger, people relied more heavily on the major roads, as opposed to the labyrinthine street network. In addition, descriptions were more detailed and elaborate for the stranger than for the in-advance versions they wrote for themselves. However, they basically contained the same types of information, that is, a similar distribution of references to landmarks, paths, actions, and so on.

Combining the evidence across various types of data gathered in this study, a novel insight emerged, as follows. Communicative purposes mean that people try to facilitate the task for somebody else. This has some effects on the way things are formulated as well as to some extent on the route chosen, which may be somewhat simpler than the route one would choose to plan for oneself. However, the main difference is between *planning in advance* and *walking directly to the goal.* These are actually two very different tasks, and involve different conceptual strategies. When planning in advance, we retrieve the basic facts about the street network from memory, and sketch the path mentally towards the goal on that basis – with a high degree of orientation towards major, more mentally accessible roads. This leads to the kinds of turn-by-turn directions that we typically give to strangers: 'Follow the main road here, then turn right when you get to the church.'

In contrast, when we are free to just walk to our goal, we do not plan these details in advance, and we do not rely on turn-by-turn information. Instead, we simply orient ourselves to where we know the goal to be. Based on our spatial knowledge of the town's layout, we have a certain sense of direction – we can point roughly to the train station from where we are. This enables us to walk there on the shortest possible path, as close as possible to the 'beeline'. However, we may not be able to describe this same path in advance to a stranger, or even to ourselves. That is because we don't have all the information readily accessible in our heads, no matter how well we know the street network. Directional knowledge of this kind may be much more central to our navigation strategies than we realise. In effect, it may be more useful than we think to simply provide the stranger on the street with this basic information: just point to where you know the goal to be, rather than trying to explain the exact route. As long as the town has a sufficiently dense network of smaller roads (and few dead ends), the stranger should be able to find their way.

To summarise this chapter, cognitive and communicative aspects work together whenever we formulate our thoughts. On the one hand, problem solving sometimes works better when we talk to another person about it. On the other hand, how we approach a problem is influenced by the communicative situation, and this will affect verbalisation in various ways. It is important to keep these effects in mind when doing CODA.

Empirical studies can be designed in such a way that either cognition or communication is in focus, or the effects of both are systematically compared. Laboratory studies that involve language are often designed to minimise the communicative aspect. However, it is unrealistic to assume that this aspect could ever entirely disappear, since language evolved to communicate. Instead of denying its presence, it may be more useful to recognise its function, and, if possible, to identify the effects of communicative purposes on a given task.

8   CODA Procedures

So far, we have looked at motivation, background, theory, and a range of possible analysis perspectives. Along with this we have seen multiple examples from previous CODA studies that illustrate how it works and what kinds of insight you might gain. This chapter is devoted to the more practical aspects of doing CODA.

Let me remind you, to start with, that CODA simply means doing discourse analysis with a focus on concepts and thought processes. CODA researchers can draw on extensive practical information available in the literature – there are many handbooks, textbooks, and research reports describing discourse analytic methods for a rich variety of purposes, and any of them may be highly useful and informative for CODA research (see also Chapter 3). In addition, there are (and will increasingly be, given rapid technological advancement) sophisticated tools available to support transcription, annotation, and corpus analysis. These are not hard to find, and researchers can flexibly make use of any of them to support the specific work in a project, once they have identified their research goals concerning linguistic data.

For this reason, the main purpose of this book is to highlight the wide range of concepts and cognition-related aspects that are reflected in language, encouraging researchers to seek relevant insights through linguistic analysis. Anyone doing that will be doing 'cognitive discourse analysis', that is, CODA, even though the label doesn't have to be there, and the exact methods for doing CODA might differ.

In this chapter, I will not attempt to reintroduce existing methods or provide extensive software tool reviews; nor do I aim to reproduce insights that are better described elsewhere (which may include the more succinct CODA introduction published in Tenbrink, 2015). Instead, the aim of this chapter is to highlight some important principles that should be kept in mind no matter which practical approach is eventually chosen. Along the way I will share some practice-based insights that have accumulated over many years of doing CODA.

Perhaps these practical tips will be of use to you, and perhaps you will prefer to do discourse analysis in a completely different way: this is entirely up to you.

This chapter is primarily intended to convey some essential methodological considerations, and it may perhaps convince you of the simplicity and accessibility of the approach: you will not need to acquire highly priced equipment, nor will you need extensive training beyond basic understanding of linguistic principles, a suitable theoretical basis for your study, and systematic thinking.

Section 8.1 will start by looking at preliminary considerations, followed by issues pertaining to experimental design and data collection in Section 8.2. Section 8.3 will take a closer look at how to elicit verbal data, Section 8.4 will discuss data preparation, and Section 8.5 describes practical steps of doing language data analysis. The two remaining sections will briefly discuss qualitative and quantitative analysis insights, respectively, in relation to CODA.

8.1   Preliminary Considerations

Before collecting data for a CODA study, it is useful to have a clear idea about initial thoughts and motivations. Why do you think linguistic analysis might be relevant for your research purposes and goals? What kinds of insights do you expect? Perhaps you have already collected language data, and now you're wondering what to do with it? Or perhaps you're about to start a research study, and are wondering how to design it so as to make the most of it? Or perhaps you wish to use publicly available language data? There's a lot out there: the Internet itself can be regarded as a corpus of language, and there are many more specific resources, collected and put together for all sorts of purposes. Don't leave this to chance – your research goals must guide all decisions concerning the data you collect or use.

Any discourse resource can be suitable for doing CODA, as all language produced by a speaker or writer reveals something about their thoughts. The language producers' concepts and way of thinking will always be represented in some way in the linguistic choices they make. For this reason, you may be able to conduct a meaningful CODA study on any data set, whatever your starting point may be. However, different starting points mean different constraints on the kinds of insights that can be expected from a CODA study.

For instance, if you look at the language use of one person in one situation, you will have nothing to compare it with. There may be many reasons why this person makes the linguistic choices the way they do. You may have trouble explaining what you find, and in the worst case you may not gain any meaningful insights from the analysis. If you wish to look at the effects of a particular factor, you will need two situations in which language is produced: one that contains this particular factor, and one that doesn't contain it or that changes it in some way. Also, your conclusions will be much stronger if linguistic data is produced by more than just one person confronted with either one of these two situations.

I personally think it's best to start from scratch, with a burning research question that pertains to language. Only then will you be in a position to collect just the kind of linguistic data that is best suited for your goals. If you have already collected data that you now wish to analyse using CODA, some design decisions that you made earlier might have been practical and useful at the time, but they may now constrain your CODA analysis in unwelcome ways. For instance, in some research contexts it may not matter much how exactly you formulate instructions to participants. So you might have explained procedures informally to them – a bit differently for each individual. However, slight changes in the instruction may lead to slight but systematic (and potentially crucial) changes in the language participants produce in a study.

If you use available data that you haven't elicited yourself, you may not have access to some important information such as speakers' gender and age, prior knowledge, motivations for producing language, situational context, discourse history, and so on, all of which may be decisive for interpretation of language in relation to thought. Again, I don't mean to suggest that CODA can only be done in studies involving specifically collected data. In fact, CODA relates closely to corpus linguistic approaches (see Chapter 9), and using existing corpora can lead to a range of fundamental insights (e.g. Egorova, Tenbrink, & Purves, 2015, 2018). However, do keep in mind that not controlling the data yourself introduces limits and considerations that you'll have to take into account during analysis.

Also, don't forget that language is not the only way in which thoughts and cognitive processes can be represented. Many insights about the human mind in the literature are not based on language; there are a broad range of methodologies in cognitive science that are suitable for addressing many different features of the human mind. This book focuses on insights that can be gained through linguistic analysis, beyond interpreting the content that is directly represented in language. The analysis perspectives discussed in this book are by no means exhaustive, but it is also clear that there are limits to what language can express (see also Chapter 1). Again, your chosen research methodology must be suitable to address your research goals.

Finally, research must always be ethical. Universities typically have an ethical board or panel that provides ethical approval for a planned study, usually guided by or similar to the APA (American Psychological Association) Ethics Code. When using publicly available data from the Internet or elsewhere, there are normally no ethical problems and no written approval will be required; however, it is fair to eliminate all personal references and names unless they are relevant to the study (as when analysing public political speeches). If you collect data yourself, make sure to adhere to ethical and data protection (GDPR)[1] principles, such as: (1) tell your participants that their participation is voluntary and they can withdraw at any time, (2) preserve participants' anonymity by using codes rather than names, (3) avoid anything that may potentially cause harm to participants, (4) treat all information confidentially, and (5) keep the data in a secure place until deletion. If you cannot find an ethically unproblematic way of eliciting data from participants, you may need to reconsider whether you really need to do the study. However, most CODA research is simple enough and straightforward in this respect – it usually doesn't harm participants to speak or write, which may be all they're asked to do, in relation to some kind of perception or thought process.

8.2 Experimental Design

If you collect data yourself, there are a range of things to consider. The experimental design is crucial to any empirical research, and controlled language data elicitation is no exception. CODA studies can be as varied as language use in real life: there are no limits to the range of potentially interesting designs. However, not every design will be suitable or useful for your research question and purpose. For this reason, it makes sense to carefully think about each step of the procedure in advance, plan all the details systematically, and document them in writing to ensure they can be consulted and reported later.

Let me just reinforce again that procedures need to be strictly consistent. All participants in an experimental group must do exactly the same task. It is unfortunately very easy to introduce small variations into the experimental task procedure, which may jeopardise the study's validity. Experimental variation must be planned and purposeful, and it should pertain to groups of participants rather than individuals. There is no value in variation that is introduced accidentally by sloppiness in the design or during data collection. So, think everything through before you start – from the moment your participants enter the room until the moment they leave it again.

Let's say you wish to find out how people describe a picture. This idea is a perfectly typical goal for a CODA study: people don't perceive pictures neutrally, as a computer might do. They ascribe meaning to what they see in the pictures, they use their experience and knowledge to interpret certain aspects, and they are influenced by their motives and professional background. With this in mind, you decide to give people pictures to describe. Because you want as much variety as possible, you ask all your friends, no matter what age or native language or whatever else, and you give each person a different picture (or several) to describe. This is legitimate, and

---

[1] https://eugdpr.org

you might get a wide range of interesting insights out of this. But let me warn you. The data that you collect in this way will be extremely varied, and it will be very hard for you to see any patterns and draw meaningful conclusions.

The goal of most empirical research is to gain generalisable insights, not simply momentary observations. If one person describes a picture in one way, and a different person with a different background describes a different picture in a different way, all you can say is that there are differences. You can point to the differences in detail, and provide an in-depth qualitative analysis of what they are. This can be useful at a certain stage of a research process, or for certain purposes. The more that is known about an area, the more detailed a qualitative analysis would have to be to provide any new insights. At a certain stage, it is far more useful to look for more general patterns, and for possible reasons behind the identified differences. This is what experimental variation, using different controlled conditions, is for.

Sometimes you might want to use just two different conditions, and sometimes there will be more. Perhaps you wish to test two different kinds of participants (such as men and women) in two different tasks, in which case you have two independent variables (or factors) that may interact with each other. Then, both of your participant groups (men and women) will need to do both tasks so that you can compare the effects of task differences as well as the effects of gender.

You can do this in either one of two ways. In what's called a *within-participants design*, each person does both tasks. This enables you to compare the effects of task differences for each individual person. This is relevant for statistics even if you don't actually compare data on a person-by-person basis. With a design like that, you need to be aware that doing one task may affect what people do on their second task. Unless this effect of task order is desirable for some reason, it is normally advisable to *balance* the order of tasks: half of the participants do one task first, and the other half do the other task first. This allows you to check for any effects of task order.

The alternative is called a *between-participants design*: one group does one task, and another group does the other. If you also wish to compare men and women, you'd need two groups of men and two groups of women, and they'd all do only one task. Since groups shouldn't be too small, it's clear that studies using a between-participants design will need to involve more people than studies using a within-participants design. However, the advantage is that you don't have to worry about effects of task order if there is only one task for each participant to do.

The one thing to avoid is to have all the men do one task and all the women do a different task. This is called conflation – two factors (gender and task) are influencing your results at the same time, and you have no way of knowing which one causes the patterns in your results. It makes sense to avoid having more than two factors, as every factor introduces further possible combinations; this makes it more difficult to see patterns and do a meaningful statistical analysis.

Sometimes it's possible to predict specific patterns in language before you even start on your study, based on the previous literature. This allows for the formulation of hypotheses in advance, and it can be very decisive in determining experimental design. However, whatever your design and motivation is, make sure you consider in advance what kinds of linguistic patterns you expect in the data that will shed light on the research question at hand.

For instance, after having read up on the topic, you might hypothesise that men use more expressive language than women, but only in informal contexts. To test this, you use two experimental groups, one consisting of men and the other of women (and of course you might use more groups, allowing you to include other gender types). Every participant is individually given one task with a formal context, and another task with an informal context. Half of the participants start with the formal one, and the other half with the informal one. This within-participants design will allow you to compare the distribution of your dependent variable (expressive language) in the collected data, in relation to the independent variables formality and gender.

Let's take a closer look at the formulation of instructions to participants. You can actually test this in a CODA study. Let's say you wish to see if people perceive and describe a picture differently depending on how the instruction is formulated. One of your experimental groups therefore gets the instruction in Example 8.1, and another gets the instruction in Example 8.2:

Example 8.1   Please could you describe what you see in this picture?
Example 8.2   Tell me what this picture shows.

Both instructions seem very similar, and it is conceivable that intuitively you might have used these formulations interchangeably, along with further variations, without being aware of possible effects of this variability. After all, you always *mean* the same – surely the participants will always understand the same, and simply provide a picture description as requested.

However, this may not be the case. At a closer look, the two instructions differ in rather decisive ways. Example 8.1 is formulated in a polite and indirect way (using *please* and a question format), whereas Example 8.2 is a simple direct command. Example 8.1 uses the verbs *describe* and *see*, as opposed to the verbs *tell* and *show* in Example 8.2. *Describing* is different from *telling someone* – it may possibly be perceived as more elaborate, and more process-oriented, whereas *telling* is a communicative process, which foregrounds the researcher as an interaction partner. And *seeing* is more subjective than *showing*, as it pertains to the speaker, whereas *showing* pertains to the picture. These semantic differences aren't as subtle as they may seem at first. Whether people perceive the instruction as the same on a pragmatic level, and provide a picture description in just the same way, is an empirical question that a CODA study would be well suited to address.

In CODA studies, participants should normally be native speakers of the language used. If you're interested in conceptual aspects reflected in speakers' choices, it makes sense for the speakers to have the full network of options at their disposal. Learners of a language have an ever-increasing range of choices, but until they are fully fluent they will have to use whatever words they already know – and this is less than the entire network of options in the language. If you are interested in how this works, you might want to design a study with two experimental groups to test this: one with native speakers, and one with non-native speakers who are learners at a similar stage and with a similar linguistic background. Both groups would receive the same task, and this would allow you to study how speakers in each group use language to express their thoughts. Keep in mind, however, that knowledge of a language is always a decisive factor. In a study looking closely at linguistic choices, it really doesn't make sense to mix native and non-native speakers in one experimental group.

In short, whenever you introduce a difference into your design that may be decisive (as most differences are, to different degrees), use different experimental groups, if at all possible. In most cases it is best to avoid differences (such as different wording or linguistic background), unless they are the target of the study – and this would have to be motivated from a theoretical perspective, based on previous research in the area.

If you cannot avoid variation, aim for a random or equal distribution. For instance, if you're not particularly interested in gender differences, try to get a balanced gender mix in each experimental group. And if you don't expect social background to matter in your study, use a random sample from the population you're interested in. In many cases the population will be undergraduate students, for convenience – these are typically easiest to find for an empirical study in academia. If that's the case, make sure you don't add one or two people who are not undergraduate students, as their educational background would introduce a variable that only applies to a small proportion of the group.

Depending on your research question, you might be interested in collecting further types of data or evidence beyond language. For instance, in a study collecting picture descriptions, you might want to record the time that participants take to describe a picture. If the temporal factor is particularly decisive for some reason, you might time the exact milliseconds that they need before they start talking after having been given the picture, as well as the pauses they make in the process, and so on. Alternatively (or in addition) you might be interested in the gestures they produce during the description, or in physiological effects that you'd need to measure using specific instruments.

As indicated by these examples, there are many different kinds of data you can collect, in addition to language. In a CODA study, language is central, but other kinds of data might add valuable information that can be used for triangulation. Most published CODA studies have used various types of evidence, addressing the research question at hand in more than one way. We will get back to the topic of triangulation in Chapter 9 and outline more broadly how CODA can be meaningfully combined with other data.

When collecting other types of data, as with language, every detail needs to be considered carefully in advance, and procedures must be clear and consistent. You will also need to make sure that you will be able to align the language with other data as required. For instance, if you ask people to do something, to perform a task in addition to producing language, you will need to keep track of what they are doing at each point while they are speaking. In most cases this will require video recording the participants' actions. As this can make analysis quite complicated, it may be worthwhile to consider in advance which aspects of the language are most interesting in relation to which kinds of action. Such considerations can influence the experimental design from the start, saving considerable effort later.

Importantly, as you decide on your experimental design and collect your data, always keep the participants' well-being in mind. As already mentioned in the previous section, you need to adhere to ethical principles, and obtain ethical consent prior to collecting data. This will ensure that you won't induce any harm to participants. In addition, it is particularly important in a CODA study that participants feel at ease, and produce language in a natural way. If they're not sure what they are doing, or feel that they are confronted with an awkward task, this will be reflected in their language. Odd and uncertain situations lead to odd and uncertain language – and this is unlikely to be your research goal. With this in mind, in the next section we will take a closer look at ways to elicit verbal data for a CODA study.

8.3 Verbal Data Elicitation

People use language in many different ways, and throughout this book we have described many examples of studies where language data was collected in different ways and formats. Let's take a look at various ways in which you might want to elicit verbal data from your experimental participants. Clearly this is an important decision to make. How you ask your participants to produce language will affect your results very strongly and constrain the analyses you can do on the data, and the conclusions you can finally draw. It therefore makes sense to spend some time thinking through the implications of different ways of eliciting verbal data. We saw some of this when discussing Examples 8.1 and 8.2. To take another example, consider the difference between the following instructions:

Example 8.3   Why did you solve the problem in the way you did?
Example 8.4   What were your thoughts during the task?
Example 8.5   Try to recall what you were thinking while solving the problem. Step by step, what were your thoughts as you solved the problem?

Imagine what people might say in response to each of these questions. Example 8.3 is a *why* question, and as such encourages the participant to look for reasons for doing what they did. These reasons may or may not correspond to the participants' actual thoughts during problem solving. People sometimes do things for a conscious reason, and sometimes things just happen, and the problem gets solved. At the very least, the response will only represent a selection of actual thoughts – people will only report those ideas that provide a reason for solving the problem.

Example 8.4 directly asks for thoughts. This might work in the way it is formulated – it doesn't create a bias towards reasons or anything else. However, the question is general and asks about any thoughts that come to mind, in any order. Example 8.5, in contrast, encourages the person to think back to the procedure of problem solving. Thoughts occur in a certain sequence during a complex cognitive task like problem solving, and you might be interested in this aspect. In support of this, Example 8.5 encourages participants to recall their problem-solving steps in their sequence, whereas Example 8.4 will probably lead to shorter, less orderly representations of remembered thoughts.

However, CODA is not only good for problem-solving tasks. Let's take a closer look at what happens during a *description* task. Descriptions are reflections of the speaker's thoughts with respect to what they describe, and can therefore be analysed in terms of *mental representations*. People can describe many things – there is no limit to the range of concepts and thoughts that can be looked at on this basis. This field is very flexible, and many CODA studies have focused on descriptions of various kinds (e.g. Cialone et al., 2018; Egorova et al., 2015, 2018; Hölscher et al., 2011; Tenbrink et al., 2017, and many more).

Let's say you are interested in people's thoughts on XYZ. Then you might ask participants to describe any of the following: XYZ itself; what they *see* with respect to XYZ; what they *remember* about XYZ; how they would *deal with* XYZ; how they *feel* about XYZ; or anything else along those lines. All of these questions trigger a specific mindset on the part of the speaker, encouraging them to think about XYZ in a particular way. Again, what exactly you ask will be decisive, as it will push the verbalisations and your subsequent analysis in a particular direction. 'Describe XYZ' is the most neutral version, but this may not always work, or you may wish to elicit more than one description. Obviously, verbalisations of *feelings about* XYZ are very different from simply *remembering* XYZ. Nevertheless, all of these questions trigger descriptions and may be of interest for a CODA study.

But what is XYZ in this instance – what could it be? Again, this opens up a wide range of possibilities. It could be anything that is somehow represented in the speaker's mind, or that the speaker currently perceives or remembers perceiving earlier: an abstract concept, a picture, an event, a scene, a path to a destination – and many more. Descriptions can be very complex, and extend over time, as in describing how a story unfolds, perhaps in a film or novel that speakers recall. On the other hand, a description may be as simple as a single sentence, if XYZ – the described item – is very simple. For instance, in Vorwerg and Tenbrink (2007) we showed participants abstract depictions of a square and one or more circles, nothing else. One of the circles was marked by an 'x'. We asked them one of two questions with respect to each picture:

Example 8.6   Where is the element that is marked by an 'x'?
Example 8.7   Which element in the picture is marked by an 'x'?

We were interested in the different responses that would be triggered by the questions. In particular, we reasoned that the question in Example 8.6 would encourage speakers to focus on the spatial *location* of the objects relative to each other, triggering fairly detailed spatial descriptions. In contrast, we expected that the question in Example 8.7 would be read as an *identification* question; responses would have to be sufficient to identify the marked element in contrast to others in the picture, but the spatial location would not be important as such. Since spatial location is frequently used to identify objects, as in 'the one on the right', the responses might still be very similar.

Following a CODA analysis of the fine details in the linguistic choices speakers made, our results showed that *where* questions (Example 8.6) did indeed trigger more precise and complex responses. If there was only one circle present in the picture, the *which* question (Example 8.7) could be simply answered by a phrase like 'the circle'; this was not possible in the case of a *where* question. More complex pictures frequently triggered spatial descriptions for *which* questions just as well as for *where* questions, but they tended to be less elaborate.

Descriptions can be very interesting to analyse, and they are simple to elicit. An everyday question like 'Please describe the picture' or 'What do you see?' may be fully sufficient for the purposes of a study, requiring no further explanation. To a high degree, descriptions represent the speaker's concepts, mediated by how the question is framed and how willing the participant is to represent their thoughts, and so they offer a varied and unlimited resource for accessing thought.

While descriptions express mental representations, they do not directly reflect thought *processes* – such as those that happen during problem solving. If you ask somebody to describe what they did when they solved a problem, they will tell you how they remember doing it, and what they *think* they did. As a mental representation of the problem-solving process, this is fine and can be very interesting. However, it is important to distinguish between a *mental representation of the process* (as reflected in a description), and the *thoughts during the process*. To access the actual thought processes during problem solving, we need to move away from description and look for a different way of eliciting verbal data.

As a matter of fact, historically the study of problem solving started out by relying on descriptions, often those of individuals. Early studies relied on the researchers' own memory of how they solved problems themselves; they aimed to identify general principles from these introspective considerations. Later, they began to ask other people, individual experimental participants, how they solved the problem. However, insights gained from these studies were increasingly criticised as being too subjective, too anecdotal. People might misremember or confabulate; they might report thought processes that never actually happened. From a current point of view, this is not surprising: after all, research then focused on *descriptions* of problem-solving processes, rather than representations of the *actual thoughts* during problem solving.

After experimenting with these concerns for several decades, Ericsson and Simon (1993) famously established their paradigm for eliciting reliable verbal data on thought processes that is still widely used in cognitive science (see Chapter 7). They suggested two main ways of eliciting data, neither of which is a description; both aim at triggering a more accurate representation of the actual thought processes, rather than a representation of what the speakers *think* they thought. The two methods differ only in one way: *when* the data are elicited – either *during* or *after* the actual problem-solving process.

Collecting verbal data *during* problem solving means that participants are asked to solve a problem, and to verbalise their thoughts as they do so. Again, it is important to note that they are not asked to 'describe what they are doing' or anything like that – we are not looking for a *description* of thoughts or actions in this case, but for a *representation* of thoughts and thought processes. Ericsson and Simon (1993) suggested a formulation similar to this one:

In our study we are interested in what you think as you perform a task that we give you. In order to do this I am going to ask you to THINK ALOUD during the whole procedure of the task. That is, I want you to say EVERYTHING you are thinking from start to finish of the task. I would like you to talk aloud CONSTANTLY. Don't try to plan out what you say and don't talk to ME. Just act as if you were speaking to yourself. It is most important that you keep talking, even though you won't get any response or feedback. Do you understand what I want you to do?

This general instruction is usually followed by a couple of warm-up practice tasks, such as:

Example 8.8   Please multiply two numbers in your head and say out loud what you are thinking as you get an answer. What is the result of multiplying 24 × 36?

Example 8.9   How many windows are there in a house you know very well, for instance the one you grew up in?

Practice tasks should be as far away from the study goals as possible. If you wish to study how people solve complex mathematical problems, Example 8.8 is not suitable as it also concerns a mathematical problem. Any kind of simple everyday problem that is not too taxing but nevertheless involves a short problem-solving process will do. Based on the instruction and practice tasks of this kind, participants normally understand what is required of them, and do not struggle with the idea of thinking aloud. Ericsson and Simon (1993) suggest that thinking aloud is a natural activity, something that we intuitively do, and that we might have done frequently as a child; it easily comes back to us in a context like this. While this may not be true for everyone, most participants are quite happy with it, and soon don't see it as an additional task. They just say out loud what is on their minds anyway.

The instruction above may sound a bit complex, but the underlying idea is really quite simple. Under circumstances that do not allow for long instructions and training, it may also work to simply ask people to *say out loud what they are thinking*. This is a shortcut to the long instruction, but it does express the entire idea. It is simple, and it avoids any bias towards description or explanation or anything else that would encourage people to express anything else than their actual thoughts.

Even though thinking aloud, if encouraged in this way, is simple and straightforward, there are a number of potential problems. There is abundant evidence in the cognitive science literature that the actual thought process may be influenced by the task of thinking aloud, in a range of ways. In some cases, verbalisation is helpful for the task. In Chapter 7, we discussed the frequent finding that some problems can be solved more easily when talking to somebody else about it (e.g. Trognon et al., 2011). In the case of thinking aloud, there is no interaction partner, but the process of verbalising itself may sometimes lead to a different organisation of thoughts, and this can support problem solving.

In other cases, verbalisation may do the opposite – it may hamper the thought process. For instance, if the task involves language in some way – perhaps solving a linguistic problem – there may be some interference between using language for verbalisation and considering language as part of the task. Also, it is possible that people are too busy thinking to express their thoughts aloud at the same time; this would then lead to silence during a decisive part of the problem-solving process. And finally, some thoughts cannot be verbalised at all. Perhaps people are not sufficiently aware of these thoughts to verbalise them; some kinds of thoughts are too subtle or low-level to be verbalised. Or perhaps people cannot put these particular kinds of thoughts into words, as not all thoughts are easily verbalisable; it might be easier to draw something or express the thoughts in a different way. Clearly, language has its limits as a representation of thought (see also Chapters 1 and 2).

These limitations don't mean that collecting think-aloud data is pointless or shouldn't be done. They simply need to be considered for the particular case at hand; the researcher needs to be aware of potential problems and interferences, and take them into account in the analysis. Also, it is always a good idea to include a control condition that does not involve thinking aloud but is otherwise identical to the think-aloud condition. This allows for a comparison between the results of a problem-solving task done while thinking aloud and without thinking aloud. For instance, in the case of a mathematical problem like multiplying 24 by 36 (as in our warm-up task in Example 8.8), you could compare the percentages of correct results in think-aloud and silent versions, as well as the time needed to get to the answer, and so on.

In spite of these limitations, thinking aloud during problem solving is clearly the most direct way of accessing thought processes as they occur. Any other kinds of verbal representations are necessarily less direct. However, Ericsson and Simon (1993) suggested that if collected in a controlled and conscientious way, *retrospective reports* are also very useful and fairly close to the actual thought process. This brings us back to the examples in the beginning of this section. If we want people to report their thoughts retrospectively, there are a number of things to consider in order to avoid meta-descriptions of what people think about their own thoughts, explanations, confabulations, and other verbalisations that lead away from the actual thought processes. Here, Ericsson and Simon (1993:378) suggested the following instruction to participants:

Now I want you to see how much you can remember about what you were thinking from the time you read the question until you gave the answer. We are interested in what you actually can REMEMBER rather than what you think you must have thought. If possible I would like you to tell about your memories in the sequence in which they occurred while working on the question. Please tell me if you are uncertain about any of your memories. I don't want you to work on solving the problem again, just report all that you can remember thinking about when answering the question. Now tell me what you remember.

It is certainly a good idea to adjust this instruction according to the needs of the current task. Also, eliminating all references to 'me' as the experimenter would make the task more similar to a think-aloud task in which there is no designated addressee. As in the think-aloud procedure, Ericsson and Simon (1993) recommended practising retrospective reports, perhaps combined with the think-aloud practice if participants are asked to do both. The practice tasks in Examples 8.8 and 8.9 work well for this.

Following Ericsson and Simon (1993), think-aloud protocols and retrospective reports are two ways of eliciting verbal data to represent thought processes as closely as possible. Descriptions, as we discussed above, are ways of accessing mental representations. Alongside these frequent and well-established methods of eliciting verbal data, there are many further options that can be useful for CODA studies. Many of these are discussed at great length in other contexts. For instance, consider interviews, focus groups, and questionnaires. All of these methods are useful for a range of purposes in social science and beyond, and all of them involve collecting verbal data of different kinds. All verbalisations are expressions of thought, mediated by the context in which they are elicited and by the way in which this happens.

Beyond the content of *what* people say in an interview, focus group, or questionnaire, CODA adds a new layer of analysis by looking at *how* they say it. In Tenbrink et al. (2012), for instance, we used CODA on a set of transcripts from previously conducted interviews with architects. The specific purpose of the analysis was to identify, on a linguistic level, how the architects expressed various perspectives during the interview. Perspective taking in architectural design had been previously identified as a relevant topic, and CODA added valuable information on the linguistic options used to express the various perspectives involved (see Chapter 4 for details on this study). This analysis was neither based on direct mental representations (as expressed in description tasks) nor on representations of complex cognitive processes (as expressed in think-aloud protocols or retrospective reports). Instead, the architects expressed their thoughts and ideas in answer to the questions given to them in the interview.

Along these lines, any kinds of verbal data may be used for CODA analysis, and may prove to be interesting resources. As long as the limitations and features of each type of verbal data are considered in the analysis, any verbalisation data can be relevant. However, some ways of eliciting data may be more useful and suitable than others in light of your research goals. If you're looking for direct representations of current thought processes, use think-aloud protocols if possible. If you wish to elicit mental representations, aim for the type of description that will suit your purposes. In all cases, the instruction should be formulated with care, and the data must be collected conscientiously and in a controlled way, making sure that all participants receive the instruction consistently in exactly the way they are supposed to.

8.4   Data Preparation

After collecting your data, you are ready to get started on your analysis. To facilitate this, you may want to transfer everything into a digital format that you can work with. If you asked your participants to type their responses into a computer (which is sometimes done in CODA studies), there is not much to do at this stage. Just make sure you have stored the data safely and consistently, and separate from any personal information such as names. Depending on the format in which the data are collected, you may need to transfer them into a different software – the choice is yours. If you collected handwritten responses, you will probably need to type them up, or at least the relevant parts; you will quickly get to the limits of what you can do on paper.

Many CODA studies involve spoken language, however, and this is when you need to make a few decisions. Transcription can be exceedingly time-consuming; can you find software that might help you, or delegate this step to assistants? As technology is changing rapidly, I will refrain from recommending any specific software here. To date, automatic transcription results are most reliable with trained systems, which specialise on one particular voice. This is unfortunately not feasible for most CODA studies, as they involve many different speakers. It helps if your data contains no interaction or dialogue, because transcription (both automatic and manual) is much easier to accomplish then. In any case, manual work will be needed to verify any automatic transcription result. If you are involved with the transcription process yourself, be prepared to spend quite some time on it. In reward, by the end of this process you will have very good knowledge of your language data, and this takes you a long way towards meaningful analysis.

Manual transcription can be assisted by useful tools that help with practical matters. Without a tool, you'd need to switch back and forth between text processing software, and the audio recording file, which can be very tedious. There are various tools available to avoid this kind of hassle. They may enable you to type what you hear directly in to the file, to scroll back automatically when you stop and start again, to insert time stamps at useful places, to slow down or accelerate the speed, and so on. Especially with lengthy transcriptions, it is advisable to spend a moment looking for a suitable transcription support tool.

Further, you may want to decide whether you actually need to transcribe everything that was recorded. This will naturally depend on your research question and empirical procedures. Some of the produced language may be directly relevant for your purposes, while other parts may have been recorded primarily as a backup. For instance, the instruction to participants must be identical in all cases, but it may still be recorded, and this provides a chance to verify that the instruction was given as intended. Such parts may not need to be transcribed. In some cases, the study may include more than one part, and it may make sense to get started by transcribing only the first one – again saving time before analysis can start.

Once you have decided what to transcribe and how to do it, the next major decision concerns the level of detail in the transcription. The range of options is rather wide here, and again the choice depends on your purposes. Journalists may tend to transcribe just the gist or the main content of what people are saying; they may not care about the exact wording at all times – and that is perfectly fine for their purposes. For CODA, the exact wording is decisive, so a rough representation or summary of content won't do. However, do you also need information on actions, postures, gestures, mimics, intonation contour, pauses, hesitations, overlaps in dialogue, and so on? This is for you to decide.

There is a trap here that is very easy to fall into. As a conscientious researcher, you may be convinced that 'everything is relevant' and you want to 'do it properly', in case it may be needed later. However, an extremely narrow transcription, which contains all of these aspects and potentially more, will be very time-consuming. In the extreme, it may take up all the time you have, leaving none for analysis. If producing a well-transcribed corpus is not the final goal of your research, it therefore makes sense to only include the kinds of information in the transcript that will actually be used in the analysis. In most CODA studies, this means transcribing exactly what the participants said, and possibly including information on pauses that last longer than a second or two, but typically not gestures, intonation, mimics, and the like.

Further, you may want to decide on a set of transcription conventions that you use on all your transcripts. This will avoid having to make spontaneous decisions or include lengthy ad hoc explanations. For instance, imagine your participant saying something that you can't hear properly on the recording. This actually happens quite frequently, and it's useful to have a short convention for this. Compare the following solutions in a transcript:

Example 8.10   How to get to, ahhhh, *this may mean Highlander Street?* errrrm maybe take a *no idea what she says!*
Example 8.11   How to get to er (inaudible) ... er maybe take a (inaudible)
Example 8.12   How to get to, uh (Highlander Street)? (2) Uhm maybe take a (...).

In Example 8.10, no conventions seem to be available, and the transcriber explains what's going on as in 'this may mean Highlander Street?' and 'no idea what she says'. The hesitation sounds are transcribed intuitively, based on what they sound like ('ahhhh' and 'errrrm'). It is not clear what punctuation markers mean in this example; the transcriber probably did not intend to suggest that the utterance was an exclamation. The transcriber's comments are distinguishable from the actual transcript by the decision to use italics, which may be fine – but italics may easily get lost in data transfer to a different file, or overlooked in the analysis process.

In Example 8.11, everything that is not clear enough to be transcribed is marked by '(inaudible)', and the convention was adopted to consistently use 'er' for hesitation. There is no punctuation except for three dots ' . . . ', which may denote a pause after the inaudible part. These simple conventions can be easily adopted and used consistently throughout transcription, but the information included is minimal.

In Example 8.12, conventions are a bit more differentiated, providing more information to the analyst without adding much complexity or confusion. The hesitation markers 'uh' and 'uhm' are distinguished by the nasal sound at the end, which may or may not be relevant for the research purposes. Both of the inaudible parts are marked by using brackets; in the first case, the transcriber's interpretation ('Highlander Street') is included, and in the second case, the convention '(. . .)' indicates that there is speech there for which there is no attempt at an interpretation. The pause after the first inaudible part is indicated by '(2)', meaning two seconds. Punctuation is used according to normal writing conventions, where a comma indicates a slight break in the intonation contour followed by continuation, a question mark indicates an intonation pattern that makes it likely that a question was intended here, and a full stop indicates the end of a sentence (or utterance unit, in this case).

As the examples indicate, transcriptions can look very different, depending on the conventions adopted. As this will affect later analysis and even inter-pretation, it makes sense to consider carefully what kinds of conventions might be most useful for the purposes at hand. With a short transcript, ad hoc conventions like Example 8.10 may be fine, but if lengthy passages are transcribed, you will probably want a cleaner-looking version like Example 8.11 or 8.12.

8.5   Practical Steps of Data Analysis

So you have collected and transcribed your data, and everything is ready in a suitable digital format. What next? Again, the most important consideration is to be systematic in what you're doing. You may start from initial intuitions, and you may be inspired by spontaneous discoveries in the language you collected – all of this is legitimate and useful. However, the main goal of CODA is to do systematic linguistic analysis, moving from observations and intuitive insights to the identification of meaningful patterns. In effect, the procedure often moves from qualitative to quantitative analysis: you expect or discover the existence of specific phenomena in the data, and then analyse systematically how often and under what circumstances they occur.

As you start your analysis, you may already have a fairly good idea of what to look for in your data. Several chapters in this book describe specific kinds of phenomena that a close linguistic analysis may unveil, and this may guide your analysis. Keep in mind, however, that the described phenomena are meant to be exemplary rather than exhaustive. The range of cognitive aspects that are reflected in language use is extensive, and it is not the intention of this book to capture all of them. As relevant reflections of concepts or thoughts may happen on different levels of language, you may need to be flexible in the way you approach your analysis. Also, you may prefer to adopt analysis procedures that you are familiar with, or have read about, which may be perfectly suitable for CODA. Here are a few practical considerations that you might find useful, depending on your background and research goals.

8.5.1 Segmentation

Before you start analysis, you may want to think about the size of each chunk of language that you analyse at a time. From a theoretical standpoint, there are no constraints: units of analysis can be as large as millions of words (in computer-assisted corpus analysis), or even smaller than a word at a time. However, not all unit sizes will be useful for you.

Sometimes your data will come in a pre-segmented way – in useful chunks that you can analyse as they are. If you give participants ten images and ask them to describe each of them briefly in a single sentence, then each image description may be a feasible and meaningful unit of analysis. And for some types of analysis, the size of the data unit to analyse does not matter. If you look for the occurrence of individual words or phrases that you can easily search for in a data set of any size, then you won't need to segment the data at all.

However, for most CODA studies, segmentation into smaller units will facilitate analysis. There are two main reasons why you may want to segment your data: for practical purposes, and for purposes of reporting patterns in the results. If segmentation serves practical purposes only, you can do this intuitively, based on what works best for you in light of the research question at hand. If you aim to report distribution patterns of segments in a publication, or if you do quantitative calculations based on the number of units, then you will need to operationalise the segmentation process to make it meaningful and reliable (see Krippendorff, 2012 for very useful discussions of this).

Very often, the idea of a sentence or independent clause (or clause complex) is a good starting point for purposes of CODA. Their size means they normally contain a limited number of features that may be interesting from a linguistic point of view. For instance, if you're looking at the kind of perspective used in a particular spatial task, you will normally be able to determine the underlying perspective used in each single sentence or clause. And if people change perspective mid-sentence, this is interesting and worth considering more closely.

In written language, sentences can easily be identified by looking at punctuation. However, it is often more useful to choose a solution that is anchored in grammar, rather than how writers happen to place their full stops. Compare the following:

Example 8.13   The hat was dirty, and the gloves he was wearing were torn.
Example 8.14   The hat was dirty. And the gloves he was wearing were torn.

Both of these are identical in their semantic content, and they may sound the same in spoken language. If this is part of a transcript, it is very much up to the transcriber to choose where to put a comma or end a sentence. From a grammatical point of view, they both contain two independent clauses. Thus, with a segmentation that is based on independent clauses, both examples would yield two separate units, whereas a sentence-based segmentation has the entire Example 8.13 in one unit.

Notice that the second independent clause has an embedded clause within it, 'he was wearing'. This clause cannot easily be separated from the main clause, as it depends directly on it. For this and similar reasons, clauses may not be a good basis for analysis; this is why I suggested focusing on independent clauses only. However, there may be reasons for looking at the clause level, using both dependent and independent clauses as separate units. Again, the decision is yours, but do aim to do this consistently.

Especially in spoken language, it is not always straightforward to identify sentences or clauses. Spoken language typically contains unfinished sentences, repetitions, hesitation markers, false starts, and other complications. In such cases, it may make sense to use the notion of a 'possible sentence' (Selting, 2000). This can be intuitive to some extent, but intuitions will be informed by syntactic, semantic, pragmatic, and intonation-based aspects. Syntactically complete sentences can always be treated as separate units.

Once you have determined your units, it makes sense to put them into separate lines or rows in the software you will be using for analysis, for instance in an Excel file. I will in the following refer to Excel as a simple example for how standard software can be used for systematic analysis. The principles are transferable to other tools. If you use Excel, put each unit of analysis into a separate row, one after the other, leaving no empty rows. If you then number the rows (which Excel can do semi-automatically), you will have a separate ID for each unit of analysis, as well as being able to see the total number of units that you will be working with.

8.5.2   Content Analysis

Before starting to take a closer look at the features of the individual units of analysis, it is essential to gain a clear understanding of their content. *What* people say is as important as *how* they say it, in terms of linguistic and conceptual features. Content (or discourse) analysis is sometimes all that is done on language data, and this can yield essential insights relevant to the purposes of the study. As Krippendorff (2012) and others offer very good insights into relevant procedures and concepts, I will focus here on practical and CODA-related aspects only.

Content analysis means taking a close look at what people say, in each unit of analysis. For most purposes, it is useful to identify a limited range of content categories, defined in light of their relevance to the research purpose. This is useful for three reasons. First, labelling different units with a short characterisation of the content provides qualitative insights into verbalisation content produced in this kind of task. This can be a valuable result in itself that may be worth reporting in a publication. Second, this analysis gives a good overview of the structure of the data, in terms of what content is produced at what time, from a sequential perspective. Again, a systematic sequential analysis of content can lead to extremely valuable results. In fact, most traditional approaches to the analysis of verbal problem-solving data target just this aspect (see, for instance, Ericsson & Simon, 1993).

However, there is a third aspect that is directly relevant to CODA. Content analysis provides a basis for specifically targeted analysis of linguistic features pertaining to certain types of content only. To start with, not all content categories may be targeted in the analysis or suitable for further linguistic scrutiny. For instance, some units may be suitably labelled as 'introduction' or 'reflections on the task' or 'off-talk', indicating that these verbalisations are not representations of the task given to participants, but rather reflect some thoughts *around* the task, in a sense. Even if relevant they do not reflect thoughts on the actual task, and so it makes sense to separate them out of the analysis, and treat them differently in subsequent analysis steps.

Further, particularly in a problem-solving task, people think of different things at different times, which is reflected in different content categories. Some linguistic analyses are best done on specific content categories only, whereas others may be meaningful for the entire data set. This should be considered carefully, in light of analysis purposes and types. If specific types of content are linguistically expressed in a limited range of ways, it may be feasible to characterise these categories on a linguistic level. This can serve to define and support the content categories, or it can be used to establish correlations.

For instance, our CODA analysis in Tenbrink and Taylor (2015) was heavily based on content analysis, supported by a range of more detailed linguistic analyses. As reported in Chapter 6, we were interested in what people said, and in what order, while solving an origami paper-folding task, and further in how their creativity was expressed in their use of spatial language. Particularly the content category 'Reformulating description without new thoughts' was based on a close look at the formulation, as we identified utterances that were almost identical to the written instruction given to the participants, but differed from it in superficial aspects such as changing 'you' to 'I'.

Other content categories were not characterised further on a linguistic level, but there was one category that was clearly associated with spatial language: 'spatial description', a subcategory of 'Additional ideas about this step' during paper folding. As expected, we found a high correlation between the frequencies of this content category and the frequency of producing new spatial terms. The spatial terms analysis was done on the entire data set, yielding a range of interesting patterns as reported in Tenbrink and Taylor (2015), and it also supported our content category 'spatial description' through consistent correlation patterns.

In Excel, content category annotation can be done simply by inserting a column next to the utterance in each row, which allows you to enter a label in the cell next to the utterance. If required, further columns next to the basic content analysis can be introduced to identify content subcategories, to the extent that this is relevant for the research purpose at hand.

8.5.3   Tool Support: Filter, Word Count, and Automatic Search for Words and Phrases

At this point, let's consider a few features that Excel, as well as many other software tools, can offer in support of systematic analysis. To start with, I mentioned in Section 8.5.2 that not all content categories may be treated in the same way. To support focusing analysis on specific categories only, a *Filter* function can be very helpful and practical, as it allows the researcher to view and work on only a subset of data at a time, filtered according to their current analysis focus.

Another useful function is to *count words*. Excel can count words in a cell, using a specific formula – as these things change, it is best to search the web for this function. Word counts are important measures for quantitative analysis, both in terms of the entire data set and in terms of words used for individual content (or other) categories. Therefore, it is often useful to allow one column for word count of the cell containing the verbal data unit.

	A	B	C	D	E	F	G	H	I	J	K
			spea					st	Reading task	no. of	Reformulating
1	Nr	par	ker	utterance	fold tim		topic	e	description	words rea	task descriptio
2	1	13	P	#00:00:16-4# okay	00:00:16	2	stem	1		0	
3	2	13	P	#00:00:18-1# put the paper in front of you	00:00:18	8	stem	1	put the paper in front of you	7	
4	3	13	P	#00:00:23-9# corner pointing towards me, okay	00:00:23	6	stem	1		0	corner pointing towards me
5	4	13	P	#00:00:33-9# okay	00:00:33	2	stem	1		0	

Figure 8.1 Screenshot of Excel-based analysis done in Tenbrink and Taylor (2015).

Figure 8.1 gives an example taken from our origami study (Tenbrink & Taylor, 2015). Column A gives the number of the unit of analysis, and column B the participant code (13). Column C captures who is speaking the utterance that is given in Column D. Since there was no interaction, this is almost always the participant (P), but there may be clarification questions answered by the experimenter (E). The utterance unit in column D contains a time stamp, contributed by the transcription software used in this study (called F4). This information is transferred to the next column, E (fold time), enabling the analyst to identify the relevant times at a glance. Column F automatically counts the number of words in column D; since this includes the time stamp, the actual number of words is that number minus 1 (this was taken into account later). Column G identifies the current task given to the participant: folding the flower's stem following the origami instructions. Since the instructions came in steps, we could also specify the utterances in relation to what the participant was working on, captured in column H, 'step'.

In column I, content analysis starts with the content category 'Reading task description'. Unit no. 2 'put the paper in front of you' was directly read from the instruction, therefore this content is copied over into cell I3. Column J automatically counts the number of words read as represented in column I, using a formula in Excel. Unit no. 3 'corner pointing towards me' was classed as 'Reformulating task description' (column K). Further word counts, content categories, and linguistic analyses were added to the right of these columns.

The use of the filter can be seen in the second row of this example. The small arrows underneath the column header appeared when clicking 'Filter'. Clicking on the arrows allows us to see only those rows within each column that correspond to a certain criterion. For instance, it is possible to show only the rows that pertain to step 1 in column H, or that contain no words read (0 in column J). This filter function can be very helpful when focusing on a subset of the data.

Many CODA studies rely heavily on the *identification of key words or phrases* that signify specific aspects of the conceptualisation or thought process at hand. It often makes sense to start from manual analysis in order to identify such key terms. But once key terms have been established, the task of identifying them in the data can be delegated to the tool, saving much valuable time.

Excel, for example, can not only count words in a cell, but also the number of occurrences of a *specific* word in a cell (using another formula that can be found on the Internet). This can be done multiple times, in different columns. So if you want to see how the pronouns 'you' and 'I' are distributed in the data, let Excel do the search for 'you' in one column and for 'I' in another. Your analysis file can contain an unlimited number of columns with automatic word searches within the verbal data unit. This takes almost no time, and it allows the analyst to view at a glance how certain key words are distributed within the data.

If the distribution of a particular word is less important than the distribution of a concept that may be expressed by several different words, it is also possible to let the software identify and count more than one word at once, within just one column. This takes up less space, and allows the researcher to update calculations more quickly if a word is added to the search within a column.

Finally, software tools are obviously very suitable for calculations of any sort. This is a clear advantage over paper-based colour coding or other manual analysis that does not involve specific software. Once the analysis is accomplished in digital format, it can easily be turned into numbers, which can be processed further in a range of ways including statistical analysis. For example, you can sum up the number of words, or of occurrences of a specific word, or of any other identified feature produced by a participant, or produced within a content category. Such summary data are best represented in a separate file or tab, with a line for each participant so that all individual results can be accessed quickly (see Section 8.7).

8.5.4   Operationalisation of Linguistic Categories

Not all linguistic features are characterised by specific key words that can be identified (more or less) automatically. For example, you might be interested in verbalised thoughts that the speakers take for granted – see our discussion of information structure and presuppositions (implicit assumptions) in Chapter 3. If no automatic procedures (parsers or software tools) are available that can identify a target structure for you, you will need to do manual coding. Be warned: this can be quite time-consuming, and it requires inter-coder reliability tests (see Krippendorff, 2012, Tenbrink, 2015, and many other resources for details of this aspect).

Annotation of linguistic features is quite the opposite of intuitive, example-based analysis. Rather than picking out particularly striking instances of a particular feature, the aim in CODA is to look for patterns. How frequently, and under what circumstances, does the feature occur? Consider the example of presuppositions. Perhaps your study is directly relevant for gaining insights on presupposition use from the outset, motivated from the previous literature or your own research. Or you might discover, while gaining a deep understanding of your data during transcription and content analysis (or while listening and reading through the materials), that some people take specific aspects for granted, while others don't.

To start with, this is just an impression, not a fact that you can report – except for quoting examples. It may be a good idea to refine this impression towards a more specific hypothesis, aiming to get crystal clear what exactly your data may be telling you. Do you think there's a particular moment in the task procedure where some people take specific things for granted? What distinguishes the moment from others? What distinguishes people who do this from those who don't? What kinds of things are taken for granted, and which aren't? There are endless possibilities here, and only one solution: you need to examine your data systematically, so you get a clearer idea of what's going on. In other words, you need to go through your data file line by line, and identify the information structure for each single unit.

This will come with a number of challenges. It is worth thinking carefully about what you wish to do, and why. Once you start annotating, you are likely to spend quite a lot of time thinking about individual cases. Make sure you really need each of the annotations and codings that you do, and make sure that you know exactly what you are doing. For this purpose, you will need a very clearly formulated operationalisation of each analysis feature. Keeping a separate sheet or document in which you clarify or define what exactly happens in each column in your analysis sheet may be helpful. Some of these will be as easy as 'Number of words in a unit', but once you get started on manual case-by-case annotation, you will need a more elaborate annotation definition.

To continue our example, the concepts of *presupposition* and *information structure* may be clear enough from a theoretical point of view, but not all of your linguistic knowledge will be easy to turn into a clear-cut annotation process. The fact that some thoughts are taken for granted can be expressed in more than one way on a linguistic level, and you may need to decide which of them are useful for you to annotate. One very simple linguistic feature indicating presupposition is the definite article, as it indicates that something is already known in the discourse context, for whatever reason. In a verbal protocol or description, the definite article therefore indicates that the speaker is not introducing this particular element as new, as in the following examples:

Example 8.15 The red flag is partially hidden in the picture.
Example 8.16 I cannot see the red flag very well.

Whatever the context of these verbalisations may be, the speaker clearly indicates that the existence of a red flag is presupposed. If it wasn't, it would have been introduced by a phrase such as *a red flag*. The definite article is therefore uniquely clear in indicating presuppositions, and can be easily annotated. In the operationalisation, it makes sense to start by identifying all definite articles (which can be done automatically as explained above), and then, in a separate step (or column), indicate the phrase that is presupposed (such as 'the red flag'). This means considering each and every instance of a definite article in terms of what it signifies. Cases of doubt may then lead to further specifications to be entered into the written operationalisation of this analysis feature.

The goal of operationalisation is to enable annotators to do exactly the same analysis consistently throughout the entire data set. Even if you are doing the entire analysis on your own, you might find that spelling out exactly what you are doing will be very helpful both during the process and for future reference. With a very clear operationalisation, you should also be able to delegate the annotation task to someone else who would get to the same results as you. This is called inter-coder reliability, and it can be evaluated by measures such as Krippendorff's Alpha (Hayes & Krippendorff, 2007). Most journals expect a high inter-coder reliability value for manually annotated data in a publication.

Once you have broken down your targeted analysis feature into operationalisable, identifiable aspects, it should be relatively straightforward to work through the entire data set. An analysis procedure that relies mostly on intuitions and ad hoc decisions is awkward and time-consuming, and will almost certainly not be reliable in the end. In effect, if you don't invest the time required to operationalise your analysis meaningfully, you will invest much more time into doing a somewhat speculative analysis that you may not be able to publish, as it lacks systematicity. It is much better to identify a suitable operationalisation that can be clearly outlined and explained to future readers.

Ideally, procedures and decisions should be grounded in the literature sufficiently to be meaningful in the context of the research undertaken. For instance, the literature on presuppositions incorporates extensive discussions of the contribution and role of the definite article. This body of research should be considered in the operationalisation. On this basis, you should be able to subcategorise instances of the definite article on the basis of what they refer to: the previous discourse (if the *red flag* was mentioned before), the situation context (the *red flag* is directly visible), uniqueness (as when talking about *the moon*), and so on.

Other cases may not be as clear-cut, and it may require some research to identify relevant resources. Sometimes creative solutions for operationalisations may be the only way, as each study will open up some kind of new area of research. Be prepared to be innovative, but always do your analysis systematically, and be clear about what you are doing.

To take another example, you may want to analyse the types of spatial terms that speakers use in your study. A range of resources that classify spatial terms are available to guide you (e.g. Bateman et al., 2010), but you will still need your own definition as to how to operationalise the categorisation of spatial terms in your study. One way to do this is to specify the range of terms that are, for the purposes of your study, classified as one of the following:

(1) Projective: Terms (typically prepositions) whose 'interpretation relies on the additional step of fixing an underlying reference system ..., defined relative to the speaker or hearer, or with respect to some object's intrinsic or imposed orientation properties ('my left' vs. 'your left', 'the front of the church', or 'in front of the rolling ball', etc.).' (Bateman et al., 2010:1030). Examples: *front, back, right, left, up, down, above, below,* ...

(2) Topological: ...

(3) Path-related: ...

(4) Compass based: ...

(5) Other

This example demonstrates three essential aspects of linguistic annotation. First, it is useful (though not always feasible) to have a clear list of options. If you annotate the spatial terms in your study, you should be able to choose from a limited range of options. So, upon encountering the phrase *to the left* in your data, you can choose the feature 'projective' in the annotation file. Second, define each option on the basis of the literature as far as possible, as well as providing examples, as done here for projective terms in (1). Third, to allow for further cases without requiring new decisions with every new word, an 'Other' category (as in (5)) is very useful. Likewise, the examples provided in (1) are not exhaustive, allowing for annotating further words in the same way if they fit the definition.

Along with this, your annotation definition file should be explicit as to whether annotation variants are mutually exclusive, or whether it is possible to attach more than one feature at a time to a word or unit. If the above list is used to annotate all spatial terms within a unit of analysis such as a sentence, then it is unlikely that the features are mutually exclusive, as spatial terms may be combined in a phrase or sentence.

Mutually exclusive features are typically preferable, as they facilitate quantitative analysis. It may take some consideration to prepare your annotation file in such a way as to enable mutually exclusive annotation. For instance, the above list of spatial terms could be broken up into different columns (if done in Excel). This allows for the number of spatial terms of a particular category (projective, topological, etc.) to be counted separately for each unit of analysis. Alternatively, you may extract individual spatial terms from your language data, and annotate them one by one, choosing from the above list. Both methods render your list of spatial terms mutually exclusive.

In sum, following a good grasp (and possibly categorisation) of the content of your language data, you will typically decide on a set of linguistic categories that may either be semi-automatically identifiable or require manual annotation. Wherever manual annotation is involved, it is most decisive to develop a clear and consistent operationalisation. This can start from intuitions, but should be iteratively developed until it reaches a state where it can be easily communicated to and adopted by other analysts.

8.6   Qualitative Insights

Most CODA studies combine qualitative and quantitative insights. As described in Section 8.5, analysts often move from the observation of a particular feature via a hypothesis as to its distribution to the identification of patterns in the data, based on systematic annotation. However, my emphasis of systematic analysis doesn't mean that qualitative insights aren't valuable, or (taking these thoughts further) that only statistically significant results should be considered. Let's take a closer look at the range of qualitative insights that can be gained from a close analysis of language data in relation to cognition.

First, the mere existence of a particular feature in the data can be a valuable result if it is unexpected or previously unreported. In Hölscher et al. (2011) (see Chapter 7), one of our research questions concerned whether people plan a route ahead if they know the environment well. Previous literature had been unclear on this point, and so it was regarded as a real possibility that the entire route plan is laid out in people's heads in advance, requiring no further planning effort during navigation. Alternatively, they might not bother to plan ahead very much at all, and simply head off in a direction, specifying the details of their route as they go.

Supporting the second alternative, we identified multiple indications of ongoing planning processes in the think-aloud protocols during navigation. All participants referred to intentions, decisions, and current planning processes as they walked to their goal. Among the relevant linguistic markers for planning processes we found modal verbs such as *could, should, might,* verbs of thinking such as *consider, think, decide,* and discourse markers such as *whether, or, if, better,* and *maybe.* These linguistic choices cannot be explained if all of the planning is completed beforehand. Since there was no comparison to be made in this regard, the *existence* of these markers was an important qualitative result in our study, and the analysis could have stopped here. However, we added detailed information on the quantitative distribution of these markers in the data, in order to be as specific as possible.

Second, it can be very interesting to scrutinise individual participants' conceptualisations and cognitive processes. Case studies of conceptualisations or thought processes can serve as illuminative examples; they demonstrate the existence or possibility of a particular way of thinking, and show in detail how this might work. In Tenbrink and Salwiczek (2016) (see Chapter 4), we set out with the sole intention to identify quantitative patterns in the linguistic features of the think-aloud data collected in our study. Much of our report does indeed represent statistical distributions, but there is also a sense of certain limitations of this approach. Some of the results simply did not fit into the overall picture, and the overall picture itself did not correspond clearly to any of the previously identified hypotheses.

To gain clarity on these issues, we needed to take a closer look at individual cases. It turned out that our participants used a wide range of cognitive strategies to solve the task given to them. The different verbalisations were highly revealing about the range of possibilities in this respect. Presenting and discussing individual case studies in our report therefore allowed us to account for the unexpected quantitative patterns in our results much more clearly.

Finally, sometimes the distribution of patterns in the data as such can be reported in (more or less) qualitative terms. The idea here is to provide a general impression or a first understanding of what is happening in the scenario at hand. Not everything can be expressed in terms of statistical significance, and not everything needs to be. Unconstrained language production data, as collected in CODA studies, are notoriously difficult as a basis for statistical analysis; there are limits to what a researcher can realistically expect in this regard. Nevertheless, a qualitative description of a certain balance in the data can be interesting and revealing, and it is likely to lead to the formulation of more specific hypotheses that can be tested in a targeted way. On this basis, reaching statistical significance in targeted follow-up studies is far more realistic.

In spite of the clear benefits of reporting qualitative findings, you might find that they are more difficult to publish, and some reviewers may advise against including observations that cannot be 'proven' statistically. There is a certain danger in assuming that a p-value can actually decide about the extent to which a particular finding is relevant for the academic audience of a publication. Statistical significance should not be confused with relevance; both are important, and have, or should have, their rightful place in academic reports.

To make a particular qualitative result relevant for a readership, it is perhaps even more important to observe the principles of rigorous analysis. It is absolutely necessary to be as specific as possible, providing details gained through in-depth analysis. It is equally essential to relate observations to the previous literature, contributing insightfully to a theoretical discussion rather than speculating about the possible relevance for it.

Perhaps the most important trap to avoid concerns unwarranted general-isations. Ad hoc individual examples picked out from a data set do not necessarily add up to a pattern. Without further analysis or a clear relation to the literature, they do not even represent a qualitative result. The mere fact that a phenomenon is found in your data does not necessarily mean much at all, if this fact doesn't answer a question, clarify a controversy, or represent a new discovery. The fact that one person uses language in a particular way does not prove that these linguistic features are predominant in your data set, or that other people in the same situation would do the same. Your impression that something happens more than something else is not enough – you will need to show this systematically, through clearly operationalised analysis that looks at the entire data set in an unbiased way. Typically, quantitative formulations like 'more' or 'rarely' in a report will invoke the natural expectation that numbers should be provided, and a statistical test should follow.

8.7   Quantitative Patterns

Moving on from qualitative insights, you may wish to identify the ways in which the observed phenomena are spread across participants. Most CODA studies involve different experimental conditions, designed to identify the influence of a specific factor on the linguistic choices that speakers make. Comparing the results in relation to conditions is therefore a natural next step once annotation is completed.

If you followed the procedures in Section 8.5, using a software tool like Excel, you will now be looking at an extensive analysis sheet with many annotations and automatically generated numbers. To get a clearer idea about patterns, you will need to transfer summary results into another sheet. Here, I would recommend allowing one row per participant, with separate columns for participant number, demographic data like gender, age, and native language, overall word count, and then the more specific analysis results: for example, word count in a particular subtask, overall count of each linguistic feature in the participant's data set, count of linguistic features in a particular subtask, and the like. There can be an unlimited number of columns, showing different summary results in overview fashion.

Figure 8.2 gives an example for an analysis spreadsheet, again (like Figure 8.1 in Section 8.5.2) from our origami study (Tenbrink & Taylor, 2015). Columns A–C give participant number and demographic data, and there are a number of further columns (not visible here) with further information pertaining to individual participants. Column S gives the total number of analysis units produced by each participant, and column T the number of words. Columns U and V reflect numbers of occurrences of individual content categories that we identified in the data (additional ideas about object quality and spatial description, respectively); for instance, participant number 1 mentioned spatial descriptions five times, but never commented on object quality.

	A	B	C	S	T	U	V
1	part. number	native language	gender	stem_ no. of units	stem_total number of words	stem_additio nal_objqual	stem_additio nal spatial desc.
2	1	English	Male	55	429	0	5
3	2	English	Female	67	408	0	0
4	3	English	Male	30	288	0	0
5	4	English	Female	48	400	0	1
6	5	English	Male	124	865	0	0
7	6	English	Male	62	335	0	0

Figure 8.2 Spreadsheet for the analysis in Tenbrink and Taylor (2015).

On this basis, you can then begin to do some easy calculations. To start with, it often makes sense to look at relative frequencies, rather than absolute numbers. Participants will vary a lot in the amount of language they produce in a task. Imagine that person A produces 150 words in a task, and person B produces 40 words. Now, if you're investigating a linguistic feature such as presuppositions, operationalised on the basis of definite articles, you might find that person A used 'the' ten times, and person B used 'the' four times. Does this mean that person A relied more on presuppositions than person B?

With this simple example, you'll probably see right away that this can't be true, as Person A used more words overall. To calculate this effect, we can simply divide the sum of definite articles by the overall number of words, and we'll find that person A used 'the' with a frequency of 10/150=0.067, as opposed to person B with 4/40=0.1 – so the frequency at which 'the' is used is higher for person B. If persons A and B were part of different conditions, we could then look at whether there is an overall pattern there: perhaps person B's condition generally leads to the use of fewer words but more presuppositions, for whatever reason.

Calculating relative frequencies on the basis of the overall word count is the simplest way of looking for patterns. However, this is not always meaningful; sometimes you may want to look at units rather than words. For instance, in Vorwerg and Tenbrink (2007) (see Section 8.3) we asked participants to describe simple pictures showing abstract object configurations, one at a time. Answers varied greatly in length, such as the following (taken from our German data set):

Example 8.17   über dem Quadrat
                [above the square]

Example 8.18   das mit einem x markierte Quadrat ist oberhalb etwas mehr
links von dem anderen Quadrat
[the square marked by an x is higher than and somewhat
more to the left of the other square]

While word count mattered in many ways, it was also important for us to look at the linguistic features within a unit, which in this study corresponded to a picture description, regardless of length or syntactical construction. Therefore, many of the calculations in our analysis were based on units rather than relative to the overall word count. Note that this decision depended on the fact that units were very clearly defined. In this study, this was easy because picture descriptions were short enough to lead to feasible units of analysis.

Overall word count and units are often useful as a basis for calculating relative frequencies, but they may not be the only options. You will need to consider carefully what kind of percentage makes sense in your case. For instance, you might wish to calculate the frequency of a particular type of linguistic feature relative to all words produced in a particular content category only, rather than all the words in the data set. Similarly, you might wish to look at the relative frequency of a certain word within all occurrences of a particular linguistic feature.

Calculating meaningful relative frequencies and comparing them will give you a first indication of possible patterns in the data. For some purposes, presenting such patterns in a descriptive way may be sufficient. However, in most cases inferential statistics will be required so as to test for significance, moving beyond a mere representation of linguistic patterns in the data. This book is not the place for introducing statistical methods – there are plenty of very useful resources for this. Once you have identified possible patterns, you should aim to find suitable statistical procedures to test them. In many cases, ANOVA, t-tests, chi-square, or regression tests will be good choices in CODA studies, but sometimes more complicated procedures may be required.

Statistical tests are most meaningful if they are based on well-founded hypotheses. With the procedures described here, you might find multiple interesting patterns in your data that may or may not be statistically significant. It is important to avoid getting lost in the data or in the wealth of possible comparisons. Typically, the best starting point for statistical analysis is the one that motivated your study. Start with the patterns and comparisons you aimed to make in the first place. Compare results between conditions, as they were designed to induce differences. Keep your research question in mind: not all patterns are meaningful from a theoretical point of view. Everything may be related to everything else, but it still doesn't make sense to look at every single possible interrelationship.

Instead, it is advisable to keep statistical tests within reasonable limits. If you do multiple calculations on a complex data set, you are likely to find some statistically significant differences – but they are not necessarily interesting. There is a non-trivial chance that some statistical tests will turn out to be *randomly* significant. For this reason, some journals require that all statistical tests that were carried out need to be reported, regardless of whether they turned out to be significant and further pursued. So it is wise to be careful. With a theoretically well-motivated study, you should be able to gain relevant statistically significant results on the basis of only a few (ideally pre-planned) calculations; and if you don't, this might be an interesting result in itself.

These considerations also relate to the idea of randomisation in your design, as mentioned in Section 8.2. Factors like sociodemographic background, gender, order of tasks, and the like will almost certainly affect your results in some way, but you cannot concentrate on all of them at the same time. If you aim for statistical comparisons on any one of those factors, make sure to design the study in such a way that this factor is a central one, implemented as an independent variable in the conditions of your study. Otherwise, if not central, keep them random. Randomised factors will normally not be targeted in your statistical analysis, other than ruling out possible distorting effects. If in doubt, do consult a statistics expert on these considerations.

Most importantly, your quantitative analysis must be motivated from a theoretical perspective, and this will be the basis for the 'story' to tell in a published report of your study. Reporting numbers as such, including potentially random statistically significant results, is rarely meaningful. However, set against a strong theoretical background, even non-significant or marginally significant patterns can make a compelling point. In that case, statistical significance can only make the effect stronger.

This chapter has laid out some of the main procedural considerations that have guided CODA studies in the past. It is worth keeping in mind that the basic idea for CODA is to analyse language use in relation to thought; the precise way in which this is done is up to the researcher and will depend on the research question at hand. In this light, this chapter may provide practical guidance for readers new to research of this kind, and it illustrates how procedures may be carried out without requiring specialist software or any other more sophisticated tools. Experienced researchers may decide to carry out a CODA study using a very different approach. Any systematic study of language use that sheds light on cognition certainly falls within the scope of 'cognitive discourse analysis', CODA.

9   Beyond CODA

Identifying thoughts and concepts through language analysis is fun and can be intensely rewarding and enlightening in itself. New discoveries, answers to questions you've had for a long time, support for an assumption that you couldn't prove before, or evidence that you've been completely wrong about something: all of these things can happen as you set out to identify patterns in discourse, making your research relevant to yourself and others.

But CODA is not necessarily a tool to be used in isolation. More often than not, CODA will be part of a larger endeavour, one analysis method alongside others. My own involvement with the method originated in the necessity to access linguistic evidence systematically in interdisciplinary projects working towards goals that were frequently practical. For instance, how can we enable a dialogue system to interact naturally with users (Cuayáhuitl et al., 2010)? How do we make a robot understand intuitive commands (Moratz & Tenbrink, 2006)? How can we make sense of people's responses to a seemingly simple behavioural task (Tenbrink & Salwiczek, 2016)? Or simply, how do we understand how people actually plan routes (Hölscher et al., 2011)?

As language is often just one way in which task-related thought processes and concepts are represented, CODA can easily be combined with other methods. Likewise, analysis results can be used for a multitude of applications and purposes, including implementation in automatic systems that support human everyday needs. This chapter will explore these kinds of extensions to CODA, using examples from earlier work to illustrate the scope. Section 9.1 looks at triangulation with other methods, and Section 9.2 outlines a range of applied purposes. Just like most insights shared in this book, there is no intention to be exhaustive; this chapter is meant for inspiration, highlighting pathways towards fruitful triangulation and innovative applications.

9.1   Triangulation: Combinations with Other Methods

CODA as a method emerged from an interest in the human mind, and as such can be regarded as one of many methods in cognitive science. At the same time, it is informed by insights and experiences from linguistics and discourse analysis, as explored in Chapter 3. In these and other ways, CODA naturally links up with various disciplines. A linguist may combine a CODA study of natural discourse with a wider discussion of grammatical phenomena, set against theories of form and function, or inspired by insights in cognitive linguistics (see Carroll & von Stutterheim, 1993, and Ferrari, 2007 for related approaches). A psycholinguist may identify patterns in linguistic choices that shed light on language production processes in the brain (Habel & Tappe, 1999; Vorwerg, 2009). A critical discourse analyst may find substantive evidence from a cognitive perspective (Hart & Lukeš, 2009; Knapton & Rundblad, 2014). And a sociologist may relate demographic patterns identified through questionnaires to a CODA analysis of natural discourse, collected through descriptions, interviews, or focus groups (Kristiansen & Dirven, 2008; Pütz, Robinson, & Reif, 2014). CODA, then, contributes one decisive part of the evidence, allowing for an in-depth discussion of the bigger picture emerging from the entire data set. Such combinations can bridge important gaps, such as those between interactional and cognitive approaches to language.

Within cognitive science, methods to access the human mind are abundant. In the following sections we will take a closer look at a few of them, to see how each plays out in combination with CODA. Section 9.1.1 will start with directly observable data such as behavioural performance, Section 9.1.2 will look at subtler cues such as reaction times, eye tracking, and neuroimaging data, and Section 9.1.3 addresses cognitive modelling. Beyond cognitive science, Section 9.1.4 will look at CODA in relation to corpus linguistics.

9.1.1   Performance and Other Observable Data

Many tasks that involve collecting language data in relation to thought also come with some kind of challenge. That challenge can typically be measured in a number of ways. People may be more or less successful in doing the task, they may solve it in more than one way, and they may be more or less efficient. In fact, this variability is frequently one of the main reasons for doing the study in the first place: what kinds of pathways do people use for solving the task, how exactly do they do it, and what is the most promising or successful pathway?

Obviously, what exactly can be measured along these lines, apart from language data, depends on the study. Having clear success criteria and defining suitable ways to assess solution pathways are among the most important design criteria for a study. Not all studies involve an element of success; this is not a necessary prerequisite for research on human thought. For instance, if people are asked to describe a film they saw or a scene they remember, there may be no clear success criteria. One may measure the number of words or of details described, or look at the time people take, or analyse the diversity of observed phenomena; all of this may shed light on the research question behind the study.

Here, I will illustrate triangulation with performance data by using another CODA study as an example. Our collaborative work in Gralla et al. (2012) was motivated by previous research that had identified two distinct ways of solving problems on the basis of analogy. Analogy is a powerful way of solving problems by comparison with other problems that one has seen before. For instance, if you are trying to solve a riddle, it will often help you to think of other riddles of a similar kind. Many problems relate to other problems in some way; the more experienced you are, the easier it will be for you to solve new problems based on analogy with known ones.

The two ways of doing this are as follows. On the one hand, the problem solver might find that the problems are similar enough to enable a simple transfer of the solution from one problem to another, with only slight adaptations to match the new problem. This is called transformational problem solving because the solution is transformed as needed. On the other hand, in derivational problem solving, the analogy lies in the problem-solving process itself. The new problem is solved by going through the solution steps one by one, solving the new problem using the solution pathway from the known one.

It seems clear from this distinction that derivational problem solving involves a deeper understanding of the problem and its solution. A simple transfer of the solution might mean that the new problem wasn't considered in depth at all. Therefore, we were interested in finding out more about when people choose which strategy, and how they could be guided towards using the derivational problem-solving strategy for problems with clear analogies.

We (Gralla et al., 2012) adopted a study design that combined the collection of language data with other methods that had previously been used to look into strategy choice. Participants were first encouraged to think of analogies through a story where one problem was solved on the basis of analogy to another problem. After reading the story, they were shown an example problem that involved identifying a complex path trajectory, given a set of constraints. The solution was explained in detail, supported by a line graph with letters indicating places (a so-called *Eulerian trail*). Next, they were presented with another problem that could be solved using a similar strategy, so they should be able to use analogy.

There were two conditions that were intended to support either the transformational or the derivational strategy. In the high-guidance condition, the initials of target words used in the second problem were identical to those in the example problem, which meant that the same letters could be used to find the solution graph. This would enable a direct transfer of the solution from one problem to the other. In the low-guidance condition, this was not the case, necessitating a more in-depth problem-solving process using the derivational strategy. Furthermore, we varied conditions with respect to the collection of language data. Whereas one-third of participants did not produce any language apart from responses to a questionnaire, two-thirds of participants were asked to do two written tasks each. In particular, altogether we collected the following data:

- Demographic data.
- Correctness of solutions.
- Overall time needed.
- Time needed specifically to map the letters onto the new problem.
- A third of the participants were asked to write planning protocols describing how they would solve the task before they actually solved it.
- After they solved the problem, these same participants were asked to write evaluations of their previous plans.
- Another third of the participants were asked to write reports on the problem-solving process after they solved it.
- Then, participants in this group were also asked to write an instruction for a friend to solve the problem.
- Finally, a questionnaire was given to all participants asking how they solved the task, containing a range of questions pertaining to transformational or derivational strategies.

These different linguistic and non-linguistic data gave us a solid basis for insights into the cognitive processes and strategies used in analogical problem solving. As expected, participants in the low-guidance condition used the derivational strategy, whereas participants in the high-guidance condition used the transformational strategy. Transformation was quicker than derivation, and questionnaires as well as the diverse types of written language data confirmed participants' strategy choice, spelling out in detail how this was achieved. In addition, the verbal data revealed that some people may have recognised the analogy but then applied the solution path in a wrong way when using the derivational strategy. As a result, solutions based on transformation tended to be better.

We can conclude from this example study that looking at other data beyond language in CODA studies does not have to be difficult, and it can be very revealing. Most CODA studies to date have used more than one type of data. Correctness and time needed plus further behavioural aspects are typical data to collect in problem-solving studies. But triangulation can also mean eliciting more than one type of linguistic data, such as the planning protocols, evaluations, reports, and instructions in our study.

9.1.2   Subtle Cues

Readily observable data such as those described in the previous section are easy to collect; accuracy of the solution, questionnaires, and time can usually be assessed without specialist equipment. However, such measures only offer part of the picture, and (like the analysis of language) are most suited to address higher-level cognitive processes. Cognitive scientists have developed a wide range of further, more subtle methods that are intended to go deeper, to provide insights about cognitive activities that remain below the threshold of participants' consciousness.

There is a lot to be gained by looking at the amount of time needed for a task, and this can often be measured with a simple everyday device. However, in some kinds of tasks this is not sufficient. In psycholinguistics, for instance, it is common to measure reaction times on the level of milliseconds. As outlined in Chapter 2, psycholinguists are interested in the cognitive processing of language, and this happens very quickly. Participants in psycholinguistic studies can be asked to read something and react to it in a particular way, or to look at a cue and produce language in relation to it. The answers will be provided within a second or two, and precise measurements are needed to identify any significant differences between conditions.

In traditional psycholinguistic experimentation, participants typically have to choose between two possible answers. This amount of experimental control means that reaction times can be directly compared. In CODA, in contrast, speakers are encouraged to make their own linguistic choices when producing language. Both approaches can be combined: subtle differences in reaction times can amount to meaningful patterns even in scenarios involving unconstrained language use. However, this kind of triangulation requires a careful design. It would have to be a very limited scenario that naturally constrains the range of things that people will spontaneously say (or write).

For example, imagine an experimental pragmaticist who is interested in examining the cognitive effort it takes to express a wish for fresh air in a room. This kind of scenario is exemplary for raising concerns about politeness and levels of formality, tapping into the communication side of language use (see Chapter 7). Participants could read an introductory scenario that describes the need for fresh air in a specific communicative context. While one may ask for a window to be opened in many different ways, it is likely that specific phrases would be preferred over others, limiting the range of things people will say. Also, specific aspects of the situation would be represented in the participants' linguistic choices, highlighting how they conceive of the situation. Measuring precise reaction times (i.e. the time needed to formulate a response after reading the scenario description) would then add to the evidence, as some linguistic choices may readily come to mind, whereas others require more time to work out.

In scenarios where participants are asked to react to visual input, it can also make sense to analyse when and how they are looking at the visuals. Eye-tracking methods are useful for the analysis of attention focus, and as such can be meaningfully combined with CODA (see Chapter 4). While speakers' linguistic choices reveal their focus of attention as expressed in language, eye-tracking data are much more fine-grained and subtle. They can therefore reveal implicit patterns of attention of which participants are rarely aware (Grant & Spivey, 2003).

Eye-tracking technology has developed rapidly in recent years and is now available at a much lower cost than previously. Also, the equipment has become less obtrusive, now causing only a little disruption to participants during experiments. Given this improved situation, research increasingly incorporates eye tracking alongside other methods. Elling, Lentz, and De Jong (2012) specifically revisited the combination of think-aloud protocols with eye tracking. They found that this kind of triangulation can be particularly useful as it means collecting two highly compatible types of evidence that can easily be matched.

In particular, Elling et al. (2012) looked at types of verbalised content that correlated with specific eye movements, as well as times when people did not speak but still looked at the visual input. While some of the categories represented in people's verbalisations could also be inferred from the eye-tracking data, further insights were gained by analysing verbalised observations and explanations. It seems only natural that the content expressed in language provides more meaningful elaboration than the information that can be gathered from what people look at. At the same time, the eye-tracking data proved particularly useful for filling the gaps when people did not speak. It turned out that silences were times when people did either one of three things: reading, scanning, or fixating. This means that they were busy taking in information from the visual input, rather than actively thinking and representing their thoughts in language.

While measuring reaction times and eye tracking involve specialist equipment and knowledge for analysis, they are still relatively accessible and widespread. Such methods are suitable for analysing subtle cues that indirectly point to cognitive processes, but they do not address the actual activities in the brain. For this, more sophisticated tools are required. The most well-known techniques are electroencephalograms (EEG), which measure electrical activity in the brain, and functional magnetic resonance imaging (fMRI), which records changes associated with blood flow. Both of these techniques provide insights on the activation of particular parts of the brain. Based on increasing knowledge about how brain activities are distributed, this kind of evidence can be used to gain insights about particular brain functions related to given tasks.

In a recent study, fMRI was used to address the extent to which thinking aloud corresponds to actual thought (Durning et al., 2013). Because jaw movements would disturb the brain imaging data, the authors had to be creative in their experimental design. Participants were trained to think aloud and then had to answer a range of multiple-choice questions in the area of medicine. Then, a phase began which the authors called 'thinking aloud' – but this was not literally true. They asked participants to formulate in their minds how they arrived at the solution, as if speaking their thoughts out loud but without actually doing so. Then, after coming out of the fMRI scanner, participants produced formal verbal reports. Thus, in effect, the authors elicited retrospective reports rather than think-aloud protocols, and they did this in two steps, the first of which yielded fMRI data related to a silent thought process.

The results of this intriguing study show various interesting patterns. There were fMRI differences between the question-answering phase and the silent think-aloud phase, but these were only gradual, rather than revealing activities in different parts of the brain. The authors account for each of these differences in detail, showing that they can be traced back to the different activities involved in question-answering and thinking aloud. Altogether, they conclude that thinking aloud can be regarded as true evidence of thought processes, which is an encouraging result given that collecting verbal data is much cheaper and easier to achieve than brain imaging.

In another intriguing study, Lutz et al. (2002) addressed the variability of EEG data by gathering additional evidence through verbal reports. Variability can be a major problem for EEG analysis, because the same electrical brain activity is hard to reproduce even with identical tasks. This is attributed to the fact that participants' thoughts will vary each time they do the task, which cannot be avoided. Lutz et al. (2002) reasoned that if people remember their thoughts each time they do a task, some generalised effects may be identified that help deal with the variability in EEG data. Their results showed, among other things, that discrepancies in the EEG patterns could be related to the extent to which participants were ready to perceive the image they were shown. This was mostly the case; being mentally ready is typically expected as part of an experimental study. However, sometimes people can be distracted, and this has direct effects on the EEG data. Participants' reports on this and other effects were systematically related to EEG variability. Again, this illustrates the value of triangulation and also supports the validity of using verbal reports as evidence for cognitive processes.

In sum, there are a range of methods that provide evidence concerning cognitive processes that are too low level to be reflected in language. Such types of data require more equipment and expertise to collect, but once available they can be extremely valuable in combination with CODA.

9.1.3   Cognitive Modelling

As we have seen in earlier chapters, one frequent motivation for doing CODA is to identify how people solve problems or make complex decisions. Results can be simply reported as such, as they provide useful insights to the field in general. However, studies of complex thought are often part of a wider endeavour that aims to capture cognitive processes on a fine-grained basis, adding up to entire theories about how the human mind works. This is called cognitive modelling, and it is done in a range of different ways, including diagrammatic and informal as well as formal ways of representing cognitive processes. Most prominently, in artificial intelligence, cognitive modelling means implementing procedures into simulations of the human mind. The resulting computational systems incorporate established insights about human cognitive processes combined with a range of mechanisms that can only be hypothesised at the current state of research.

As outlined in Chapter 2, language can represent many cognitive processes, but certainly not all of them. Much of what goes on in our minds happens at a very low level and does not reach consciousness, and therefore doesn't get to be verbalised. Cognitive modelling typically aims to capture just those low-level cognitive processes, which means that gaps in the existing evidence need to be filled based on theory. As such, cognitive models cover the full range of cognitive processes from conscious human decisions and strategies through to neural activities. The result of a computationally implemented cognitive model can then be compared with observable insights from various sources, including language data, feeding back into improved models. Thus, new insights gained on the basis of linguistic analysis can be very useful for filling in gaps or correcting erroneous assumptions in existing cognitive models.

Verbal reports as data provide the general structure of a thought process to be modelled. If speakers differ in their verbalised strategies, joint patterns can be extracted as far as possible with the aim of developing a consistent cognitive model. Alternatively, several different solution paths can be modelled and their results compared, such as thought processes in novices as opposed to experts. Either way, the more detailed cognitive processes are typically still underdetermined and could be implemented in various different ways. At the same time, the overall cognitive model can serve to explain differences in the verbalisations, as people may have different strategies for verbalising their thoughts. In that sense, triangulation works both ways, with each method complementing and informing the other.

Aspects that will not be verbalised include motor actions, visual processing, knowledge retrieval, and the like. We can report or talk about what we do, but not exactly how we do it. We can say *I am lifting my arm* and *I see a car* and *I remember doing this before* – but the neural activities that result in the arm being lifted aren't accessible to us, and we can't explain how we recognise the car as a car, or what our eyes are doing, or how we activated the memory that we refer to. Here cognitive modelling can help make predictions about the non-verbalised steps and cognitive processes, since there may be more than one possibility, but the number of computational models that generate similar results as in humans will be far more limited.

Cognitive models can represent the different ways in which problems can be solved in terms of cognitive shortcuts or solution paths. For instance, imagine a child trying to solve an addition like 3 + 4. The child won't have a ready solution in their head, and so will have to put various types of knowledge together to reach the answer. In contrast, adults can retrieve the solution directly by simply accessing knowledge built up from previous experience. Along these lines, conscious cognitive processes become automatised implicit processes over time.

One of the most established and long-standing cognitive modelling architectures that is suitable for capturing these and many other phenomena is called ACT-R (Adaptive Control of Thought – Rational; Anderson & Lebiere, 1998). ACT-R was initiated by John Anderson at Carnegie Mellon University and has been continuously developed since the 1970s. The architecture covers mechanisms and procedures across all cognitive levels and modules, ranging from low-level processes far beyond a person's awareness to high-level decisions that can be easily reported in language. More recent approaches may increasingly use other techniques such as Hidden Markov or Bayesian models, but still often relate to insights gained through the more traditional ACT-R architecture (e.g. Zhang, Walsh, & Anderson, 2018).

Some ACT-R models are based directly on verbal reports. For example, Gugerty and Rodes (2007) presented an ACT-R model of the strategies and cognitive processes involved in cardinal direction judgements. They gave participants a quite demanding task where they looked at a scene from above, as if from an airplane, and had to match the scene with a north-aligned map. Then, they were asked to state the compass direction between two places that they saw from above, such as a parking lot located *to the west* of a building. Verbal protocols revealed that participants used diverse kinds of strategies to solve this problem. Gugerty and Rodes (2007) combined this evidence with further insights in the literature about human direction concepts and other processes that were not directly reported by participants. On this basis, they developed a cognitive model in ACT-R that plausibly demonstrates how humans get to a solution for this kind of problem.

Other approaches focus on the sequential steps to reach a target directly, without dealing with the lower-level cognitive processes. Such so-called process models can be expressed in semi-formal representations such as the one in Figure 9.1, which may or may not be implemented computationally. Verbal protocols are very informative in this regard, and content analysis is typically sufficient to account for the sequential steps very well. However, think-aloud protocols often contain a range of hypotheses that turn out to be false, and other trains of thought that are not pursued any further. Process models may or may

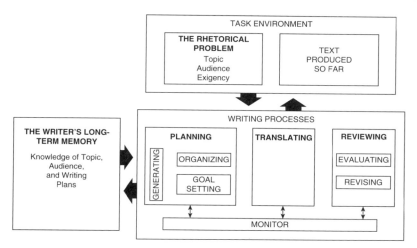

Figure 9.1 A process model of writing (Flower & Hayes, 1981).

not include such false leads, depending on how authentic they aim to be. Linguistic analysis can provide very clear accounts of thought sequences, particularly if the temporal order is considered rather than treating the data as an undifferentiated corpus (see Chapter 8). For instance, false starts and hesitations at certain decisive moments may be indicative of specific cognitive steps.

Cognitive modelling researchers are typically experts on the modelling side of things, rather than on the analysis of verbal protocols. As a result, models may be built on somewhat limited evidence, such as insights gained from a single person rather than on a controlled language elicitation design that would be more typical for CODA studies. An in-depth under-standing of one person's cognitive processes as a case study can be highly informative, but it is unclear to what extent such insights can be general-ised. Also, most existing approaches are informed by the directly obser-vable content of verbal protocols only, extracting whatever seems relevant for the modelling purposes at hand.

Combination with CODA can enhance this approach, ranging from refining the experimental design via more systematic content analysis to the identifica-tion of in-depth linguistic aspects. For instance, linguistic analysis can associ-ate cognitive steps with linguistic structure, and confirm content-based evidence by linguistic theory. Such additional evidence provides a more solid basis for analysis, allowing for enhanced confidence in the annotation proce-dure as well as well-informed data interpretation.

As with any CODA studies, it will be important to narrow the scope of linguistic feature analysis down to those aspects that are particularly decisive for the purposes at hand, in this case cognitive modelling. The analyst might focus on particularly interesting steps in a cognitive process and identify the variability of linguistic markers for specific aspects rather than aiming at representing the entire process, which would not realistically be feasible in most cases. Possible analysis foci include investigating the level of granularity with which the speakers conceive of a problem-solving step, how certain they are, or which perspective on a situation they adopt (see previous chapters).

Also, it can be worthwhile to take a closer look at 'non-sequiturs', that is, conclusions that aren't based on previously verbalised thoughts, or other kinds of jumps in the verbal report's logic. People verbalising their thoughts are asked to simply express what they are thinking, so they don't necessarily make sure that their line of argument is solid and obvious. However, the way they formulate any 'jumps' in the argument might reveal how they got from one thought to the other. There may be instances of presupposition or specific discourse markers that shed some light on the underlying train of thought that didn't get to be verbalised completely (see Chapter 3). Also, there may be traces in the language that indicate the sources of new insights. The analyst may identify the speaker's information status and attention focus at a decisive point in time, leading to a possible explanation of non-sequential conceptual aspects.

Computational procedures have become increasingly sophisticated and accessible to non-computer experts. As a result, the implementation of insights on complex cognitive processes in computational modelling approaches offers a growing resource for a wide range of applications and purposes. CODA-based insights can contribute decisively in this regard, as they build a bridge between directly verbalised content and more intricate conceptual aspects that are reflected in language only implicitly.

9.1.4   Corpus Linguistics

In terms of a final example for triangulation, we will have a brief look at corpus linguistics. This well-established approach has many applications, some of which are related to cognitive aspects. As noted in Chapter 2, corpus linguistic studies tend to be on the other side of the scale with respect to experimental control, compared to typical CODA studies. In corpus-based studies, language data are collected across scenarios and speaker categories. The resulting corpora are analysed with respect to general patterns in language use, for instance in a language (like English) as a whole or within a specific dialect or sociolect (like Scouse or Cockney). However, more specific applications are also possible, as corpus linguistic methods can be rather varied.

Corpus linguistic research draws on a range of sophisticated software tools, such as WordSmith or the UaM corpus tool. Such tools can identify word frequencies, collocations, grammatical distributions, and the like, and they can be used to compare different corpora, or different parts of the same corpus, to each other. The Internet offers ample information on these and other tools, as well as rich resources of linguistic corpora that are readily available for analysis (the LINGUIST List website is an excellent starting point: https://linguistlist .org). One well-known example is the British National Corpus (BNC), which contains 100 million words from a rich diversity of sources and has been regarded as representative for British spoken and written language for a long time. Unfortunately, as the corpus is getting older, it is no longer unanimously recognised as up to date. For American English, a rich and regularly updated freely available resource is the COCA corpus, with more than 560 million words that fall into various categories.

Any corpus linguistic study will need to investigate carefully what kind of resource is most suitable for current research purposes. Corpora vary not only with respect to their age and size, but each of them comes with further features. Some of the available corpora were collected for very specific purposes, or even within a controlled scenario (see Danino, 2018). For instance, our 'Dolldialogue' study on furnishing a doll's house (Tenbrink et al., 2017) resulted in a small corpus of about 85,000 words, which is now available online (http://dolldialogue.space) along with photographs of the furnished houses and anonymised participant information. Naturally it is always possible to collect or compile a new corpus for the purposes of a study that requires a specific type of linguistic data.

This is where CODA and corpus linguistics meet. Like traditional corpus linguistic approaches, CODA examines the features of language data in linguistic data sets. It does so with respect to the mind, based on controlled scenarios, and it uses a range of analysis methods beyond those available through corpus software. Despite these differences to traditional corpus approaches, some aspects of CODA can definitely benefit from corpus tools. For instance, if the occurrence of specific words or phrases has been identified as relevant in the collected data, their distribution and collocations can be investigated meaningfully using corpus tools.

Also, it can be very enlightening to compare their occurrence in a small CODA corpus with a larger reference corpus. If people use a specific phrase frequently in the context in which the data for the CODA study were collected, this may either mean that the phrase is decisive for this particular scenario, or it may simply be a frequently used phrase in the language the speakers use in general. A systematic comparison with a reference corpus (ideally with millions of words) provides evidence in either direction.

Using corpus tools for CODA analysis means treating the data as a corpus –
and this typically means using the resource like 'a bag of words', without
attending to discourse structure or temporal development. In most discourse
analytic approaches, in contrast, it is particularly important to identify how the
discourse unfolds over time. CODA can benefit from both perspectives,
depending on current purposes. Treating a think-aloud protocol as a corpus
may obscure the main features of gradually developing trains of thought in
a certain sequence. However, in other cases the order in which thoughts or
concepts are mentioned, or the specific moment at which they are mentioned,
may not be as decisive.

In some cases, collecting data in a controlled scenario is not feasible at all.
Danino (2014) was interested in how people talk about an event they do not
fully understand, as was the case in the 9/11 attack on the World Trade Center in
New York City. She compiled a corpus from CNN's live broadcast on the day in
order to analyse diverse speakers' productions in the face of shocking but
barely comprehensible perceptions. Looking at the discourse produced during
this unique, deeply troubling event enabled her to trace how language reflected
the speakers' attempts to put into words what they were seeing. This work
exemplifies the value of going beyond everyday situations, addressing discourse used under extraordinary circumstances. In this case, no controlled
study could have achieved the same level of authenticity.

Also focusing on language outside most people's everyday life, though less
troubling, we (Egorova et al., 2015) set out to analyse the language used in
mountaineering. Much previous research had been invested on route descriptions in urban contexts, yielding a wide range of valuable insights about the
ways in which we conceptualise space. Mountains provide a very different
setting, in which only a few of the environmental features that we use in urban
contexts are available. If you explain to your friend how to reach the summit of
Mount Everest, it seems unlikely that you use any of the following stereotypical
route description phrases:

Example 9.1   Turn right at the second intersection.
Example 9.2   Follow the road for 300 metres until you reach the supermarket,
               then turn left.
Example 9.3   Carry on for a few minutes, then your destination is the huge
               building on the right.

What might be the equivalent for intersections, roads, supermarkets, and other
typical route direction elements on mountains? Would it make sense to refer to
a temporal estimation like 'a few minutes', and how easy would it be to rely on
chunks such as 'the second intersection' or '300 metres'? Intuitively, the
language of mountaineering descriptions will be very different to this, and it

will therefore reveal very different concepts of space. But how can we collect route descriptions in mountains? Even the concept of a route description, as such, does not seem to apply very well, as people aren't likely to stop strangers on a mountain to ask for the way to the summit. Also, not everybody has climbed mountains. Whereas route description research in street networks can be conducted easily with various kinds of settings and speakers, participant recruitment on mountains comes with considerable challenges.

To work around these obstacles, Egorova (2018; Egorova et al., 2015) decided to take a different approach, namely to use existing language data to investigate the features of mountaineering discourse. She compiled a small corpus of nineteen texts of about 400 words each from an online resource that provided route descriptions in alpine contexts. In contrast to more typical CODA approaches, this method did not allow for controlling parameters such as which mountain was described, what exactly the purpose of the description was, and so on. Egorova couldn't formulate a well-designed instruction to the participants, but instead had to use what was available. However, the website allowed her to restrict the selection in some ways, such as the estimated difficulty of the route.

Since the corpus was very small and restricted to the specific context of mountaineering, we (Egorova et al, 2015) were able to adopt CODA principles in many other respects. Crucially, we achieved an in-depth analysis of linguistic features that are prominent in this kind of setting, which we could then compare with what is known from urban route instruction contexts. For instance, we found that the locomotion itself is far more prominent in alpine contexts than in a city. This is reflected in a broader variety of verbs such as *climb* and *ascend* in addition to the more common *go* or *walk*, and in frequent references to safety measures such as *climbing shoes*, *helmet*, *boots*, *ice axe*, and the like. Landmarks are prominent in mountains just as well as in cities, but they can look very different. Instead of buildings, one might refer to *where the snow begins* – in a city, such a reference would hardly be regarded as permanent enough to make it into a route description.

Taking this in-depth linguistic analysis as a starting point, Egorova (2018) went on to explore automatic methods towards a corpus linguistic approach. She aimed at developing rules for identifying and extracting spatial concepts from larger text resources in alpine contexts. Her focus was on concepts of 'fictive motion' – descriptions such as *the ridge descends for two miles*. The motion verb *descends* normally applies to people who are moving in a downward direction, but here it is used to describe a ridge's slope; in this sense, the motion is fictive. Egorova (2018) specified precisely how cases such as these can be extracted automatically, using a natural language processing engine, from a large text corpus that is tagged for parts of speech (verbs, nouns, etc.). In this way, she successfully transferred insights from CODA-based analysis into the efficient handling of much larger quantities of language data.

Altogether, corpus linguistics overlaps with CODA in a range of ways, and expertise in corpus analysis methods can be very useful in connection with CODA studies. Corpus tools are most useful for quantitative aspects in the data, based on automatic analysis and extraction processes. Since quantitative aspects are important for CODA (see Chapter 8), the approaches are highly compatible.

9.2   Practical Purposes within and outside Academia

The way we speak reveals crucial aspects about the way we think, and this insight motivates a broad range of CODA studies serving many different purposes. Verbal protocols and linguistic descriptions are pervasive in many areas of research, basic as well as applied, reaching as far as the marketing-oriented research procedures employed in commerce. Very often, the aim in such studies is to understand human intuitions better in order to support their goals in everyday life. A close, well-informed look at the language used in such data, and the significance of its features, opens up many practical opportunities with potential impact on society.

In this section, we will have a look at some of these avenues to exemplify and illustrate the scope of collaborative, purpose-oriented research. Section 9.2.1 starts by looking at artificial intelligence and interactions between humans and automatic systems. Section 9.2.2 outlines CODA in relation to architectural design, and Section 9.2.3 discusses visualisation tools. Section 9.2.4 concludes the book by opening up further visions beyond research already done or underway.

9.2.1   CODA and AI: Understanding Humans in Order to Develop Intuitive Systems

Artificial intelligence (AI) is an exciting field of research with enormous impact on the world around us and the society we live in. The idea of manufacturing artificial agents that resemble humans is as controversial as it is fascinating. Progress over recent decades has opened up many opportunities for developing smart and adaptive machines, for designing dialogue systems that can interact with humans, for constructing artificial brains, and much more. Applications of AI have long since reached our everyday life, despite a growing worry that we might be creating something that we could end up being unable to control. The main reason for this worry is that one of the main current AI methods, machine learning, enables automatic systems to develop beyond the programmers' direct steering. However, even with this method, systems can only use the input they receive, and they won't be able to creatively work towards sinister ulterior motives. It therefore remains, as ever, the responsibility of the programmer to equip (or 'feed', if you will) the system with the kinds of information that will be beneficial, rather than harmful, for the purposes at hand.

Despite best efforts and significant breakthroughs in AI research, automatic systems remain very unlikely to ever be able to truly understand humans, or to simulate the ways in which humans draw on intuitions and common sense. This kind of understanding can only be gained from humans themselves. The better we understand how humans think and talk, the more specific insights in this regard can be implemented in a system. With intelligent programming that is informed by relevant insights on human cognition, artificial systems become increasingly intuitive and can play to human strengths and intelligence in the most supportive way.

The idea of supporting the users' strengths in an intuitive way is especially central for assistance systems that are designed to help humans achieve their goals, rather than doing entire tasks for them. Imagine you are planning to go on holiday with your friends, and you wish to develop a route plan in advance. What kind of system would help you with this? You will certainly require a wide range of information, which a system could provide. Then, you might appreciate support with the complexity of the task, given that there are a range of constraints to consider: not to travel too far on any single day, to avoid a succession of boring days, to have places to stay overnight, and much else. Nevertheless, you probably wouldn't want an automatic system to plan the entire route for you – you want to stay in control, to make the final decisions about every part of the route.

As outlined in Chapter 7, we (Tenbrink & Seifert, 2011) examined how humans plan complex holiday routes in advance. Our CODA study revealed a range of cognitive strategies – ways of thinking about space that humans intuitively use during planning. Some of these insights were used for implementation in a travel planning assistance system (Seifert, 2008). For instance, one of the strategies that humans use to reduce task complexity is to think of the travel environment in terms of regions. Dividing the space up into smaller areas, in a non-rigid way, helps with focusing on subtasks rather than having to consider everything and everywhere at once. Thus, thinking of regions supports solving the spatial planning task in a hierarchical way. While the overall trajectory connects the regions at a high level of granularity, detailed planning is carried out one region at a time. Seifert (2008) designed a travel assistance system that supports this cognitive strategy while enabling the user to make all relevant decisions in an informed way.

Scenarios that involve actions in the real world impose further challenges. In robotics, traditional approaches have typically been motivated from an engineering rather than a cognitive perspective. Industry robots can relatively easily be programmed to carry out very specific, predefined tasks; they will do the exact movements and actions determined by their specification. This may involve interaction with tools and objects, and sometimes with humans. The main issue here is that without humanlike concepts, robots will remain very inflexible – everything needs to be programmed beforehand, there is little room for diversity. Along with this, there is little room for verbal human instructions that change depending on the features of a specific scenario.

Addressing these challenges requires cognition-related research in two major, interrelated respects. On the one hand, we need to understand how humans *think* in order to equip robots with similar flexibility. On the other hand, we need to understand how humans *talk* in order to enable robots to talk naturally with humans – to use language in a flexible and context-dependent way. Although there are plenty of automatic dialogue systems on the market, and in use even within our households, their flexibility is still fairly limited. The main reason for this lies in the very link between thought and language. As long as automatic systems cannot *think* like a human, they will have difficulty *talking* to a human, especially about constantly changing aspects in the immediate environment. These need to be perceived and referred to adequately in order to establish a meaningful dialogue that is appropriate for the situation at hand.

Research on these issues has made significant progress over the past decades, but there are still significant gaps. Here, CODA can be applied to gain decisive insights about human thought and language use. In our research, a robot was enabled to understand instructions like *Go to the object on the right* (Moratz & Tenbrink, 2006); this involved implementing a cognitive model that allowed for an adequate interpretation of human spatial concepts, as well as a dialogue system that dealt with the language itself. We also applied CODA to identify specific features of human–computer (Tenbrink et al., 2010) and human–robot interaction (Winterboer, Tenbrink, & Moratz, 2013), and to support the development of an intuitive dialogue system for indoor wayfinding (Cuayáhuitl et al., 2010).

In all of these areas, it is important to identify what people say intuitively with respect to different kinds of scenarios, and also how these intuitions change when their interaction partner is an automatic system. We don't talk to a system in the same way as to a human, because we don't expect the system to be able to understand our thoughts in the same way. Although this general assumption is of course correct, our intuitions as to how to talk to the system may not always be accurate. A smart dialogue system therefore needs to be designed in such a way as to account for human expectations about dialogue systems as well as their intuitive ways of speaking and thinking.

9.2.2 CODA and Architectural Design: Towards Intuitive Building Design

As seen in various examples throughout this book, CODA has been used in many studies that involved various tasks and research questions related to space. One of the main driving questions of spatial cognition research concerns what can be done to improve wayfinding in people's everyday life, both in indoor and outdoor settings. For outdoor navigation areas such as street networks, there are now plenty of navigation aids available, both for planning a route in advance, and for navigating en route based on ubiquitous GPS signals. In contrast, navigation within complex buildings remains a challenge in many ways. The GPS signal isn't reliable indoors, and far fewer maps or automatic systems are normally available to guide people to their destination within buildings.

Complex public buildings are often designed to impress and to fascinate, but not necessarily to navigate easily. Architectural design is a multilayered process that involves various challenges in terms of cognition and communication (Tenbrink et al., 2014; see Chapter 4). Architects have to consider the building's functionality and aesthetic aspects against constraints imposed by the client, by financial limitations, and by the available space. Ease of navigation is therefore just one aspect among many, and it is certainly not always a priority.

However, it does not have to be difficult to improve architectural design so that buildings are more intuitive and facilitate wayfinding. Sometimes simple considerations and adjustments are sufficient to make a considerable difference for the users of a building. To achieve this, it can be useful to think, for a moment, like a person trying to find their way inside the building. What would be a likely purpose of their visit, what will they need, what intuitions or expectations will they bring in, and what would confuse them as they look for their destination?

Research in this area has led to several decisive insights in this regard. For instance, in terms of intuitions and expectations, people may be open-minded when they enter a new building, but they aren't entirely naïve; they have been in public buildings before and can draw on this previous experience in a new situation. If they are looking for a place within the building that is likely to be frequently visited by many people, it is unlikely that they would choose narrow or semi-dark hallways if they are unsure of the route. Typically, hallways with long lines of sight are preferred choices. Likewise, attractive objects serve as navigation aids at intersections, and they can influence decisions as to which direction to choose (Frankenstein et al., 2010).

CODA informs this line of research in various ways, for instance by identifying features that consistently appear in verbalisations, or by highlighting the diversity of navigation strategies reflected in language. The study by Tenbrink et al. (2011a), reported in Chapter 5, is a case in point. When we asked participants who were new to a building how they might find their way to the nearest exit, they reported a range of highly suitable navigation strategies. CODA enabled us to establish the relationship between these strategies and more standard turn-by-turn route directions. Also, the verbalisations revealed the ways in which users related to the building's features; for instance, they used prominent places such as the main staircase and certain staircase towers as decisive orientation aids. These findings are in line with previous studies within complex buildings in which people were asked to verbalise their navigation strategies (Hölscher et al., 2006).

Research in this area is ongoing, and there are various questions still to be asked. For instance, how do wayfinding strategies change with age; how would a home for the elderly need to be designed to be helpful? O'Malley et al. (2018) found that elderly people who suffer from memory loss have significant difficulties finding their way around. Moving into a communal retirement development is meant to be a way to support them in their everyday needs; however, getting a clear idea about where places are in this new environment can be a major challenge. If a building is not designed to be helpful, the result can be a persistent feeling of disorientation for new tenants. This can easily be the case if all hallways look the same, or if any pictures or other objects intended to give the building a fresh look are nondescript and non-distinctive. All people, not only those suffering from memory loss, require salient landmarks in the environment for orientation. Keeping a residence for the elderly neutral and indistinctive clearly imposes a major navigation challenge on the very people it is designed for.

Independent of the users' age or memory capacities, it is clear from previous research that complex buildings must strike a balance between distinctiveness and simplicity. The overall concept of the building should be clearly understandable, which is helped by long lines of sight. At the same time, there must be sufficiently salient features to enable the users to orient themselves, to know where they are. These features must be distinct and ideally unique, rather than being repeated in several locations. Getting this balance right may be tricky, but it is certainly achievable. Research involving a combination of navigation tasks and verbalisations, such as interviews and think-aloud data that can be systematically analysed using CODA, can inform these endeavours decisively.

9.2.3   *CODA and Visualisation Tools: Making Insights Intuitively Accessible*

As we saw at the start of this book, language is just one way of representing thoughts and insights. Another well-established way is through the use of diagrams and other visualisations (such as Figure 9.1 earlier in this chapter). Some concepts and relationships can be expressed better in a visuospatial way than through words (Larkin & Simon, 1987). One main reason for this is that language is sequential – you read or hear a message in a certain temporal order. This is not always ideal; complex relationships that involve more than one dimension may be best expressed through a representation medium that uses more than one dimension. Standard diagrams or pictures are two-dimensional, and you can focus your attention on certain aspects in any order you prefer, whatever makes most sense to you. Some modern displays use three-dimensional designs, and dynamic visualisations can even represent a fourth dimension, showing developments over time.

Another advantage is that visualisations often use figurative and analogous elements, as opposed to the abstract nature of language. The word *dog* doesn't look like a dog, but a visualisation can incorporate a schematic representation of a typical dog. Especially in spatial contexts, this aspect can become quite crucial. We have only a limited range of words in our everyday language to express spatial directions, and usually happily content ourselves with vague or qualitative concepts like 'to the right', even in cases where the angle isn't exactly ninety degrees. In contrast, a schematic representation can represent the angle more accurately, allowing for more information to be conveyed without adding complexity to the message.

Taken together, these main advantages allow for representing relevant aspects of the depicted concepts or situations in an efficient and relatively simple way. Facilitated by ever-improving software tools, visualisations are fairly ubiquitous in modern times. They not only serve to illustrate facts and enhance the content of accompanying text, but further guide the observer towards certain conclusions or decisions based on what the visualisation suggests. But what exactly happens in this process – what do we take from a visualisation, and how do we know what other people would understand from it?

When looking at a picture or diagram, humans do not perceive all features and elements equally or objectively, as a computer might do. Instead, the perception of visual information is guided by a combination of relevance and salience principles. The perceiver's attention is drawn towards aspects that visually stand out and are therefore particularly salient (Fine & Minnery, 2009) just as well as towards elements that relate directly to current task purposes (Henderson, Malcolm, & Schandl, 2009). As a consequence, some parts of a visualisation may remain entirely outside the perceiver's consciousness. It is very easy, and very human, to miss seemingly irrelevant aspects if they don't stand out in any particular way.

Understanding these principles is vital for designing visualisations in such a way that they work well in supporting humans in the way they are supposed to. Simply including relevant information in and of itself is not sufficient if perceivers don't notice and understand it easily. They might not only miss vital information but could also easily misinterpret the message intended by the designer. For instance, they might confuse accidental features of a diagram as representing actual states or relationships in the real world. If a map represents a forest in a dark brown colour, the map user may infer that the forest has predominantly dark brown trees. This may not be a conscious inference – people may not even notice that they have come to this kind of conclusion. Nevertheless, they will work on the basis of this false assumption until they realise their mistake.

In this respect, conventions and expertise play a major role. We understand language because we use it all the time in line with the conventions in our communities, which involve certain rules of grammar as well as accepted usage at more pragmatic levels. Likewise, we understand diagrams better if they follow certain conventional principles, and regular users of a particular type of visualisation will be less likely to be misguided than first-time observers. However, visualisations are far less conventionalised or standardised than language is, and therefore the risk for miscommunication is generally stronger. The intuitive and pictorial nature of visualisations goes a long way towards alleviating this problem, but there will always be abstract or schematic elements or features that can be misinterpreted.

In expert domains, this issue can become quite crucial. Visualisations are often generated as part of an effort to enable experts to quickly extract relevant information for a purpose. The ability to do this efficiently strongly depends on experience (Jee et al., 2009). To a degree, perceivers of displayed information are biased by their background as well as by how they judge aspects of relevance in a given context. This will affect the conclusions and decisions that they will make on the basis of visualised information, leading to either desired or undesired outcomes.

These effects are complex, and they are based on cognitive processes on the part of the people perceiving visualisations. Something goes on in the minds of the people perceiving visualisations, and it is vital to understand how this works, as visualisations are becoming increasingly widespread. In recent years, various endeavours have been undertaken to address these issues, for example through the analysis of diagram users' eye movements (Çöltekin, Fabrikant, & Lacayo, 2010), or by testing the usability of different versions in the field (Sarjakoski & Nivala, 2005).

Another way to learn about users' understanding of visualisations is through language. When we perceive a diagram, we will to a certain extent be able to express our understanding of the diagram in words. Although much can be learned by interviewing people concerning their thoughts, simply asking questions may not be sufficient. Often, information gathered this way does not make its way into scientific reports, even if it serves to inform researchers on an informal basis.

Here, as with other research on cognitive processes, CODA is a way to systematise the insights that can be gained on the basis of language (Tenbrink, 2014). CODA can highlight users' understanding of visualisations in every respect outlined in this book. Perhaps the most decisive aspect concerns attention (Section 4.1); what are the kinds of things people attend to as they try to interpret a visualisation? It is part of the design process for a visualisation to consider how users' attention can be drawn towards the most relevant aspects. A CODA analysis of attention patterns can verify the extent to which this is successful, and identify undesired shifts of attention towards non-central aspects of a visualisation. This can be combined with eye-tracking data, as discussed earlier in this chapter.

Furthermore, users can perceive visualisations from different conceptual perspectives (Section 4.2), depending on the situation or task at hand. Imagine you're an expert in ocean sciences, and you're looking at a diagram showing flooded areas across Britain as part of a research article. How you look at it, and what you take from it, might be very different depending on your purpose in reading the article. Are you aiming to increase your knowledge in the field? Are you looking for something to relate your own research to? Do you wish to draw on this information to alert the people in Britain to imminent dangers, and to start a campaign for building better flood defences? Or is the visualisation something you might use for your own teaching purposes, in which case you'd have to consider its suitability for students?

Each of these aims would lead to different perspectives on the visualisation, and further perspectives will be employed by people with yet different aims. Non-experts will perceive it differently from experts, and other people might have very different purposes – such as seeking evidence *against* flood protection, or against the notion of global warming. A CODA study of verbalised perceptions in different situations and by different people can highlight this diversity and identify the effects it has on people's understanding of the visualisation.

Similar considerations apply for each of the other levels of analysis suggested in earlier chapters. People may understand visualisations at different levels of granularity (Section 5.1), and they may be more or less certain about the meanings and insights conveyed (Section 5.2). They may make different kinds of inferences (Section 6.1), depending on how the visualisation triggers their thoughts. Visualisations may – and often do – enable users to transform things in the real world (Section 6.2), as is the case with illustrations of steps in a manual. People often communicate about visualisations (Section 7.1), for instance to discuss the implications of the insights conveyed. Also, understanding the message of a visualisation can be a problem, or it can be part of a problem-solving task; in this case, the problem-solving process can be analysed on a sequential basis (Section 7.2). Apart from these central layers of analysis as outlined in this book, further analysis perspectives can be adopted in the spirit of CODA, all of which lead to a better understanding of how people understand visualisations.

9.3   Conclusion

How much can we learn from the way we talk, and what can we do with this knowledge? As I hope I have shown in this final chapter, the scope for combinations with other methods as well as for applications within and outside academia is extremely wide. The reason for this is very simple: language is the primary medium of communication and representation of thought, and it is hard to imagine a situation in which it plays no role at all. As long as there is something to put into words in relation to a question at hand, you can get participants to speak, or you can add an element of verbalisation to a study you're already planning, and you'll be able to gain systematic insights from the discourse through CODA.

This sounds simple, and in a sense it is. The idea for CODA as well as the basic procedures are actually very straightforward, as long as a few basic parameters are considered (see Chapter 8). It is all about taking language seriously as a representation of thought, and analysing it systematically, with a clear awareness of the underlying concepts and states of mind that lead the speaker to make their linguistic choices in the way they do. It matters whether people say *the car is green* or *here is a Mercedes with an odd grass-like colour.* There is a reason for the diverse differences here, and also for the many indications of doubt in an utterance like *Oh, I really cannot say for sure, but, uh, perhaps I could place the, um, teacup on the, well, on the table?*

Differences and markers such as these are obvious once you start looking at language closely. You don't need to be an expert on language to understand their significance. All it takes is an analyst's mindset. The linguistic features may seem subtle or irrelevant to start with, and indeed they are easily overlooked in everyday conversation. We do not normally pay conscious attention to the exact ways in which we formulate things, neither in speaking nor in listening or reading. We understand the content and take things further from there: act on what we've heard, respond to it, and so on. However, just because we don't normally pay attention to the specifics of how things are said doesn't mean that we cannot do it. This is, in a nutshell, the idea for CODA. You don't need to be an expert in linguistics to recognise significant linguistic features, but you do need to adopt the mindset and systematicity of an analyst to work them out properly.

There are a range of areas that still await further exploration. For instance, consider relations between input and output. How does the *production* of language interact with the *comprehension* of language? How are linguistic features in the produced language affected by the features of the language presented to participants? Empirical studies that involve the production of language, such as descriptions of some observed phenomenon, or verbal protocols of a problem-solving process, typically also involve instructing the participants through language. Using language is almost inevitable in academic research. But clearly this also affects participants, and it is important to be aware of this. Most of all, as emphasised in Chapter 8, it is essential to keep the instruction constant, and not vary it randomly across participants.

As shown in Chapter 7, it is clear from previous research that input affects output in many important ways. We align our utterances to those of our interaction partner, and we can be primed by certain constructions or word choices towards using similar ones. Inevitably, the linguistic input that participants receive in an academic study will influence the language they produce. This fact can be addressed as a specific target in CODA research. For instance, different participants could get differently worded instructions with a similar content, enabling the analyst to focus on the effect of the instruction's formulation.

In Tenbrink and Taylor (2015; see Chapter 6) we were interested in how people follow written origami instructions, and to what extent their thoughts diverged from those instructions. To identify the divergence, we closely attended to the instructions' wording, and compared it to the wording used by the participants as they verbalised their thoughts. This input–output comparison enabled us to identify a range of cognitive strategies that people follow in relation to written information.

However, there is much more to be learned about the relationship between language input and subsequent linguistic output. In a current collaboration with Alice Bell at Sheffield Hallam University, we are addressing reader responses to a novel. This line of research relates to research in literature studies, with its focus on the effects of literature on the reader. Typically, in reader response research, readers' reactions are addressed through questionnaires containing Likert scales and open questions. These responses are not normally investigated from a linguistic point of view. However, we found indications that the novel's features may have had an effect on the linguistic features in the readers' responses, especially concerning aspects relating to their thoughts. This opens up exciting avenues for future research in literature studies and beyond, looking at the effects of what we read or hear on our thoughts and the ways in which we express those thoughts through language.

Taking this train of thought further, consider users' understanding of manuals that contain visual or textual instructions, or both. Manuals play an important role in human everyday life, and misunderstanding them can have severe consequences, depending on circumstances. Our research in Tenbrink and Maas (2015) revealed that the link between visual and textual elements is particularly tricky, as it is not always clear how the text relates to the accompanying visuals. If visuals are only poorly understood in relation to text, it must be even more difficult to transfer the visualised information to the object in the real world that the manual is aiming to explain. Research in this direction could aim to develop a set of guidelines for improving user manuals, making them more intuitive and avoiding ambiguities.

As a long-term vision, this strand of research may help to improve the communication of complex insights in general. Understanding how people express their thoughts, using CODA, can help to facilitate the two-way communication between humans. Getting thoughts across from one mind to another is one important function of discourse, independent of the mode of communication. CODA can be used to address the success of this aspect, to identify the most suitable ways of formulating thoughts in such a way that the addressee can easily follow them. Our dialogue work in Tenbrink et al. (2017) is a case in point, but there is still much more to discover.

Research has brought us a long way towards understanding how language works as a system, and how we use it in discourse. As technology develops, it increasingly opens up further ways to incorporate this knowledge – through new communication media, in automatic dialogue systems and intelligent agents, and much more. CODA, as an idea or general approach, is simple and flexible enough to remain available despite major changes in the medium it addresses. This book was written with the aim of making the method easily accessible to researchers across disciplines; it is my hope that this will spark further ideas about how discourse can help us understand human thought.

Register of Linguistic Features

This section lists key linguistic features that have been mentioned throughout the book, and which may be of interest to researchers using CODA. While there is no intent to be exhaustive, the features listed here have all been identified in the literature as being indicative of specific cognitive aspects in some way, and so they can serve as starting points for CODA studies. As in this book as a whole, English is assumed as a starting point but the linguistic features should usually be represented in other languages as well.

In the following, →arrows tell you that you can access more information about this concept in this list.

Absence of content or features. Introduction; Sections 5.1.1; 7.1.1. If some specific content or linguistic feature is not represented in a linguistic data set, this may have many reasons. Some of these reasons may be uncovered by analysing patterns of linguistic features in relation to the conditions in which language was produced. If a feature is frequent in one condition but absent in another, there must be a reason for this pattern. Otherwise, if an expected cognitive aspect is completely absent, it may mean that this aspect is not or cannot be represented in language, even though it may be present in the mind.

Adjectives. Sections Sections 3.1.1; 4.1.2; 5.1.2; 7.2.4. Like →Nouns and (to a lesser extent) →Verbs, adjectives can be key indicators of semantic fields and conceptual domains. Further, they are particularly powerful in expressing perceived object features (as in *the blue car*), as well as attitudes and evaluations in different degrees of intensity (such as *good* or *dreadful*).

Certainty markers. Sections 1.3.2; 5.2. Language can express levels of certainty through →Modality, →Pauses and hesitations, and →Verbs (such as *know*) that explicitly indicate certainty, through hedges (such as *in a sense* and *probably*), and in many other ways.

Conjunctions. Sections 1.2.4; 2.3.6. Conjunctions (also called discourse markers) such as *because* or *after* explicitly indicate →Discourse relations, or relations between elements within a clause.

Discourse relations. Sections 1.2.3; 3.2.3; 3.3.5; 5.1.2; 7.2.3. Clauses often relate to each other, in various ways, such as causally or temporally.

251

Such relations are frequently but not necessarily made explicit by →Conjunctions. This aspect concerns how the speaker conceives of the interconnections between the elements described.

Discourse structure. Sections 1.2.3; 2.3.6; 7.1.3. The way a particular piece of discourse is structured can be revealing when analysed relative to the situation context. For instance, in think-aloud protocols, discourse structure reflects the temporal order of thoughts; in dialogue, communication partners react to each other's contributions in structured ways.

Grammatical case and function. Sections 1.1.2; 3.3.3; 4.1.2. The form and function of a →Noun, or noun phrase, within a clause indicate what role the speaker assigns to them – for instance whether a person is an agent or a beneficiary in a transaction.

Granularity. Sections 3.2.4; 5.1; 5.2.1. Descriptions of processes, states, or objects can be more or less elaborate and reflect different levels of detail. This is related (but not identical) to →Precision and can be traced, among other aspects, by analysing the features of →Nouns and →Verbs.

Inferences. Sections 2.3.1; 3.2.3; 6.1. Inferences are not directly expressed on the linguistic surface; however, a close look at what was said against the information available to the speaker can reveal any inferences that the speaker has made.

Information structure. Sections 3.2.2; 3.3.4; 4.1.2; 8.5.4. The way a sentence is structured reflects to some extent which aspects are assumed to be already known and which are represented as new. Typically, in English, clauses start with given information and present new information at the end. However, aspects of information structure such as contrast and focus can also be expressed by other means, such as tonal stress and intonation contour.

Metaphors and transferred meanings. Sections 2.1.2; 3.1.5. Many linguistic expressions are not meant in their literal sense, but reflect some kind of meaning transfer. For instance, *good times ahead* uses the spatial domain to describe a temporal phenomenon.

Modality. Sections 1.2.1; 3.3.2; 5.2.2; 6.2.2; 8.6. Modal verbs such as *could*, *should*, *would*, and *might* indicate possibilities and alternative worlds that the speaker conceives of in various ways, related (but not restricted) to →Certainty.

Mood. Sections 3.3.1; 3.3.2. Mood denotes whether a clause represents a question, command, or statement, reflecting whether speakers convey conceptualised facts (as in *The window is open*) or aim to achieve a certain discourse goal (as in *Could you open the window?*).

Nouns. Sections 1.1.2; 1.2.1; 3.1.2; 3.2.4; 3.3.3; 6.1; 6.2.2; 7.2.2; 7.2.4. Every object or person can be referred to or categorised in more than one way. The term we use for reference in a given situation indicates the conceptual level of detail and associated features – for instance, whether we say *shoes* or *high* *heels*. The lexical choices for nouns also indicate semantic fields and conceptual domains; e.g. *shoes* belong to the domain of clothing and *violin* to the domain of music. Other lexical choices in the co-text (including other forms such as →Verbs) further contribute to building up a semantic field.

Pauses and hesitations. Sections 1.3.3; 3.2.1; 5.2.2; 8.4. Spoken discourse typically contains many instances of pauses and hesitation markers such as *uhm, uh, mh*. There may be many reasons underlying these delays in speech fluency, including lack of →Certainty, high cognitive load (i.e. too busy thinking to talk), or problems finding the right words. Because it can be very time-consuming to transcribe pauses accurately, it makes sense to identify beforehand to what extent these aspects can be analysed meaningfully.

Perspective. Sections 1.2.3; 1.3.2; 4.2; 7.1.1; 7.1.4. All utterances reflect the underlying conceptual perspective in some ways; this is often, but need not be, the speaker's own stance. Spatial perspective determines the interpretation of descriptions like *to the right of the chair* (see also →Spatial reference systems).

Precision. Sections 1.3.2; 3.2.4; 5.2.3; 8.3. Descriptions can be more or less precise or vague, which can reflect degrees of knowledge or →Certainty, or the speaker's current focus of attention.

Prepositions. Sections 1.2.4; 3.1.2; 4.1.2; 6.2.3; 8.5.4. Although seemingly small and irrelevant, prepositions are powerful representations of underlying concepts. For instance, rather than simply representing a vertical direction (as in *on the table*), the preposition *on* indicates an underlying notion of location control (as exemplified by *on the wall*). Prepositions are frequently used in a transferred sense, as part of a conventionalised →Metaphor; here, as well, there are subtle but meaningful differences between prepositional choices (compare *on time* and *in time*).

Presuppositions. Sections 1.2.4; 3.2.2; 8.5.4; 9.1.3. Many utterances implicitly point to underlying assumptions that are presupposed by the speaker. For instance, reference to *the white horse* presupposes that there is a white horse that is somehow accessible to the speaker (and hearer where applicable).

Pronouns. Sections 1.2.1; 4.2.3; 8.5.3. Pronouns are used to represent recurring elements in a discourse that are known and do not need to be reintroduced by name. It can be revealing to identify patterns in the use of first- or second-person pronouns, or to trace the referents of third-person pronouns.

Spatial reference systems. Sections 1.1.2; 3.1.4; 4.2.2. We can refer to space in several different ways; spatial reference systems are the concepts underlying our choices – for instance, *north of me* as opposed to *on the table's right*. Speakers' assignments of the roles of locatum and relatum as well as the spatial relationship expressed (typically) by a →Preposition can be highly revealing of their spatial conceptualisations.

Syntax. Sections 3.1.3; 3.1.4; 4.1.2. The syntax of a clause reflects a range of abstract meaning structures as well as attention focus through →Information structure, →Grammatical case, and more.

Verbs. Sections 2.3.6; 3.2.4; 3.3.3; 7.2.1; 7.2.2; 7.2.4; 9.1.4. Similar to lexical choices for →Nouns, the verbs used to express a particular action or process highlight the underlying conceptualisation. Some verbs are fairly direct indicators of processes related to cognition, such as perceptual verbs (*see*, *feel*, *hear*) or verbs expressing conceptual states or goals (e.g. *search*, *know*, *focus on*).

References

Adesope, O. O., Lavin, T., Thompson, T., & Ungerleider, C. (2010). A systematic review and meta-analysis of the cognitive correlates of bilingualism. *Review of Educational Research 80*(2), 207–45.

Afflerbach, P. & Johnston, P. (1984). On the use of verbal reports in reading research. *Journal of Reading Behavior 16*, 307–22.

Aitchison, J. (1983). *The Articulate Mammal: An Introduction to Psycholinguistics* (2nd ed.). London: Hutchison.

Allen, G. L. (2000). Principles and practices for communicating route knowledge. *Applied Cognitive Psychology 14*, 333–59.

Altmann, G. T. (2001). The language machine: Psycholinguistics in review. *British Journal of Psychology 92*, 129–70.

Anderson, J. R. (2009). *Cognitive Psychology and Its Implications* (7th ed.). New York: Worth Publishers.

Anderson, J. R. & Lebiere, C. (1998). *The Atomic Components of Thought*. Mahwah, NJ: Lawrence Erlbaum Associates.

Anderson, M. L. (2003). Embodied cognition: A field guide. *Artificial Intelligence 149* (1), 91–130.

Andonova, E., Tenbrink, T., & Coventry, K. R. (2010). Function and context affect spatial information packaging at multiple levels. *Psychonomic Bulletin and Review 17*, 575–80.

Antaki, C., Billig, M. G., Edwards, D., and Potter, J. A. (2003). Discourse analysis means doing analysis: A critique of six analytic shortcomings. *Discourse Analysis Online 1*(1). https://extra.shu.ac.uk/daol/articles/open/2002/002/antaki2002002 -paper.html

Arnold, J. E. (2008). Reference production: Product-internal and addressee-oriented processes. *Language and Cognitive Processes 23*(4), 495–527.

Arts, A. (2004). *Overspecification in Instructive Texts*. Nijmegen: Wolf Publishers.

Atit, K., Shipley, T. F., & Tikoff, B. (2013). *Cognitive Processing 14*, 163–73.

Bartl, C. & Dörner, D. (1998). Sprachlos beim Denken – Zum Einfluß von Sprache auf die Problemlöse- und Gedächtnisleistung bei der Bearbeitung eines nichtsprachlichen Problems. *Sprache und Kognition 17*, 224–38.

Bateman, J., Hois, J., Ross, R. R., & Tenbrink, T. (2010). A linguistic ontology of space for natural language processing. *Artificial Intelligence 174*, 1027–71.

Bavelas, J., Gerwing, J., & Healing, S. (2017). Doing mutual understanding. Calibrating with micro-sequences in face-to-face dialogue. *Journal of Pragmatics 121*, 91–112.

Bégoin-Augereau, S. & Caron-Pargue, J. (2003). Linguistic criteria for demarcation and hierarchical organization of episodes in a problem solving task. In F. H. van Eemeren, J. A. Blair, C. A. Willard, & F. Snoeck Henkemans (eds.), *Proceedings of the Fifth Conference of the International Society for the Study of Argumentation*, pp. 81–7. Amsterdam: Sic Sat.

Bégoin-Augereau, S. & Caron-Pargue, J. (2009). Linguistic markers of decision processes in a problem solving task. *Cognitive Systems Research 10*, 102–23.

Biber, D., Conrad, S., & Reppen, R. (1998). *Corpus Linguistics: Investigating Language Structure and Use*. Cambridge, UK: Cambridge University Press.

Bierwisch, M. & Schreuder, R. (1992). From concepts to lexical items. *Cognition 42*, 23–60.

Boren, M. & Ramey, J. (2000). Thinking aloud: Reconciling theory and practice. *IEEE Transactions on Professional Communication 43*(3), 261–78.

Brennan, S. E. & Clark, H. H. (1996). Conceptual pacts and lexical choice in conversation. *Journal of Experimental Psychology: Learning, Memory and Cognition 22*(6), 1482–93.

Brösamle, M. & Hölscher, C. (2012). Architectural gestures: Conserving traces of design processes. In C. Hölscher & M. Bhatt (eds.), *Proceedings of SCAD Spatial Cognition for Architectural Design*. Report No. 029–08/2012 Report Series of the Transregional Collaborative Research Center SFB/TR 8 Spatial Cognition, pp. 215–23. Bremen: Bremen University.

Brown, P. and Levinson, S. C. (1993). 'Uphill' and 'downhill' in Tzeltal. *Journal of Linguistic Anthropology 3*, 46–74.

Brown, R. (1958). How shall a thing be called? *Psychological Review 65*(1), 14–21.

Brunyé, T. T., Ditman, T., Mahoney, C. R., Augustyn, J. S., & Taylor, H. A. (2009). When you and I share perspectives: Pronouns modulate perspective taking during narrative comprehension. *Psychological Science 20*(1), 27–32.

Bugmann, D., Coventry, K. R., & Newstead, S. E. (2007). Contextual cues and the retrieval of information from cognitive maps. *Memory and Cognition 35*(3), 381–92.

Butler, C. S. & Gonzálvez-García, F. (2014). *Exploring Functional-Cognitive Space* (Vol. 157). Amsterdam: John Benjamins Publishing Company.

Canas, J., Quesada, J., Antolí, A., & Fajardo, I. (2003). Cognitive flexibility and adaptability to environmental changes in dynamic complex problem-solving tasks. *Ergonomics 46*(5), 482–501.

Carlson, L. A., Hölscher, C., Shipley, T. F., & Dalton, R. C. (2010). *Getting Lost in Buildings. Current Directions in Psychological Science 19*(5), 284–9.

Carlson, L. A. & van der Zee, E. (eds.) (2005). *Functional Features in Language and Space: Insights from Perception, Categorization and Development*. Oxford: Oxford University Press.

Caron-Pargue, J. & Caron, J. (1989). Processus psycholinguistiques et analyse des verbalisations dans une tâche cognitive. *Archives de Psychologie 57*, 3–32.

Caron-Pargue, J. & Caron, J. (1995). La fonction cognitive des interjections. *Faits de Langues 6*, 111–20.

Caron-Pargue, J. & Caron, J. (2000). Les interjections comme marqueurs du fonctionnement cognitif. *Cahiers de praxématique 34*, 51–76.

Caron-Pargue, J. & Gillis, S. (eds.) (1996). *Verbal Production and Problem Solving*. Antwerp Papers in Linguistics 85, University of Antwerp.

Carroll, M. & von Stutterheim, C. (1993). The representation of spatial configurations in English and German and the grammatical structure of locative and anaphoric expressions. *Linguistics 31*, 1011–41.

Carston, R. (1998). Informativeness, relevance and scalar implicature. In R. Carston & S. Uchida (eds.), *Relevance Theory: Applications and Implications*, pp. 179–236. Amsterdam: John Benjamins.

Carston, R. (2002). *Thoughts and Utterances: The Pragmatics of Explicit Communication*. Oxford: Blackwell.

Chi, M. T. H. (2006). Two approaches to the study of experts' characteristics. In K. A. Ericsson, N. Charness, P. J. Feltovich, & R. R. Hoffman (eds.), *The Cambridge Handbook of Expertise and Expert Performance*, pp. 21–30. Cambridge, UK: Cambridge University Press.

Chi, M. T. H., Glaser, R., & Rees, E. (1982). Expertise in problem solving. In R. Sternberg (ed.), *Advances in the Psychology of Human Intelligence*, pp. 7–75. Hillsdale, NJ: Erlbaum.

Chomsky, N. (1972). *Studies on Semantics in Generative Grammar*. The Hague: Mouton Publishers.

Chomsky, N. (1980). *Rules and Representations*. New York: Columbia University Press.

Cialone, C., Tenbrink, T., & Spiers, H. J. (2018). Sculptors, architects, and painters conceive of depicted spaces differently. *Cognitive Science 42*, 524–53.

Clark, D. R., Li, D., & Shepherd, D. A. (2018). Country familiarity in the initial stage of foreign market selection. *Journal of International Business Studies 49*(4), 442–72.

Clark, H. H. (1996). *Using Language*. Cambridge, UK: Cambridge University Press.

Clark, H. H. & Krych, M. (2004). Speaking while monitoring addressees for understanding. *Journal of Memory and Language 50*, 62–81.

Clark, H. H. & Wilkes-Gibbs, D. (1986). Referring as a collaborative process. *Cognition 22*, 1–39.

Cleland, A. A. & Pickering, M. J. (2003). The use of lexical and syntactic information in language production: Evidence from the priming of noun phrase structure. *Journal of Memory and Language 49*, 214–30.

Çöltekin, A., Fabrikant, S. I., & Lacayo, M. (2010). Exploring the efficiency of users' visual analytics strategies based on sequence analysis of eye movement recordings. *International Journal of Geographical Information Science 24*(10), 1559–75.

Corley, M. & Scheepers, C. (2002). Syntactic priming in English sentence production: Categorical and latency evidence from an internet-based study. *Psychonomic Bulletin and Review 9*(1), 126–31.

Corteen, R. S. & Wood, B. (1972). Autonomic responses to shock-associated words in an unattended channel. *Journal of Experimental Psychology 94*(3), 308.

Couclelis, H. (1996). Verbal directions for way-finding: Space, cognition, and language. In J. Portugali (ed.), *The Construction of Cognitive Maps*, pp. 133–53. Dordrecht: Kluwer Academic Publishers.

Coventry, K. R. & Garrod, S. C. (2004). *Saying, Seeing and Acting: The Psychological Semantics of Spatial Prepositions*. London: Psychology Press.

Cuayáhuitl, H., Dethlefs, N., Richter, K.-F., Tenbrink, T., & Bateman, J. (2010). A dialogue system for indoor wayfinding using text-based natural language.

International Journal of Computational Linguistics and Applications 1(1–2), 285–304.

Culpeper, J. & Kytö, M. (2010). *Early Modern English Dialogues: Spoken Interaction as Writing*. Cambridge, UK: Cambridge University Press.

Dąbrowska, E. (2012). Different speakers, different grammars: Individual differences in native language attainment. *Linguistic Approaches to Bilingualism 2*(3), 219–53.

Danino, C. (2014). Language production and meaning construction mechanisms in the discourse on an ongoing event: the case study of CNN's live broadcast on 9/11. PhD dissertation, University of Poitiers, France.

Danino, C. (2018). Introduction: Les Petits Corpus. *Corpus 18*. http://journals .openedition.org/corpus/3099

Denis, M. (1997). The description of routes: A cognitive approach to the production of spatial discourse. *Current Psychology of Cognition 16*, 409–58.

Denis, M., Pazzaglia, F., Cornoldi, C., & Bertolo, L. (1999). Spatial discourse and navigation: An analysis of route directions in the city of Venice. *Applied Cognitive Psychology 13*(2), 145–74.

Durning, S. J., Artino, A. R. Jr, Beckman, T. J., et al. (2013) Does the think-aloud protocol reflect thinking? Exploring functional neuroimaging differences with thinking (answering multiple choice questions) versus thinking aloud. *Medical Teacher 35*(9), 720–6.

Edwards, D. & Potter, J. (1992). *Discursive Psychology*. London: Sage.

Egorova, E. (2018). From text to space: Spatial discourse in alpine route directions and narratives. PhD dissertation, University of Zurich.

Egorova, E., Tenbrink, T., & Purves, R. S. (2015). Where snow is a landmark: Route direction elements in alpine contexts. In S. I. Fabrikant, M. Raubal, M. Bertolotto, C., et al. (eds.), *Spatial Information Theory*, pp. 175–95. Berlin: Springer.

Egorova, E., Tenbrink, T., & Purves, R. S. (2018). Fictive motion in the context of mountaineering. *Spatial Cognition and Computation 18*(4), 259–84.

Ehrich, V. & Koster, C. (1983). Discourse organization and sentence form: The structure of room descriptions in Dutch. *Discourse Processes 6*, 169–95.

Elling, S., Lentz, L., & De Jong, M. (2012). Combining concurrent think-aloud protocols and eye-tracking observations: An analysis of verbalizations and silences. *IEEE Transactions on Professional Communication 55*(3), 206–20.

Ericsson, K. A. & Simon, H. A. (1993). *Protocol Analysis: Verbal Reports as Data* (2nd ed.). Cambridge, MA: Bradford Books/MIT Press.

Ericsson, K. A. & Simon, H. A. (1998). How to study thinking in everyday life: Contrasting think-aloud protocols with descriptions and explanations of thinking. *Mind, Culture, and Activity 5*(3), 178–86.

Evans, V. (2009a). *How Words Mean: Lexical Concepts, Cognitive Models and Meaning Construction*. Oxford: Oxford University Press.

Evans, V. (2009b). Semantic representation in LCCM Theory. In V. Evans and S. Pourcel (eds.), *New Directions in Cognitive Linguistics*, pp. 27–55. Amsterdam: John Benjamins.

Fan, Y. & Heeman, P. A. (2010). Initiative conflicts in task-oriented dialogue. *Computer Speech and Language 24*, 175–89.

Fairclough, N. (1995). *Critical Discourse Analysis*. London: Longman.

Feldman, J. (2010). Embodied language, best-fit analysis, and formal compositionality. *Physics of Life Reviews* 7(4), 385–410.

Ferrari, F. (2007). Metaphor at work in the analysis of political discourse: Investigating a 'preventive war' persuasion strategy. *Discourse and Society* 18(5), 603–25.

Filipi, A. & Wales, R. (2004). Perspective-taking and perspective-shifting as socially situated and collaborative actions. *Journal of Pragmatics* 36(10), 1851–84.

Fine, M. S. & Minnery, B. S. (2009). Visual salience affects performance in a working memory task. *Journal of Neuroscience* 29(25), 8016–21.

Finke, R. A., Pinker, S., & Farah, M. J. (1989). Reinterpreting visual patterns in mental imagery. *Cognitive Science* 13(1), 51–78.

Fischer, M. H. & Zwaan, R. A. (2008). Embodied language: A review of the role of the motor system in language comprehension. *Quarterly Journal of Experimental Psychology* 61(6), 825–50.

Flower, L. & Hayes, J. R. (1981). A cognitive process theory of writing. *College Composition and Communication* 32(4), 365–87.

Fodor, J. A. (1983). *The Modularity of Mind.* Cambridge, MA: Bradford Books.

Fontaine, L., Bartlett, T., and O'Grady, G. (eds.) (2013). *Systemic Functional Linguistics: Exploring Choice.* Cambridge, UK: Cambridge University Press.

Frankenstein, J., Büchner, S., Tenbrink, T., & Hölscher, C. (2010). Influence of geometry and objects on local route choices during wayfinding. In C. Hölscher, T. Shipley, M. Olivetti Belardinelli, J. Bateman, & N. Newcombe (eds.), *Spatial Cognition VII: International Conference, Spatial Cognition 2010, Mt. Hood/ Portland, OR, USA, August 15–19, 2010*, pp. 41–53. Berlin/: Springer.

Franklin, N., Henkel, L. A., & Zangas, T. (1995). Parsing surrounding space into regions. *Memory and Cognition* 23, 397–407.

Freksa, C. (1981). Linguistic pattern characterization and analysis. Dissertation, University of California, Berkeley.

Garrod, S. & Pickering, M. J. (2004). Why is conversation so easy? *Trends in Cognitive Sciences* 8(1), 8–11.

Gee, J. P. (2010). *An Introduction to Discourse Analysis: Theory and method.* London: Routledge.

Gee, J. P. (2013). Discourse versus discourse. In C. A. Chapelle (ed.), *The Encyclopedia of Applied Linguistics.* Oxford: Blackwell. www.geez.byethost17.com/pdfs/Big%20 D%20Discourse.pdf?i=1

Gentner, D. (2010). Bootstrapping the mind: Analogical processes and symbol systems. *Cognitive Science* 34(5), 752–75.

Gentner, D., Levine, S., Dhillon, S., & Poltermann, A. (2009). Using structural alignment to facilitate learning of spatial concepts in an informal setting. In B. Kokinor, K. Holyoak, & D. Gentner (eds.), *Proceedings of the Second Analogy Conference*, pp. 175–82. Sofia, Bulgaria: NBU Press.

Giles, H. & Coupland, N. (1991). *Language: Contexts and Consequences.* Milton Keynes: Open University Press.

Goldberg, A. (1995). *Constructions: A Construction Grammar Approach to Argument Structure.* University of Chicago Press.

Gralla, L. (2013). Linguistic representation of problem solving processes in unaided object assembly. PhD dissertation, Bremen University, Germany.

Gralla, L. & Tenbrink, T. (2013). 'This is a wall' – assigning function to objects. In M. Knauff, M. Pauen, N. Sebanz, & I. Wachsmuth (eds.), *Proceedings of the 35th Annual Meeting of the Cognitive Science Society: CogSci 2013*, pp. 513–18. Austin, TX: Cognitive Science Society.

Gralla, L., Tenbrink, T., Siebers, M., & Schmid, U. (2012). Analogical problem solving: Insights from verbal reports. In N. Miyake, D. Peebles, & R. P. Cooper (eds.), *Proceedings of the 34th Annual Conference of the Cognitive Science Society*, pp. 396–401. Austin, TX: Cognitive Science Society.

Gramann, K., Müller, H. J., Eick, E. M., & Schönebeck, B. (2005). Evidence of separable spatial representations in a virtual navigation task. *Journal of Experimental Psychology: Human Perception and Performance* 31(6), 1199–223.

Grant, E. R. & Spivey, M. J. (2003). Eye movements and problem solving: Guiding attention guides thought. *Psychological Science 14*, 462–6.

Grice, H. P. (1975). Logic and conversation. In P. Cole, & J. Morgan (eds.), *Syntax and semantics* (Vol 3), pp. 41–58). New York: Academic Press.

Grosz, B. J. & Sidner, C. L. (1986). Attention, intentions and the structure of discourse. *Computational Linguistics 12*(3), 175–204.

Gugerty, L. & Rodes, W. (2007). A cognitive model of strategies for cardinal direction judgments. *Spatial Cognition and Computation 7*(2), 179–212.

Gülşen, T. T. (2016). You tell me in emojis. In T. Ogata & T. Akimoto (eds.), *Computational and Cognitive Approaches to Narratology*, pp. 354–75. Hershey, PA: IGI Global.

Habel, C. & Tappe, H. (1999). Processes of segmentation and linearization in describing events. In R. Klabunde & C. von Stutterheim (eds.), *Representations and Processes in Language Production*, pp. 117–53. Wiesbaden: Springer.

Haddington, P. (2010). Turn-taking for turntaking: Mobility, time and action in the sequential organization of junction-negotiations in cars. *Research on Language and Social Interaction* 43(4), 372–400.

Halliday, M. A. K. & Matthiessen, C. M. I. M. (2014). *Halliday's Introduction to Functional Grammar* (4th ed.). London: Routledge.

Hanna, J. E., Tanenhaus, M. K., & Trueswell, J. C. (2003). The effects of common ground and perspective on domains of referential interpretation. *Journal of Memory and Language 49*(1), 43–61.

Hart, C. & Lukeš, D. (eds.) (2009). *Cognitive Linguistics in Critical Discourse Analysis: Application and Theory*. Newcastle upon Tyne: Cambridge Scholars Publishing.

Hayes, A. F. & Krippendorff, K. (2007). Answering the call for a standard reliability measure for coding data. *Communication Methods and Measures 1*, 77–89.

Henderson, J. M. & Ferreira, F. (eds.) (2004). *The Interface of Language, Vision, and Action: Eye Movements and the Visual World*. New York: Psychology Press.

Henderson, J. M., Malcolm, G. L., & Schandl, C. (2009). Searching in the dark: Cognitive relevance drives attention in real-world scenes. *Psychonomic Bulletin and Review 16*(5), 850–6.

Hobbs, J. R. (1995). Sketch of an ontology underlying the way we talk about the world. *International Journal of Human–Computer Studies 43*(5/6), 819–30.

Hoffman, R. R., Trafton, G., & Roebber, P. (2005). *Minding the Weather: How Expert Forecasters Think*. Cambridge, MA: MIT Press.

Holsanova, J. (2008). *Discourse, Vision, and Cognition*. Amsterdam: Benjamins.

Hölscher, C., Meilinger, T., Vrachliotis, G., Brösamle, M., & Knauff, M. (2006). Up the down staircase: Wayfinding strategies and multi-level buildings. *Journal of Environmental Psychology 26*(4), 284–99.

Hölscher, C., Tenbrink, T., & Wiener, J. (2011). Would you follow your own route description? *Cognition 121*, 228–47.

Jee, B. D., Gentner, D., Forbus, K., Sageman, B., & Uttal, D. H. (2009). Drawing on experience. In N. A. Taatgen & H. van Rijn (eds.), *Proceedings of the 31st Annual Meeting of the Cognitive Science Society*, pp. 2499–504. Austin, TX: Cognitive Science Society.

Johnson-Laird, P. N. (1983). *Mental Models.* Cambridge, MA: Harvard University Press.

Johnstone, B. (2008). *Discourse Analysis* (2nd ed.). Hoboken, NJ: Blackwell Publishers.

Kahneman, D. (1973). *Attention and Effort.* Englewood Cliffs, NJ: Prentice-Hall.

Kastens, K. A., Agrawal, S., & Liben, L. S. (2009). How students and field geologists reason in integrating spatial observations from outcrops to visualize a 3-D geological structure. *International Journal of Science Education 31*(3), 365–93.

Klabunde, R. & von Stutterheim, C. (eds.) (1999). *Representations and Processes in Language Production.* Wiesbaden: Springer.

Klein, W. (1979). Wegauskünfte (Route descriptions). *Zeitschrift für Literaturwissenschaft und Linguistik* (LiLi) 33, 9–57.

Klippel, A. (2003). Wayfinding choremes. In W. Kuhn, M. Worboys, & S. Timpf (eds.), *Spatial Information Theory: Foundations of Geographic Information Science*, pp. 320–34. Berlin: Springer.

Knapton, O. & Rundblad, G. (2014). Public health in the UK media: Cognitive discourse analysis and its application to a drinking water emergency. In C. Hart & P. Cap (eds.), *Contemporary Critical Discourse Studies*, pp. 559–82. London: Bloomsbury.

Krahmer, E. & Ummelen, N. (2004). Thinking about thinking aloud: A comparison of two verbal protocols for usability testing. *IEEE Transactions on Professional Communication 47*(2), 105–17.

Krippendorff, K. (2012). *Content Analysis: An Introduction to Its Methodology* (3rd ed.). London: Sage.

Kristiansen, G. & Dirven, R. (eds.) (2008). *Cognitive Sociolinguistics: Language Variation, Cultural Models, Social Systems* (Vol. 39). Berlin: Walter de Gruyter.

Kuipers, B. J. & Kassirer, J. P. (1984). Causal reasoning in medicine: Analysis of a protocol. *Cognitive Science 8*, 363–85.

Kuipers, B. J., Moskowitz, A. J., & Kassirer, J. P. (1988). Critical decisions under uncertainty: Representation and structure. *Cognitive Science 12*, 177–210.

Ladd, R. D. (1996). *Intonational Phonology.* Cambridge, UK: Cambridge University Press.

Lakoff, G. & Johnson, M. (1980). *Metaphors We Live By.* University of Chicago Press.

Lakoff, G. & Johnson, M. (1999). *Philosophy in the Flesh: The Embodied Mind and Its Challenge to Western Thought.* New York: Basic Books.

Langacker, R. W. (1986). An introduction to cognitive grammar. *Cognitive Science 10*, 1–40.

Langacker, R. W. (2000). A dynamic usage-based model. In M. Barlow & S. Kemmer (eds.), *Usage-Based Models of Language*, pp. 1–64. Stanford, CA: CSLI Publications.

Langacker, R. W. (2002). *Concept, Image, and Symbol: the Cognitive Basis of Grammar.* Berlin: Mouton de Gruyter.

Larkin, J. H. & Simon, H. A. (1987). Why a diagram is (sometimes) worth ten thousand words. *Cognitive Science 11*, 65–99.

Le Guen, O. (2011). Speech and gesture in spatial language and cognition among the Yucatec Mayas. *Cognitive Science 35*(5), 905–38.

Leow, R. P., Grey, S., Marijuan, S., & Moorman, C. (2014). Concurrent data elicitation procedures, processes, and the early stages of L2 learning:· A critical overview. *Second Language Research 30*(2), 111–27.

Levinson, S. C. (1997). From outer to inner space: Linguistic categories and non-linguistic thinking. In J. Nuyts & E. Pederson (eds.), *Language and Conceptualization*, pp. 13–45. Cambridge, UK: Cambridge University Press.

Levinson, S. C. (2003). *Space in Language and Cognition.* Cambridge, UK: Cambridge University Press.

Linde, C. & Labov, W. (1975). Spatial networks as a site for the study of language and thought. *Language 51*, 924–39.

Lindsey, A. E., Greene, J. O., Parker, R. G., & Sassi, M. (1995). Effects of advance message formulation on message encoding: Evidence of cognitively based hesitation in the production of multiple-goal messages. *Communication Quarterly 43*(3), 320–31.

Lutz, A., Lachaux, J. P., Martinerie, J., & Varela, F. J. (2002). Guiding the study of brain dynamics by using first-person data: Synchrony patterns correlate with ongoing conscious states during a simple visual task. *Proceedings of the National Academy of Sciences 99*(3), 1586–91.

Maes, A., Arts, A., & Noordman, L. (2004). Reference management in instructive discourse. *Discourse Processes 37*(2), 117–44.

Martin, J. R. & Rose, D. (2003). *Working with Discourse: Meaning beyond the Clause.* London: Continuum International Publishing Group Ltd.

Mast, F. W. & Kosslyn, S. M. (2002). Visual mental images can be ambiguous: Insights from individual differences in spatial transformation abilities. *Cognition 86*(1), 57–70.

McManus, I. C., Zhou, F. A., l'Anson, S., et al. (2011). The psychometrics of photographic cropping: The influence of colour, meaning, and expertise. *Perception 40*(3), 332–57.

Meilinger, T. & Knauff, M. (2008). Ask for your way or use a map: A field experiment on spatial orientation and wayfinding in an urban environment. *Spatial Science 53*(2), 13–24.

Mercier, H. & Sperber, D. (2011). Why do humans reason? Arguments for an argumentative theory. *Behavioral and Brain Sciences 34*(2), 57–74.

Montague, R. (1970). Universal grammar. *Theoria 36*(3), 373–98.

Montello, D. R. (1993). Scale and multiple psychologies of space. In A. Frank & I. Campari (eds.), *Spatial Information Theory: A Theoretical Basis for GIS*, pp. 312–21. Berlin: Springer.

Moratz, R. & Tenbrink, T. (2006). Spatial reference in linguistic human-robot interaction: Iterative, empirically supported development of a model of projective relations. *Spatial Cognition and Computation 6*(1), 63–106.

Moray, N. (1959). Attention in dichotic listening: Affective cues and the influence of instructions. *Quarterly Journal of Experimental Psychology 11*(1), 56–60.

Neisser, U. & Becklen, R. (1975). Selective looking: Attending to visually specified events. *Cognitive Psychology 7*, 480–94.

Nissen, M. J. & Bullemer, P. (1987). Attentional requirement of learning: Evidence from performance measures. *Cognitive Psychology 19*, 1–32.

Newell, A. & Simon, H. A. (1972). *Human Problem Solving*. Englewood Cliffs, NJ: Prentice-Hall.

Newman, E. L., Caplan, J. B., Kirschen, M. P., et al. (2007). Learning your way around town: How virtual taxicab drivers learn to use both layout and landmark information. *Cognition 104*(2), 231–53.

Norman, D. A. & Shallice, T. (1980). Attention to action: Willed and automatic control of behavior. In R. J. Davidson, G. E. Schwartz, & D. Shapiro (eds.), *Consciousness and Self-Regulation*, pp. 1–15. New York: Plenum.

Noveck, I. A. & Sperber, D. (2006). *Experimental Pragmatics*. London: Palgrave Macmillan.

Nuyts, J. & Pederson, E. (eds.) (1997). *Language and Conceptualization*. Cambridge, UK: Cambridge University Press.

Olloqui Redondo, J., Tenbrink, T., & Foltz, A. (2019.) Effects of animacy and linguistic construction on the interpretation of spatial descriptions in English and Spanish. *Language and Cognition 11*(2), 256–84.

O'Malley, M., Innes, A., Muir, S., & Wiener, J. M. (2018). 'All the corridors are the same': A qualitative study of the orientation experiences and design preferences of UK older adults living in a communal retirement development. *Ageing and Society 38* (9), 1791–816.

Pashler, H. (1984). Processing stages in overlapping tasks: Evidence for a central bottleneck. *Journal of Experimental Psychology: Human Perception and Performance 10*(3), 358–77.

Piaget, J. (1952). The Origins of Intelligence in Children. New York: International Universities Press.

Pick, H. L., Heinrichs, M. R., Montello, D. R., Smith, K., & Sullivan, C. N. (1995). Topographic map reading. In P. A. Hancock, J. M. Flach, J. Caird, & K. J. Vicente (eds.), *Local Applications of the Ecological Approach to Human-Machine Systems* (Vol. 2), pp. 255–84. Hillsdale, NJ: Lawrence Erlbaum Associates.

Pickering, M. & Garrod, S. (2004). Toward a mechanistic psychology of dialogue. *Behavioral and Brain Sciences 27*, 169–226.

Purcell, T. & Gero, J. S. (1998). Drawings and the design process: A review of protocol studies in design and other disciplines and related research in cognitive psychology. *Design Studies 19*(4), 389–430.

Pütz, M., Robinson, J. A., & Reif, M. (eds.) (2014). *Cognitive Sociolinguistics: Social and Cultural Variation in Cognition and Language Use* (Vol. 59). Chicago: John Benjamins.

Ranyard, R., Crozier, W. R., & Svenson, O. (eds.) (1997). *Decision Making: Cognitive Models and Explanations*. London: Routledge.

Rasinger, S. (2010). Research questions in linguistics. In L. Litosseliti (ed.), *Research Methods in Linguistics*, pp. 49–67. London: Continuum.

Reason, J. (1990). *Human Error*. Cambridge, UK: Cambridge University Press.

Riecke, B. E. & Wiener, J. M. (2007). Can people not tell left from right in VR? Point-to-origin studies revealed qualitative errors in visual path integration. In W. R. Sherman,

M. C. Lin, & A. Steed (eds.), *Proceedings of IEEE Virtual Reality 2007*, pp. 3–10. Washington: IEEE Computer Society.

Röder, B. & Rösler, F. (2003). Memory for environmental sounds in sighted, congenitally blind and late blind adults: Evidence for cross-modal compensation. *International Journal of Psychophysiology 50*(1), 27–39.

Rosch, E. (1978). Principles of categorization. In E. Rosch & B. B. Lloyd (eds.), *Cognition and Categorization*, pp. 27–48 Hillsdale, NJ: Lawrence Erlbaum Associates.

Rosch, E., Mervis, C. B., Gray, W. D., Johnson, D. M., Boyes-Braem, P. (1976). Basic objects in natural categories. *Cognitive Psychology 8*, 382–439.

Roth, T. (1985). Sprachstatistisch objektivierbare Denkstilunterschiede zwischen 'guten' und 'schlechten' Bearbeitern komplexer Probleme. *Sprache und Kognition 4*, 178–91.

Russo, J. E., Johnson, E. J., & Stephens, D. L. (1989). The validity of verbal protocols. *Memory and Cognition 17*, 759–69.

Sachs, J. S. (1974). Memory in reading and listening to discourse. *Memory and Cognition 2*(1), 95–100.

Sacks, H. (1992). *Lectures on Conversation*. Oxford: Blackwell.

Sacks, O. (2010). *The Mind's Eye*. New York: Knopf.

Sanders, T. (1997). Semantic and pragmatic sources of coherence: On the categorization of coherence relations in context. *Discourse Processes 24*, 119–47.

Sarjakoski, L. & Nivala, A. M. (2005). Adaptation to context: A way to improve the usability of mobile maps. In L. Meng, A. Zipf, & T. Reichenbacher (eds.), *Map-Based Mobile Services, Theories, Methods and Implementations*, pp. 107–23. Berlin: Springer.

Schiffrin, D. (1987). *Discourse Markers*. Cambridge, UK: Cambridge University Press.

Schlobinski, P. (1996). *Empirische Sprachwissenschaft*. Berlin: Springer.

Schober, M. F. (1995). Speakers, addressees, and frames of reference: Whose effort is minimized in conversations about location? *Discourse Processes 20*(2), 219–47.

Schober, M. F. (1998). Different kinds of conversational perspective-taking. In S. R. Fussell & R. J. Kreuz (eds.), *Social and Cognitive Psychological Approaches to Interpersonal Communication*, pp. 145–74. Mahwah, NJ: Lawrence Erlbaum.

Schober, M. F. & Brennan, S. E. (2003). Processes of interactive spoken discourse: The role of the partner. In A. C. Graesser, M. A. Gernsbacher, & S. R. Goldman (eds.), *Handbook of Discourse Processes*, pp. 123–64. Mahwah, NJ: Lawrence Erlbaum Associates.

Schönebeck, B., Thanhäuser, J., & Debus, G. (2001). Die Tunnelaufgabe: Eine Methode zur Untersuchung kognitiver Teilprozesse räumlicher Orientierungsleistungen (The tunnel task: A method for the investigation of cognitive subprocesses of spatial orientation performance). *Zeitschrift für Experimentelle Psychologie 4*, 339–64.

Schooler, J. W., Ohlsson, S., & Brooks, K. (1993). Thoughts beyond words: When language overshadows insight. *Journal of Experimental Psychology: General 122*(2), 166–83.

Seifert, I. (2008). Spatial planning assistance: A cooperative approach. Dissertation, Bremen University, Germany.

Selting, M. (2000). The construction of units in conversational talk. *Language in Society* *29*, 477–517.

Senft, G. (1994). Spatial reference in Kilivila: The Tinkertoy Matching Games – A case study. *Language and Linguistics in Melanesia 25*, 55–93.

Shepard, R. N. & Metzler, J. (1971). Mental rotation of three-dimensional objects. *Science 171*(3972), 701–3.

Shi, H., Ross, R. J., Tenbrink, T., & Bateman, J. (2010). Modelling illocutionary structure: Combining empirical studies with formal model analysis. In A. Gelbukh (ed.), *Computational Linguistics and Intelligent Text Processing*, pp. 340–53. LNCS 6008. Berlin: Springer.

Sholl, M. J. (1988). The relationship between sense of direction and mental geographic updating. *Intelligence 12*(3), 299–314.

Siegel, A. W. & White, S. H. (1975). The development of spatial representations of large-scale environments. In H. W. Reese (ed.), *Advances in Child Development and Behavior*, pp. 9–55. New York: Academic Press.

Siegler, R. S. & Stern, E. (1998). Conscious and unconscious strategy discoveries: A microgenetic analysis. *Journal of Experimental Psychology: General 127*(4), 377–97.

Simon, H. A. (1956). Rational choice and the structure of the environment. *Psychological Review 63*(2), 129–38.

Sitter, S. & Stein, A. (1996). Modeling information-seeking dialogues: The conversational roles model. *Review of Information Science 1*(1), 165–80.

Smagorinsky, P. (1998). Thinking and speech and protocol analysis. *Mind, Culture, and Activity 5*, 157–77.

Smith, W. & Dror, I. E. (2001). *Psychonomic Bulletin and Review 8*, 732–41.

Spenader, J. (2002). Presupposed propositions in a corpus of dialogue. In K. van Deemter & R. Kibble (eds.), *Information Sharing: Reference and Presupposition in Language Generation and Interpretation*. Stanford, CA: CSLI Publications.

Sperber, D. & Wilson, D. (1986). *Relevance: Communication and Cognition*. Cambridge, MA: Harvard University Press.

Spiers, H. J. & Maguire, E. A. (2008). The dynamic nature of cognition during wayfinding. *Journal of Environmental Psychology 28*(3), 232–49.

Sternberg, R. J. & Ben-Zeev, T. (2001). *Complex Cognition: The Psychology of Human Thought*. Oxford: Oxford University Press.

Steube, A. (ed.) (2004). *Information Structure: Theoretical and Empirical Aspects*. Berlin: Mouton de Gruyter.

Talmy, L. (2000). *Toward a Cognitive Semantics*. Cambridge, MA: MIT Press.

Talmy, L. (2007). Attention phenomena. In D. Geeraerts & H. Cuyckens (eds.), *Handbook of Cognitive Linguistics*, pp. 264–93. Oxford: Oxford University Press.

Taylor, J. (1989). *Linguistic Categorization*. Oxford: Clarendon.

Taylor, H. A. & Tversky, B. (1996). Perspective in spatial descriptions. *Journal of Memory and Language 35*, 371–91.

Tenbrink, T. (2007). Space, Time, and the Use of Language: An Investigation of Relationships. Berlin: Mouton de Gruyter.

Tenbrink, T. (2008). The verbalization of cognitive processes: Thinking-aloud data and retrospective reports. In W. Ramm & C. Fabricius-Hansen (eds.), *Linearisation and*

Segmentation in Discourse. Multidisciplinary Approaches to Discourse 2008 (MAD 08), pp. 125–35. Oslo: Oslo University Press.

Tenbrink, T. (2011). Reference frames of space and time in language. *Journal of Pragmatics 43*(3), 704–22.

Tenbrink, T. (2014). Cognitive discourse analysis for cognitively supportive visualisations. Proceedings of DECISIVe 2014, Open Access Repository, University of Konstanz.

Tenbrink, T. (2015). Cognitive discourse analysis: Accessing cognitive representations and processes through language data. *Language and Cognition 7*(1), 98–137.

Tenbrink, T., Andonova, E., & Coventry, K. R. (2008). Negotiating spatial relationships in dialogue: The role of the addressee. In J. Ginzburg, P. Healey, & Y. Sato (eds.), *Proceedings of LONDIAL*, pp. 201–8. London: Queen Mary University.

Tenbrink, T., Andonova, E., Schole, G., & Coventry, K. R. (2017). Communicative success in spatial dialogue: The impact of functional features and dialogic strategies. *Language and Speech 60*(2), 318–29.

Tenbrink, T., Bergmann, E., Hertzberg, C., & Gondorf, C. (2016). Time will not help unskilled observers to understand a cluttered spatial scene. *Spatial Cognition and Computation 16*(3), 192–219.

Tenbrink, T., Bergmann, E., & Konieczny, L. (2011a). Wayfinding and description strategies in an unfamiliar complex building. In C. H. Carlson & T. F. Shipley (eds.), *Proceedings of the 33rd Annual Conference of the Cognitive Science Society*, pp. 1262–7. Austin, TX: Cognitive Science Society.

Tenbrink, T., Brösamle, M., & Hölscher, C. (2012). Flexibility of perspectives in architects' thinking. In C. Hölscher & M. Bhatt (eds.), *Proceedings of SCAD Spatial Cognition for Architectural Design*. Report No. 029–08/2012 Report Series of the Transregional Collaborative Research Center SFB/TR 8 Spatial Cognition, pp. 215–23. Bremen: Bremen University.

Tenbrink, T., Coventry, K. R., & Andonova, E. (2011b). Spatial strategies in the description of complex configurations. *Discourse Processes 48*, 237–66.

Tenbrink, T., Hölscher, C., Tsigaridi, D., & Conroy Dalton, R. (2014). Cognition and communication in architectural design. In D. R. Montello, K. E. Grossner, & D. G. Janelle (eds.), *Space in Mind: Concepts for Spatial Learning and Education*, pp. 263–80. Cambridge, MA: MIT Press.

Tenbrink, T. & Maas, A. (2015). Efficiently connecting textual and visual information in operating instructions. *IEEE Transactions on Professional Communication 58*(4), 346–66.

Tenbrink, T., Ross, R. R., Thomas, K. E., Dethlefs, N., & Andonova, E. (2010). Route instructions in map-based human-human and human-computer dialogue: A comparative analysis. *Journal of Visual Languages and Computing 21*(5), 292–309.

Tenbrink, T. & Salwiczek, L. (2016). Orientation and metacognition in virtual space. *Journal of Experimental Psychology: Human Perception and Performance 42*(5), 683–705.

Tenbrink, T. & Schilder, F. (2003). (Non)temporal concepts conveyed by before, after, and then in dialogue. In P. Kühnlein, H. Rieser, & H. Zeevat (eds.), *Perspectives on Dialogue in the New Millennium*, pp. 353–80. Amsterdam: Benjamins.

Tenbrink, T. & Seifert, I. (2011). Conceptual layers and strategies in tour planning. *Cognitive Processing 12*(1), 109–25.

Tenbrink, T. & Taylor, H. A. (2015). Conceptual transformation and cognitive processes in Origami paper folding. *Journal of Problem Solving 8*(1), 2–22.

Tenbrink, T. & Wiener, J. (2009). The verbalization of multiple strategies in a variant of the traveling salesperson problem. *Cognitive Processing 10*(2), 143–61.

Tenbrink, T. & Winter, S. (2009). Variable granularity in route directions. *Spatial Cognition and Computation 9*, 64–93.

Tomasello, M. (2003). *Constructing a Language: A Usage-Based Theory of Language Acquisition*. Cambridge, MA: Harvard University Press.

Toulmin, S. (1958). *The Uses of Argument*. Cambridge, UK: Cambridge University Press.

Trognon, A., Batt, M., & Laux, J. (2011). Why is dialogical solving of a logical problem more effective than individual solving? A formal and experimental study of an abstract version of Wason's task. *Language and Dialogue 1*(1), 44–78.

Tversky, B. (1999). Spatial perspective in descriptions. In P. Bloom, M. A. Peterson, L. Nadel, & M. F. Garrett (eds.), *Language and Space*, pp. 109–69. Cambridge, MA: MIT Press.

Tversky, B. & Hard, B. M. (2009). Embodied and disembodied cognition: Spatial perspective-taking. *Cognition 110*, 124–9.

Tversky, B. & Lee, P. (1999). Pictorial and verbal tools for conveying routes. In C. Freksa & D. M. Mark (eds.), *Spatial Information Theory: Cognitive and Computational Foundations of Geographic Information Science* (COSIT '99), pp. 51–64. Berlin: Springer.

Tyler, A. & Evans, V. (2003). *The Semantics of English Prepositions: Spatial Sciences, Embodied Meaning, and Cognition*. Cambridge, UK: Cambridge University Press.

van Deemter, K. & Kibble, R. (eds.) (2002). *Information Sharing: Reference and Presupposition in Language Generation and Interpretation*. Stanford, CA: CSLI Publications.

van Deemter, K. & Peters, S. (eds.) (1996). *Semantic Ambiguity and Underspecification*. Stanford, CA: CSLI Publications.

van Dijk, T. A. (2000). Cognitive discourse analysis: An introduction. www .discursos.org/unpublished%20articles/cogn-dis-anal.htm

van Dijk, T. A. (2008). *Discourse and Power*. Houndsmills: Palgrave-MacMillan.

van Someren, M. W., Barnard, Y. F., & Sandberg, J. (1994). *The Think Aloud Method: A Practical Guide to Modelling Cognitive Processes*. London: Academic Press.

Vorwerg, C. (2009). Consistency in successive spatial utterances. In K. Coventry, T. Tenbrink, & J. Bateman (eds.), *Spatial Language and Dialogue*, pp. 40–55. Oxford: Oxford University Press.

Vorwerg, C. & Tenbrink, T. (2007). Discourse factors influencing spatial descriptions in English and German. In T. Barkowsky, M. Knauff, G. Ligozat, & D. Montello (eds.), *Spatial Cognition V: Reasoning, Action, Interaction*, pp. 470–88. Berlin: Springer.

Wachsmuth, I., de Ruiter, J., Jaecks, P., & Kopp, S. (eds.) (2013). *Alignment in Communication: Towards a New Theory of Communication*. Amsterdam: John Benjamins.

Warren, P. (2005). Patterns of late rising in New Zealand English: Intonational variation or intonational change? *Language Variation and Change 17*(2), 209–30.

Wen, W., Ishikawa, T., & Sato, T. (2013). Individual differences in the encoding processes of egocentric and allocentric survey knowledge. *Cognitive Science 37*, 176–92.

Whorf, B. L. (1941). The relation of habitual thought and behavior to language. In L. Spier (ed.), *Language, Culture, and Personality: Essays in Memory of Edward Sapir*, pp. 75–93. Menasha, WI: Sapir Memorial Publication Fund.

Wilson, M. (2002). Six views of embodied cognition. *Psychonomic Bulletin and Review 9*(4), 625–36.

Winterboer, A., Tenbrink, T., & Moratz, R. (2013). Spatial directionals for robot navigation. In M. Dimitrova-Vulchanova & E. van der Zee (eds.), *Motion Encoding in Spatial Language*, pp. 84–101. Oxford: Oxford University Press.

Wittgenstein, L. (1953). *Philosophical Investigations*. New York: Macmillan.

Yang, S. C. (2003). Reconceptualizing think-aloud methodology: Refining the encoding and categorizing techniques via contextualized perspectives. *Computers in Human Behavior 19*, 95–115.

Zacks, J. M., Tversky, B., & Iyer, G. (2001). Perceiving, remembering, and communicating structure in events. *Journal of Experimental Psychology: General 130*, 29–58.

Zhang, Q., Walsh, M. M., & Anderson, J. R. (2018). The impact of inserting an additional mental process. *Computational Brain and Behavior 1*(1), 22–35.

Index

accommodation, 174
ACT-R, 234
adaptation, 173
addressee, 24, 56, 152, 169, **170**, 207, 250
adjective, 97, 118, 124
analysis
    qualitative, 19, 27, 30, 109, 110, 114, 119,
        121, 138, 140, 161, 165, 198, 211, 213,
        220–2, 245
    quantitative, 19, 34, 42, 131, 138, 140, 161,
        211, 214, 219, 220, 222–5, 240
analysis perspective, 23, 33, 40, 49, 83, 84, 152,
    171, 236
Anderson, John Robert, 33, 93, 95, 234
annotation, 22, 24, 53, 124, 126, 184, 194, 214,
    216–17, 218, 219–20, 222, 235
applications, 47, 226, 248
article
    definite, 23, 24, 78, 217, 218, 223
    indefinite, 77
assembly, 160
attention, 2, 31, 83, **92**, 116, 182, 187, 190,
    230, 236
awareness, 11, 43, 48, 52, 94, 132, 150,
    172, 234

back-channelling, 172, 176
behavioural data, 47, 138, 186, 187

certainty, 86, **128**, 132, 137, 161
choice, 3, 12, 13, 15, 18, 28, 34, 38, 40, 64, 65,
    81, 83, 84, 97, 98, 113, 171, 195, 200,
    222, 230
Chomsky, Noam, 58, 64
clause, 13, 68, 85, 87, 88, 89, 90, 124, 211–13
cognition
    complex, 14, 20, 26, 156, 181, 182, 186, 187,
        190, 202, 207, 236
    human, 2, 10, 11, 142, 146, 241
    spatial, 16, 23, **35**, 122, 243
cognitive load, 136, 174
cognitive strategy, 46, 185, 190–3, 241

common sense, 143, 241
communication, 8, 10, 14, 31, 34, 46, 56, 78,
    93, 100, 114, 125, 135, 150, 151, 160, **169**,
    171, 173, 176, 190, 230, 250
concept, 10, 11, 22, 36, 38, 58, 61, 63, 81, 82,
    99, 103, 113, 122, 123, 145, 174, 188, 194,
    211, 216, 226, 245
conceptual aspect. *See* analysis perspective
conceptual perspective, 64, 103, 110–16,
    180, 247
conceptual strategy, 30, 31, 192
conjunction, 22–3, 100, 116
content, 3, 21, 22, 23, 49, 53, 54, 74, 84, 124,
    166, 181, 183, 184, 196, 213, 220, 235
content analysis, 21, 22, 26, 54, 184, 213–14,
    215, 217, 234, 235
content category, 21, 22, 54, 164, 165, 166,
    181, 184, 185, 213–14, 215, 216, 222, 224
conversation analysis, 77
Coventry, Kenny R., 16, 17, 19, 26, 29, 40, 179,
    202, 237

Dąbrowska, Ewa, 26
data collection, 38, 49, 197
decision making, 14, 20, 25
demonstrative, 161, 162, 172
detail, 13, 17, 28, 43, 76, 81, 99, 117, 118, 119,
    123, 130, 141, 149, 173, 227
dialogue, 37, 39, 48, 55, 100, 107, 149, 168,
    171, 172, **173**, 175, 178, 179, 180, 191,
    208, 237, 250
dialogue system, 171, 178, 226, 240, 242,
    250
discourse
    relations, 79, 80
    structure, 53, 99, 100, 132, 238
discourse analysis, 32, 56, **72**, 77, 78, 80, 83,
    91, 152, 194, 227
distribution pattern, 211, 221

EEG, 231, 232
elaboration, **123**, 125, 126, 151

empirical, 28, 29, 33, 67, 155, 168, 171, 197, 200
Ericsson, K.A., 21, 22, 28, 30, 44, 46, 47, 48, 49, 50, 52, 53, 56, 163, 181, 182, 184, 190, 204, 205, 206, 207
ethics, 196
Evans, Vyvyan, 11, 59, 60, 70, 71
experience, 9, 35, 36, 38, 59, 65, 72, 93, 95, 100, 119, 120, 123, 125, 131, 144, 145, 146, 149, 156, 179, 197, 234, 246
experimental design, 15, 28, 38, 39, 40, 46, 197–201, 231, 235
expertise, 27, 56, 61, 102, 128, **129**, 132, 137, 141, 153, 246
explicit, 22, 25, 49, 80, 122, 143, 144, 150, 152
extensions, 226

fMRI, 231, 232
focus group, 207, 227

generalisability, 30
Goldberg, Adele, 71
grammar
    cognitive, 64–5, 97
    functional, 32, 68, 79, 83–91, 132, 133, 134, 136, 169
granularity, **117**, 117–28, 236, 241, 247
Grice, Paul, 121, 150

Halliday, Michael, 22, 24, 78, 79, 83, 85, 86, 88, 89, 98, 124, 132, 134, 136, 169, 175, 176, 178
hesitation. *See* pause

implicit, 1, 29, 79, 80, 97, 107, 120, 122, 124, 145, 152, 161, 216, 231, 234, 236
indicator, 2, 25, 54, 108, 134, 181, 185, 190
inference, 19, 43–4, 79–80, 83, 121, 122, **142**, 142–55, 166
information structure, 73, 77–8, 90, 217
instruction, 29, 39, 47, 52, 156, 163, 187, 196, 200, 202, 205, 207, 209, 249
intelligence, artificial, 240–3
interaction, 14, 48, 98, 103, 107, 137, 162, 169, 170, 174, 179, 191, 208, 242
interview, 42, 46, 55, 56, 74, 102, 114, 116, 207, 227, 244, 246
intonation contour, 76, 209, 210

Johnson, Mark, 8, 11, 69, 70

Lakoff, George, 8, 11, 69, 70, 113
Langacker, Ronald, 64, 65, 68, 96–7
LCCM, 59–60
Levinson, Stephen, 10, 66, 67, 68, 104, 105

Likert scale, 249
limit, 30, 31, 35, 42, 59, 60, 92, 117, 131, 147, 169, 173, 196, 197, 202, 206, 207, 213, 230
linguistics, cognitive, 15, 32, 57–72, 95, 113, 227
linguistics, corpus, 34, 179, 196, 211, 227, 240
linguistics, systemic functional, 15

machine learning, 240
marker
    certainty, 129, 132–7
    discourse, 22, 54, 55, 73, 79–80, 181, 220, 236
    hesitation, 30, 135, 136, 162
    orientation, 140, 141
    politeness, 170
    uncertainty, 27, 28, 137, 138, 140, 141
mental rotation, 157, 158
metaphor, 11, 69–72, 73, 113, 115
modality, 13, 55, 86, 133, 161, 162, 170, 190, 220
model
    cognitive, 227, 232–6
mood, 13, 83–4, 85–6, 170, 175–6

neuroscience, cognitive, 30
non-sequitur, 236
noun, 64, 98, 113, 161, 239

observable, 142, 227
operationalisation, 21, 126, 138, 154, 181, 189, 211, **217**, **222**
orientation, 18, 19, 92–116, 157, 165, 192, 219, 244

pattern, usage, 69, 71
pause, 30, 135, 136, 209, 235
performance, 10, 46, 48, 52, 95, 129, 157, 158, **228**
perspective, 16, 17, 18, 29, 31, 36, 65, 66, **103**, 103–16, 118, 207, 212
Piaget, Jean, 159
Pinker, Steven, 157
preposition, 70–1, 165, 219
presupposition, 24–5, 73, 78, 216, 217, 218, 223, 236
principles, 2, 43, 63, 83, 143, 148, 150, 175, 178, 181, 194, 197, 204, 212, 221, 245
problem solving, 14, 20, 21, 23, 42, 44, 47, 52, 53–6, 130, 163, 202, 204–7, 213–14, 227–9, 236, 248, 249
procedures, 21, 54, 74, 148, 184, 197, 208, 211, 213, 216, 222, 224, 236, 248
pronoun, 13, 79, 90, 115, 161, 172

protocol, verbal, 20–1, 22, 45, 46, 49, 50, 52,
53–6, 131, 152, 168, 171, 181–93, 201–8,
217, 232, 233, 234, 235, 249
prototype theory, 62–3
psycholinguistics, 15, 16, 32, 37–41, 227, 230
psychology, cognitive, 20, 32, 50, 53–6, 108,
129–32, 181

questionnaire, 50, 51, 207, 227, 229, 249

reaction times, 38, 44, 230
referential communication, 40
reliability, 26, 216
report, retrospective, 21, 25, 46, 49, 52, 55, 109,
187, 190, 206, 207, 232
representation, 10, 245
linguistic, 7, 15, 24, 31, 32, 46, 90, 124, 169,
188, 202, 204
mental, 14, **15**, 19, 33, 38, 89, 97, 142, 183,
202, 204
research
goal, 15, 195, 196, 201, 207, 211
purpose, 33, 195, 210, 213, 214, 237
robot, 177, 226, 241, 242
Rosch, Eleanor, 62, 63
route description. *See* wayfinding

scale, 29, 67, 75, **119**, 124
science
cognitive, 3, 31, 45, 48, 92, 93, 95, 99, 117,
137, 168, 181, 184, 196, 204, 226, 227
social, 174, 207
segmentation, 211
semantics, cognitive, 63–4
signal, linguistic, 45, 54, 77, 78, 80, 101, 141,
172, 174
Simon, Herbert A., 20, 21, 22, 28, 30, 44, 46,
47, 48, 49, 50, 52, 53, 56, 147, 163, 181,
182, 184, 190, 204, 205, 206, 207
statistics, 27, 34, 198, 199, 216, 221, 224
study, 16–19, 22, 25, 39, 53–4, 101–3, 114–16,
137–41, 148–9, 153–5, 159–67, 171,

179–81, 183, 186, 187, 188–90, 191–3,
203, 207, 228–9, 231–2, 239–40
syntax, 13, 64–6, 82, 173, 224
system, spatial reference, 16, 17–19, 35, 66–8,
103–10, 219
systematic, 2, 5, 12, 14, 21, 24, 29, 36, 46, 48,
55, 57, 63, 77, 129, 130, 184, 210,
218, 249

Talmy, Leonard, 63, 64, 65, 97, 98
Taylor, Holly A., 106, 107, 109, 144, 157, 163,
164, 166, 214, 215, 222, 249
Tenbrink, Thora, 16, 18, 19, 23, 24, 25, 28, 29,
30, 40, 48, 49, 101, 104, 107, 109, 114,
115, 116, 122, 125, 126, 128, 137, 141,
144, 147, 153, 155, 156, 160, 163, 164,
166, 171, 179, 180, 183, 185, 186, 188,
194, 196, 202, 203, 207, 214, 215, 216,
219, 221, 222, 223, 226, 228, 237, 238,
239, 241, 242, 243, 244, 247, 249, 250
think-aloud, 22, 25, 30, 46, 47, 48, 49, 53, 109,
135, 138, 162, 163, 166, 186, 206, 207,
220, 231, 232, 238, 244
Tomasello, Michael, 8, 68, 69, 100
transcription, 74–7, 182, 194, 208–10
transferred meaning. See metaphor
transformation, **155**, 155–67, 228, 229
triangulation, 201, 226–40
Tversky, Barbara, 9, 19, 36, 106, 107, 109
Tyler, Andrea, 11, 70, 71

validation, 21
variability, 31, 37, 60, 136, 227, 232, 236
verb, 54, 64, 68, 71, 87–9, 97, 134, 161, 162,
183, 185, 189, 220, 239
verbalisability, 7, 30, 44, 206
verbosity, 131

wayfinding, 9, 10, 36, 37, 47, 125, 128, 138,
140, 147, 190–3, 238, 242, 243, 244
Whorf, Benjamin, 11, 101
Wittgenstein, Ludwig, 61–2